The Principles of Educational Leadership and Management

Education at SAGE

SAGE is a leading international publisher of journals, books, and electronic media for academic, educational, and professional markets.

Our education publishing includes:

- accessible and comprehensive texts for aspiring education professionals and practitioners looking to further their careers through continuing professional development

- inspirational advice and guidance for the classroom

- authoritative state of the art reference from the leading authors in the field

Find out more at: **www.sagepub.co.uk/education**

The Principles of Educational Leadership and Management

Second Edition

Edited by
Tony Bush, Les Bell and
David Middlewood

Los Angeles | London | New Delhi
Singapore | Washington DC

First published 2002
Reprinted 2003, 2005, 2006, 2007, 2009

SAGE Publications Ltd
1 Oliver's Yard
55 City Road
London EC1Y 1SP

SAGE Publications Inc.
2455 Teller Road
Thousand Oaks, California 91320

SAGE Publications India Pvt Ltd
B 1/I 1 Mohan Cooperative Industrial Area
Mathura Road
New Delhi 110 044

SAGE Publications Asia-Pacific Pte Ltd
33 Pekin Street #02-01
Far East Square
Singapore 048763

Library of Congress Control Number: 2009938214

British Library Cataloguing in Publication data

A catalogue record for this book is available from the British Library

ISBN 978-1-84860-209-0
ISBN 978-1-84860-210-6 (pbk)

Typeset by C&M Digitals (P) Ltd, Chennai, India
Printed in Great Britain by CPI Antony Rowe, Chippenham, Wiltshire
Printed on paper from sustainable resources

Contents

Preface

This book is a sequel to a highly successful volume (Bush and Bell, 2002) and, like that book, addresses the key features of an increasingly important field in education, that of educational leadership and management. However, this volume is in many respects very different from its predecessor. Most significantly, the term 'leadership' has been added to the title. This is because, as the editors explain in Chapter 1, there is now a much greater recognition of the importance of this concept within the broad field of educational management, administration and leadership. There is a growing recognition, at the level of policy and practice, that schools and other educational organisations need to be led capably as well as being managed competently. The differences between leadership and management are discussed in Chapter 1.

We have also set out to provide a more broadly based international perspective, with authors drawn from five countries and an author 'brief' to address a global audience. Many of the authors are acknowledged leaders in the field of educational leadership and are some of the foremost scholars and writers in their fields. Many are 'new' in that they did not contribute to the first edition while others are 'new' in that they are young researchers who are developing important perspectives on emerging themes. Collectively, they represent a truly global perspective, working within and across a variety of international boundaries. The contents, therefore, represent a considerably updated picture of some of the research, theorising and practical applications of approaches to educational leadership. The combination of authors largely reflects the modified orientation of the book, notably its focus on leadership, and its global perspective is crucial as the importance of leadership in education is acknowledged in both developed and developing countries. We believe you will be satisfied with the outcomes.

The first section sets the context by exploring some of the current key principles and practice. If leadership makes a difference, it needs ultimately to be reflected in outcomes for students and this section therefore begins by considering this fundamental issue. The next chapter argues that the underlying purposes of education should have ethical or moral dimensions. As new models and ideas about effective leadership emerge, the next two chapters in this section describe and debate some of these.

Theories and models of leadership are of no practical value unless there is a supply of effective leaders made available and their effectiveness when in post is maintained and, if possible, improved by continuous development. Section II therefore locates a discussion of leadership development within a consideration of the contested notion of teacher professionalism and its implications for professional development. The section goes on to consider the preparation of prospective leaders , their recruitment and the support needed and offered when in post, as well as their responsibility for the next generation of leaders.

While learning is clearly central to educational institutions, the relationship between leadership and that learning is not always apparent or straightforward. Section III examines the links between leadership and learning and also explores the importance of appropriate cultures, both societal and organisational, in influencing the way in which leaders foster effective learning within the institutions for which they are responsible. A further crucial aspect of effectiveness in learning is the way in which resources are managed within an institution and Chapter 11 in this section describes and analyses recent models of leadership approaches to this important issue.

One significant shift in several countries has been to move away from the notion of educational leadership being seen exclusively as leadership of a single organisation, into a wider area of responsibility involving several institutions, the community at large, or indeed with a remit to influence whole areas of society through an enhanced emphasis on diversity. Policies embodied in such legislation as No Child Left Behind (2001) in the USA and Every Child Matters (2004) in England and Wales were major indicators of this wider approach. Section IV deals with this new development, with chapters on the notions of diversity and inclusion, on the special factors involved in leading educational partnerships and on the leadership aspects of networking. The final chapter discusses how educational leadership involves engaging with the wider community, emphasising again the moral responsibility of those in leadership roles.

We believe this book will be of great help and interest to a wide range of readers through its updated picture of some of the research, theorising and practical applications of educational leadership. Students on Master's and taught Doctorate programmes will find that the book offers an excellent updated insight into a number of key elements of educational leadership and management. Current practitioners, including practising principals and those aspiring to principalship, will find both the models and the case studies provide food for thought and, in some instances, for action. Since leadership can be found at all levels in an institution, middle leaders and those aspiring to such positions will also wish to reflect on several aspects of this book's contents, in formulating their own leadership approaches, as they draw on their own experiences and those of others. Additionally, academic writers and researchers should find much to reflect upon in these chapters. All these chapters were specifically commissioned for this volume with the exception of some parts of Chapter 6, which are based on ideas developed by the late Ray Bolam in Bush and Bell (2002). The inclusion and further development of these ideas by a co-author is both a tribute to Ray and a testament to the enduring nature of his insights.

The editors are most grateful to all the authors for their scholarship and care in preparing their chapters for this volume. We also express our thanks to all those at Sage Publications who have helped us, and to our respective families for their constant support. We believe the book will be a valuable contribution to the developing literature on educational leadership and management.

Tony Bush, Les Bell and David Middlewood
September 2009

References

Bush, T. and Bell, L. (eds) (2002) *The Principles and Practice of Educational Management.* London: Paul Chapman Publishing.

Notes on Editors

Tony Bush is Professor of Educational Leadership at the University of Warwick, UK, having previously held similar posts at the Universities of Leicester, Reading and Lincoln. He is also Visiting Professor at the University of The Witwatersrand, Johannesburg, South Africa. He has extensive experience of research on school leadership, including directing ten projects for the National College for School Leadership (NCSL) and six such projects in South Africa. He has published more than 30 books and many refereed journal articles. Tony is the current editor of the leading international journal, *Educational Management, Administration and Leadership*, and a vice-president of The British Educational Leadership, Management and Administration Society (BELMAS). He was presented with the Society's Distinguished Service Award in 2008. He is a board member of the Commonwealth Council for Educational Administration and Management (CCEAM) and was elected as a CCEAM Fellow in 2008.

Les Bell   taught in primary and secondary schools before becoming a member of the Education Department at the University of Warwick, UK. From 1994 to 1999, he was Director of The School of Education and Community Studies at Liverpool John Moores University, UK, where he later became Dean of Education, Health and Social Studies. He joined the University of Leicester in 1999 as a Professor of Educational Management, directing the Doctoral pro-gramme in UK and South East Asia, retiring from there in 2006. Les has written extensively on educational management and leadership and given keynote addresses in many parts of the world. His most recent publication is *Perspectives on Educational Management and Leadership*, published by Continuum Press (2007)

David Middlewood   had extensive experience in a wide range of schools and colleges, including nine years as headteacher of an 11–18 all-ability school. He joined the University of Leicester, UK, in 1990, becoming director of school-based programmes and Deputy Director of the Centre for Educational Leadership and Management there. After a period at the University of Lincoln, he joined the University of Warwick, UK, where he is currently a research fellow. David has been a visiting professor in New Zealand and South Africa and led programmes in school leadership in Seychelles and Greece. His research interests include appraisal, inclusive schools, support staffing, and leadership teams. He has published more than a dozen books, including his most recent on *Leading and Managing Extended Schools* (with Richard Parker), published by Sage (2009), and has been a series editor for Sage.

Notes on Contributors

Tracey Allen is Senior Lecturer at the London Centre for Leadership in Learning, Institute of Education, University of London, UK, after several years' experience in teaching and research within education. She has co-directed and worked on a range of projects for leading research agencies, government and most recently for ESRC, exploring multi-agency partnerships and young people's perceptions. She has written on issues such as leadership and innovation in schools, equality and diversity in the education workforce and new models such as extended schools, Every Child Matters policy and pupil voice. She has led various research and training programmes for school leaders, local authority practitioners and young people

Stephen E. Anderson is an associate professor in the Educational Administration Program, Ontario Institute for Studies in Education, University of Toronto, and member of the International Centre for Educational Change. His research and consulting activities focus on education policy and program change, school improvement, in-service teacher development, and education leadership in Canada, the United States, Africa, Pakistan, and Chile. His publications appear in such journals as *School Effectiveness and School Improvement, the International Journal of Educational Development, Curriculum Inquiry, the Canadian Journal of Education, the Journal of School Leadership*, and the *Journal of Staff Development*. He is editor and a contributing author to a book on school improvement in East Africa, co-author of a research-based book on whole school reform projects in the U.S., and co-author of two national studies and reports of leadership and approaches to school district and school level improvement in the U.S.

Paul T. Begley is a Professor of Education at Nipissing University in North Bay, Ontario, Canada, having previously been Professor of Educational Leadership at Pennsylvania State University, USA, and Executive Director of the D.J. Willower Centre for the Study of Leadership and Ethics. He was also Director of the Pennsylvania School Study Council which focuses on professional development and research liaison between university and school districts. Some of his research interests are in the influence of values and ethics on school leadership, ethics and procedures of performance appraisal and state of the art pre-service and in-service for school leadership development (including on-line education). His research has been in Ontario, Canada's Northwest Territories, Sweden, Hong Kong and Australia. Recent publications include *The Ethical Dimensions of School Leadership*, published by Kluwer Press (2003).

Ray Bolam was Director of the National Centre for School Management at University of Bristol, UK, for seven years before becoming Professor of Education at the University of Swansea in Wales. He moved to the University of Cardiff as Professor of Education and Head of School of Education, as well as Director of the NPQH Centre for Wales. He was a consultant for the Organisation for Economic Co-operation and Development (OECD), British Council and European Commission as well as working in Africa, Asia and North America. He was continuing to work part-time at Cardiff University when he died suddenly in August 2006.

Ann Briggs taught in secondary schools and tertiary colleges before joining the University of Leicester, UK. She is Emeritus Professor of Educational Leadership at Newcastle University, UK, having retired from her Newcastle chair in 2009. She was Chair of BELMAS from 2007–2009. Ann has published widely on research methods, middle leadership, 14–19 education and especially on management structures in post-compulsory institutions.

Mark Brundrett worked in secondary, middle and primary schools prior to entering higher education. Subsequently, he worked in a number of university departments as lecturer, senior lecturer and professor of education. He is currently Professor of Educational Research in the Faculty of Education, Community and Leisure at Liverpool John Moores University.

Peter Gronn is Professor of Education at the University of Cambridge, UK, and a fellow of Hughes Hall. At Cambridge, he works in the area of leadership and school improvement. Previously, he held chair appointments at the University of Glasgow and at Monash University in Australia.

Alma Harris is Pro-Director (leadership) and Director of the London Centre for Leadership in Learning at the Institute of Education,

University of London, UK. Previously, she was Professor of Education and Director of the Institute of Education at the University of Warwick, after working at the Universities of Nottingham, Bath, and the Open University. She was previously the editor of the journal *School Leadership and Management*. Alma's research has focused on organisational change and she is internationally known for her work on school improvement, especially on how leadership can contribute to this. She is committed to working with schools in challenging circumstances, with some of her 23 books published being on this subject. Her latest book, *Distributed Leadership: Developing Tomorrow's Leaders* (2008) is in a second edition and a special edition of the *Journal of Educational Administration* (vol. 46, no. 2), edited by Alma, received an award at the American Education Research Association conference in 2009.

Rosalind Levačić is Emeritus Professor of Economics and Finance of Education in the Department of Quantitative Social Science at the Institute of Education, University of London, UK. She has researched and taught on school finance for 20 years and has considerable experience as an international consultant on school finance for the World Bank, and various Ministries of Education in Eastern Europe and Central and Southern Asia. She has published widely on school resources and financial management and on the relationship between student outcomes and resources. She is also vice-chair of governors for a school with extended services in Milton Keynes, UK.

Kenneth Leithwood is Professor of Educational Leadership and Policy at OISE/University of Toronto, Canada. His most recent books include *Distributed Leadership According to the Evidence* (Routledge 2008) and *Leading with Teachers Emotions in Mind*, (Corwin 2008). Professor Leithwood is the recent recipient of the University of Toronto's Impact on Public Policy Award and a Fellow of the Royal Society of Canada.

Jacky Lumby is Professor of Education and Head of School at the University of Southampton, UK. She taught in a range of educational settings, including secondary/high schools and further/technical education colleges. She also worked for a Training and Enterprise Council in developing leaders across public and private sectors. She has researched and published widely on management and leadership in the UK and internationally. Her work on leadership encompasses a range of perspectives including diversity, comparative and international perspectives, and leadership in upper secondary education.

Blair Mascall is Associate Professor in the Department of Theory and Policy Studies at the Ontario Institute for Studies in Education, University of Toronto, Canada. His current research is divided between an empirical study to establish the outcomes of distributed leadership in schools and school districts in Canada, and a large-scale project to define the impact of leadership on student achievement in the USA. His most recent book (with Kenneth Leithwood and Tiiu Strauss) is *Distributing Leadership According to the Evidence*, (Routledge 2009).

Christopher Rhodes worked in schools and colleges for 14 years prior to entering higher education. He was Director of Postgraduate Studies in the School of Education at the University of Wolverhampton, UK. He is currently Senior Lecturer in Educational Leadership in the School of Education at the University of Birmingham, UK.

Tiiu Strauss is a project director working with Kenneth Leithwood in the Department of Theory and Policy Studies at the Ontario Institute for Studies in Education at the University of Toronto, Canada. She has published in the areas of leader problem-solving and distributed leadership, and is involved in research projects related to leadership in turnaround schools.

Andrew Townsend is Assistant Professor in Educational Enquiry in the Institute of Education at University of Warwick, UK, where he is primarily concerned with supporting practitioners studying at Master's level. Previously, he worked as a consultant researching, supporting and evaluating professional development and action research projects, following a ten-year teaching career. Andrew's recent work has included researching and publishing on processes and outcomes of collaborative and networked enquiry, and also supporting student voice projects. He has also used action research in externally funded research, establishing groups of practitioners as partners in research.

Allan Walker is Chair Professor of International Educational Leadership and Head of the Department of Education Policy and Leadership at the Hong Kong Institute of Education. He is also Co-Director the new Asia Pacific Centre for Leadership and Change. Allan has experience as a teacher, principal, university teacher and administrator, and consultant in a range of international settings, including Australia, Singapore and Hong Kong. He has also researched and led development programmes in North America and the Asia-Pacific Region. His research interests include principal preparation and selection, cultural influences on leaders, school improvement and professional learning communities. His most recent research involves the work lives of vice-principals and the 'learning bridges' needed to prepare for principalship.

Section I

Leadership Principles and Practice

CHAPTER 1

Introduction: New Directions in Educational Leadership

Tony Bush, Les Bell and David Middlewood

Introduction: from management to leadership

The labels used to define the field within which this book is located have changed from 'educational administration' to 'educational management' and, more recently, to 'educational leadership' (Gunter, 2004). In England, this shift away from administration and management is illustrated most strongly by the opening of the National College for School Leadership (NCSL) in 2000, described as a paradigm shift by Bolam (2004). However there are many different conceptualisations of leadership, leading Southworth (1993) to term leadership a contested concept and Yukl (2002: 4–5) to argue that 'the definition of leadership is arbitrary and very subjective'. He adds that 'most definitions of leadership reflect the assumption that it involves a social influence process whereby intentional influence is exerted by one person [or group] over other people [or groups] to structure the activities and relationships in a group or organisation (Yukl, 2002).

Bush (2008) agrees that the central concept is *influence* rather than authority, noting that influence and authority are dimensions of power but pointing out that the former could be exercised by anyone in the school or college, while the latter tends to reside in formal positions, such as principal or headteacher. Leadership is independent of positional authority while management is linked directly to it.

The process of leadership is also *intentional*, in that the person seeking to exercise influence is doing so in order to achieve certain purposes. The notion of 'influence' is neutral in that it does not explain or recommend what goals or actions should be pursued. However, leadership is increasingly linked with values. Leaders are expected to ground their actions in clear personal and professional values. Greenfield and Ribbins (1993) claim that leadership begins with the 'character' of leaders, expressed in terms of personal values, self-awareness, and emotional and moral capability. These values underpin leadership actions and contribute to determining leaders' sense of purpose.

Leadership is often associated with 'vision', which provides the essential sense of direction for leaders and their organisations. Southworth (1993) argues that heads are motivated to work hard because their leadership is the pursuit of their individual visions. However, an over-emphasis on vision may be problematic. Fullan (1992: 83) notes that 'vision building is a highly sophisticated dynamic process which few organizations can sustain'. Hoyle and Wallace (2005: 11) are particularly critical of the contemporary emphasis on vision in England: 'Visionary rhetoric is a form of management speak that has increased very noticeably in schools since the advent of educational reforms'. They contrast the 'visionary rhetoric' with 'the prosaic reality' experienced by staff, students and parents. They add that visions have to conform to centralised expectations and to satisfy Office for Standards in Education (OFSTED) inspectors; 'any vision you like, as long as it's central government's' (Hoyle and Wallace, 2005: 139).

Distinguishing educational leadership and management

As the terminology used to describe the organisation of educational bodies, and the activities of their principals and senior staff, has evolved from 'administration', which is still widely used in North America and Australia, for example, through 'management', to 'leadership', the question arises as to whether these are just semantic shifts or whether they represent a more fundamental change in the conceptualisation of headship (Bush 2008)? Hoyle and Wallace (2005: viii) note that 'leadership' has only recently overtaken 'management' as the main descriptor for what is entailed in running and improving public service organisations. However, Bell and Stevenson (2006) argue that this change in nomenclature is neither a product of semantics nor of changes in fashion. It reflects deep-rooted and significant developments in educational policy over five decades. As a consequence of these developments, the roles of headteachers and other school leaders have undergone a series of fundamental changes in the extent of their autonomy, the levels and patterns of their accountability, and the very nature of their responsibilities (Bell, 2007). Nevertheless, there remains an important differentiation between management and leadership.

Cuban (1988) provides one of the clearest distinctions, linking leadership with change and management with 'maintenance'. He also stresses the importance of both dimensions of organisational activity:

> By leadership, I mean influencing others' actions in achieving desirable ends. Leaders are people who shape the goals, motivations, and actions of others. Frequently they initiate change to reach existing and new goals ... Leadership ... takes ... much ingenuity, energy and skill ... Managing is maintaining efficiently and effectively current organizational arrangements. While managing well often exhibits leadership skills, the overall function is toward maintenance rather than change. I prize both managing and leading and attach no special value to either since different settings and times call for varied responses. (Cuban, 1988: xx)

Bush (1998) links leadership to values or purpose while management relates to implementation or technical issues. Leadership and management need to be given equal prominence if schools and colleges are to operate effectively and achieve their objectives. While a clear vision may be essential to establish the nature and direction of change, it is equally important to ensure that innovations are implemented efficiently and that the school's residual functions are carried out effectively while certain elements are undergoing change.

> Leading and managing are distinct, but both are important ... The challenge of modern organizations requires the objective perspective of the manager as well as the flashes of vision and commitment wise leadership provides. (Bolman and Deal, 1997: xiii–xiv)

The dichotomy in Britain and elsewhere is that, while leadership is normatively preferred, notably through the establishment and activities of the NCSL, governments are encouraging a technical–rational approach to school management through their stress on performance management and public accountability (Glatter, 1999; Gunter, 2004). In practice, schools and colleges require both visionary leadership, to the extent that this is possible with a centralised curriculum, *and* effective management. That is why we have retained 'management' in the title of this volume. However, it is important to stress the need for managing towards clear educational purposes, rather than regarding management as an end in itself. The latter may lead to 'managerialism', managing to excess.

The impact of leadership

Global interest in educational leadership and management has grown during the past few years and there is widespread recognition that leadership is second only to classroom practice in terms of impact on school and student outcomes. For many years, it was assumed that the scope of leadership was modest, perhaps explaining no more than 5–7 per cent of variation in learning outcomes. More recently, Leithwood et al. (2006) and Robinson (2007) have demonstrated that this impact can be much greater, particularly where leaders engage directly with teachers to enhance classroom practices. In Chapter 2, Ken Leithwood, Stephen E. Anderson, Blair Mascall and Tiiu Strauss examine the evidence for the impact of leadership on student outcomes and propose four 'pathways' of influence. Significantly, one of these is the 'family' path, providing the potential for leaders to impact on the external variables which often strongly influence learner outcomes. This broad interpretation of leadership contrasts with the narrow scope of the role in some countries, for example in South Africa, where principals may be largely office-bound and be concerned more with meeting the demands of the external bureaucracy than with addressing the needs of learners (Bush et al., 2009). Paul T. Begley, in Chapter 3, addresses the ethical and moral foundations of educational leadership. He argues that leadership must not only be implemented with a clear sense of educational purpose, but also be based on a strong ethical and moral stance. The basic premise of this chapter is that effective as well as moral school leaders need to keep the fundamental purposes of education at the forefront of their administrative practices. Whether articulated as leadership for moral literacy, ethical leadership practices or leadership with moral purpose, the common foundation is purpose-driven educational leadership.

We noted earlier that the influence process is independent of formal authority. This means that notions of leadership can be loosened from headship or other senior formal roles. It may be exercised by anyone in the organisation, regardless of position, although principals retain considerable power. This links to the contemporary emphasis on 'distributed leadership'. As Alma Harris notes in Chapter 4, few ideas have provoked as much attention, debate and controversy as this concept. In essence, distribution relates to multiple sources of influence and is based on expertise rather than formal authority. However, she also comments that distributed leadership requires the support of principals. This leads Peter Gronn, in Chapter 5, to argue for a 'hybrid' model of leadership, which aligns individual and distributed leadership. While he is persuaded of the merits of distributed leadership, he also asserts that individual action accords with the reality of practice in many educational settings. New leadership configurations are required to align distributed and individual leadership.

Developing teachers and leaders

School leaders are invariably drawn from the wider teaching profession. Given the centrality of leadership for learning, noted earlier, it is essential for school principals and other leaders to have substantial professional experience. In practice, of course, the journey from teacher to leader is an incremental process, which generally involves the gradual substitution of leadership and management activities for classroom teaching. Middle leaders may have an 80 per cent teaching commitment, while senior leaders may teach for 50 per cent of their time and principals often have no regular teaching load. An important factor, therefore, in enabling leaders to develop and inculcate a sense of purpose in their schools, and to facilitate school improvement, is the recognition of the need for ongoing development of teachers and leaders. The nature and pace of change make it inevitable that initial teacher education will need to be supplemented by additional professional development to enhance subject knowledge and pedagogy. This is the central focus of Chapter 6, by Les Bell and the late Ray Bolam. These authors stress the impact of reforms on the nature of teacher professionalism and note the challenges involved in maintaining professional discretion while interpreting and implementing externally mandated change. They also note the centrality of continuing professional development (CPD) if teachers are to improve their skills and knowledge. They conclude that CPD should enhance teacher professionalism and not simply relate to 'mechanistic' implementation of national policies.

In many countries, however, there is no specific preparation or development for school leaders. There is an implicit assumption that professionally qualified teachers would be able to 'assume' leadership roles with no specific training. This stance fails to recognise the very different role of school leaders, as Tony Bush stresses in Chapter 7. As the scope and impact of leadership are increasingly acknowledged, the need for specialised preparation, for principals if not often for other leaders, is being recognised. Development programmes are available in countries as diverse as England, Singapore, South Africa and the USA and, increasingly, principals cannot be appointed without such qualifications. While professional development is essential to school improvement, David Middlewood shows, in Chapter 8, that this does not diminish the clamour for improved educational performance. Most performance management systems have been relatively unsuccessful in having much impact on 'under-performing' teachers and it is possible that more straightforward measures will be required in some cases, such as the teachers' licence being considered in 2009 by the British Department for Children, Schools and Families (DCSF). Middlewood stresses that high-quality teaching begins with the recruitment and selection process and continues through support, guidance and development. He also emphasises the need to provide feedback to teachers if they are to improve.

Leadership for learning

The need for leadership and management to be underpinned by a clear sense of educational purpose has been recognised earlier in this chapter. While schools and colleges also have responsibility for many aspects of child and student well-being, their primary and unique purpose is to promote learning. In the twenty-first century, this has been conceptualised as 'leadership for learning', replacing the previous emphasis on 'managing the curriculum' or 'instructional leadership'. In Chapter 9, Christopher Rhodes and Mark Brundrett explore the origins of this notion and explain its relevance, starting with the view that learning is the reason why schools exist. Leaders need to influence classroom practice if they are to make a real difference to student learning. One of the weaknesses of much current practice in South Africa, for example, is that leaders rarely engage with the learning process. The separation between leadership and learning is damaging to student outcomes, which remain stubbornly low (Bush et al., 2009). Significantly, Rhodes and Brundrett also show that there is a clear positive relationship between leadership distribution and learning outcomes.

The relationship between leadership and learning is extended in Chapter 10 by Allan Walker's treatment of learning cultures. He distinguishes between 'big picture' national or societal culture and organisational culture. Even within the latter, subcultures may exist, focused around subject departments or interest groups. He stresses the significance of learning-oriented cultures illustrated through such constructs as 'communities of practice' and 'professional learning communities'. He also argues that a learning culture requires conditions that promote and encourage learning as a way of professional life; in other words, it becomes ingrained in the norms and behaviours of the school. This links to the earlier discussion of values but Walker emphasises the need to align purpose and practice if leadership is to be effective in building and sustaining learning cultures.

From the late 1980s, many developed countries began to devolve greater powers to schools, often through governing bodies or boards. An important dimension of this process was provision for self-management, which usually involved responsibility for aspects of finance. Much of the early discussion about funding involved essentially technical issues such as how to construct budgets, and the need to appoint bursars so that school principals could avoid some of the more detailed operational aspects of financial management, although they retained a strategic overview. More recently, there has been a closer alignment between resources and learning, recognising, as Rosalind Levačić stresses in Chapter 11, that the purpose of resource management is to maximise student learning within given funding constraints. She emphasises the importance of the 'resource mix', the ability of site-based leaders to determine the ways in which resources are combined to support learning. Devolved budgeting is based on the assumption that site-based leaders are more likely to be able to determine the most appropriate 'mix' than officials based in national, provincial or local departments and is underpinned by professional judgements about what is best to support student learning.

Leadership for diversity

A recurrent theme of this chapter has been the centrality of educational purpose when conceptualising or enacting leadership. An increasingly important aspect of this theme is the need to manage diversity. In Chapter 12, Jacky Lumby defines diversity as 'the range of human characteristics which result in socially constructed advantage and disadvantage'. This may arise from gender, ethnicity, disability or a combination of these or other features. In many countries, women are under-represented in leadership positions even though they usually form a majority of the teaching profession (Coleman, 2002). Similarly, black and ethnic minority teachers and leaders are often under-represented when compared to the demographic composition of the community served by the school or college (Bush et al., 2006).

Lumby argues that the responsibility for diversity should be located at a high level in organisations and not be seen as a 'bolt on' to the main activities of the school or college. The argument for embracing and celebrating diversity is partly ethical, because discrimination is unacceptable, and partly pragmatic, because under-representation leads to a potential waste of human talent. As Lumby stresses, there is a 'gulf' between recognition of inequality and enacting effective change to address such problems.

Ann Briggs, in Chapter 13, extends this broad idea of diversity to include notions of partnership between and across schools and colleges. In England, these linkages include federations of schools, school improvement partnerships and 14–19 collaborations, all of which require some form of collective decision-making. Similarly, Andrew Townsend's treatment of networks in Chapter 14 illustrates the fluid nature of leadership within and beyond individual schools. He argues that, because leadership is dependent on interactions between people, it is inevitably concerned with networks, although not always explicitly. In Chapter 15, Tracey Allen discusses the growing importance of community-oriented schooling in enhancing the resonance and relevance of the curriculum by bridging community and school cultures more effectively. She goes on to explore key conceptual issues that underpin community leadership and orientation. This group of chapters, taken collectively, demonstrates that our understanding of the concept of leadership has moved a long way from the study of headship to a wider appreciation of the potential for leadership to infuse every aspect of schools and colleges.

Conclusion

Interest in educational leadership has never been greater. The emerging evidence that the impact of leadership on learning outcomes is greater than previously thought has led to enhanced recognition of the importance of leadership and leadership development. Leadership may be independent of formal position and relies on an influence process. It may also reside in groups and teams as well as in individuals. This knowledge has led to a weakening of 'great man' theories, which assumed the vital importance of singular leadership, usually located in the role of principal or headteacher. Instead, distributed leadership is in vogue, linked to recognition that there can be greater 'purchase' if leadership involves the many rather than the few.

Another major development in the twenty-first century is the enhanced focus on leadership for learning. Predominant among the plethora of demands placed on schools and their leaders is their pre-eminent responsibility to promote learning. Other leadership and management responsibilities, such as managing budgets and staff, should be seen as contributing to this overarching objective. In many countries, schools and colleges serve diverse populations and leaders need to ensure that their programmes, and their staff, fully reflect their local communities.

As the scope of leadership has increased, through devolution to site level in many countries and the increasing recognition of their power to enhance learning, the need to provide specialised preparation for leaders has been acknowledged and, in some countries, translated into customised development opportunities for aspiring and practising principals. Ongoing learning for teachers and leaders provides the best prospect of school improvement.

References

Bell, L. (2007) *Perspectives on Educational Management and Leadership*. London: Continuum Books.

Bell, L. and Stevenson, H. (2006) *Policy in Education: Process, Themes and Impact*. London: RoutledgeFalmer.

Bolam, R. (2004) 'Reflections on the NCSL from a historical perspective', *Educational Management, Administration and Leadership*, 32(3): 251–68.

Bolman, L. and Deal, T. (1997), *Reframing Organisations: Artistry, Choice and Leadership*. San Francisco, CA: Jossey-Bass.

Bush, T. (1998) 'The National Professional Qualification for Headship: the key to effective school leadership?', *School Leadership and Management*, 18(3): 321–34.

Bush, T. (2008) 'From management to leadership: semantic or meaningful change?', *Educational Management, Administration and Leadership*, 36(2): 271–88.

Bush, T., Glover, D. and Sood, K. (2006) 'Black and minority ethnic leaders in England: a portrait', *School Leadership and Management*, 26(4): 289–305.

Bush, T., Joubert, R., Kiggundu, E. and Van Rooyen, J. (2009) 'Managing teaching and learning in South African schools', *International Journal of Educational Development*, 30(2): 162–8.

Coleman, M. (2002) *Women as Headteachers: Striking the Balance*. Stoke-on-Trent: Trentham Books.

Cuban, L. (1988) *The Managerial Imperative and the Practice of Leadership in Schools*. Albany, NY: State University of New York Press.

Fullan, M. (1992) *Successful School Improvement*. Buckingham: Open University Press.

Glatter, R. (1999) 'From struggling to juggling: towards a redefinition of the field of educational leadership and management', *Educational Management and Administration*, 27(3): 253–66.

Greenfield, T. and Ribbins, P. (eds) (1993) *Greenfield on Educational Administration: Towards a Humane Science*. London: Routledge.

Gunter, H. (2004) 'Labels and labelling in the field of educational leadership', *Discourse – Studies in the Cultural Politics of Education*, 25(1): 21–41.

Hoyle, E. and Wallace, M. (2005) *Educational Leadership: Ambiguity, Professionals and Managerialism*, London: Sage.

Leithwood, K., Day, C., Sammons, P., Harris, A. and Hopkins, D. (2006) *Seven Strong Claims about Successful School Leadership*. London: Department for Education and Skills.

Robinson, V. (2007) *School Leadership and Student Outcomes: Identifying What Works and Why*. Melbourne. Australian Council of Leaders.

Southworth, G. (1993) 'School leadership and school development: reflections from research', *School Organisation*, 12(2): 73–87.

Yukl, G.A. (2002) *Leadership in Organizations*. 5th edn. Upper Saddle River, NJ: Prentice-Hall.

CHAPTER 2

School Leaders' Influences on Student Learning: The Four Paths

Kenneth Leithwood, Stephen E. Anderson, Blair Mascall and Tiiu Strauss

Introduction

This chapter rests on two fundamental assumptions about educational leadership. First, such leadership is about the exercise of influence and, second, the effects of such influence on student learning are mostly indirect. Premised on these two assumptions, we draw on recent evidence to describe four distinct paths along which the influence of successful leadership practices flow in order to improve student learning. As Figure 2.1 indicates, these are the rational, emotional, organisational and family paths.

Each path is populated by distinctly different sets of variables, each with a more or less direct impact on students' experiences. Such variables might include those relating to school culture, teachers' practices, teachers' emotional states, or parents' attitudes. Selecting the most promising of these variables and improving their status are two of the three central challenges facing leaders intending to improve learning in their schools. As the status of variables on each path improves, through influences from leaders and other sources, the quality of students' school and classroom experiences are enriched, resulting in greater learning. Since exercising leadership influence along one path alone, or just one path at a time, has rarely resulted in demonstrable gains for students, alignment of leadership influence across paths is the third leadership challenge.

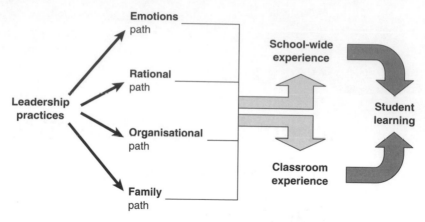

Figure 2.1 Four paths of leadership influence on student learning

Selection and improvement of variables, the first two leadership challenges, are addressed in the next four sections of this chapter, each section focuses on one path. Using the results of recent research, some of the most powerful variables located on each path are identified. One or two of these variables are explored in more detail; evidence of their impact on students is summarised, and leadership practices likely to influence their status in a positive direction are outlined. Alignment of leadership influence across paths is taken up in the fifth section. Hattie's (2009) remarkably comprehensive synthesis of meta-analyses is frequently used to estimate the impact on student learning of selected variables found on three of the four paths; these estimates are reported as effect sizes (or 'd').[1]

We are not the first to offer a conceptualisation of varying strategic orientations to leadership for school improvement. House (1981), for example, distinguished technical, political, and cultural perspectives on the implementation of educational change, each characterised by differing change agent assumptions and strategies for mobilising and supporting change. This framework has proven useful as a way of describing and comparing change facilitator assumptions and strategies for mobilising and supporting specific educational change initiatives (see Corbett and Rossman, 1989; House and McQuillan, 1998; Rolheiser-Bennett and Anderson, 1991–92). However, scholars applying the framework have not explicitly linked the different perspectives or paths and associated leadership practices to any research-based conception of variables that are likely to make a difference, directly or indirectly, in the quality of teaching and learning. Here we not only propose four paths through which school leaders can influence student learning, we offer an evidence-based interpretation of what key variables within each path are most susceptible to leadership action and influence. We argue that effective leadership is not a matter of choosing one path over the other, rather that leaders should be simultaneously attending wisely and strategically to relevant variables within each of the paths.

The rational path

Variables on the rational path are rooted in the knowledge and skills of school staffs about curriculum, teaching and learning. In general, exercising a positive influence on these variables calls on school leaders' knowledge about the 'technical core' of schooling, their problem-solving capacities (Robinson, in press), and their knowledge of relevant leadership practices.

Selecting variables to influence

The rational path includes both classroom- and school-level variables. Since there is now a considerable amount of evidence available about the effects on student learning of many such variables, school leaders are able to prioritise for their attention, those known to have the greatest chance of improving their students' learning. In the classroom, Hattie's (2009) synthesis of evidence implies that school leaders carefully consider the value of focusing their efforts on improving, for example, the extent to which teachers are providing students with immediate and informative feedback ($d = 0.73$), teachers' use of reciprocal teaching strategies ($d = 0.74$), teacher–student relations ($d = 0.72$), the management of classrooms ($d = 0.52$), and the general quality of teaching in the school. Effect sizes for these variables are among the highest reported for all classroom-level variables, whereas some variables currently the focus of considerable effort by school leaders have much smaller effect sizes (for example, individualised instruction has an effect size of $d = 0.23$).

Many school-level variables have reported effects on student learning as large as all but a few classroom-level variables. Both academic press[2] and disciplinary climate[3] stand out among these especially consequential variables. Of the more than 20 empirical studies which have been published since about 1989, by far the majority have reported significant, positive and at least moderate relationships between academic press and student achievement, most often in the area of mathematics, but extending to other subjects such as writing, science, reading and language (for example, Goddard et al., 2000).

Similarly consistent and positive evidence has also been reported about the contribution of disciplinary climate. A large proportion of this research has used very large data-sets and sophisticated statistical methods (Ma and Klinger, 2000), features that add to the confidence we can have in these findings. Hattie's (2009) synthesis of evidence estimates that 'decreasing disruptive behavior' (p. 103) has a moderate effect size ($d = 0.53$) on student learning.

Influencing selected variables

Knowing which variables on the rational path hold the greatest promise for improving student learning still leaves leaders with the problem of figuring out how to improve the status of those variables in their schools. There may well be differences in the specific leadership practices or their enactments depending on which variables are chosen for attention.

About disciplinary climate, a small amount of evidence recommends flexible rather than rigid responses by leaders to disciplinary events, and engagement of staff and other stakeholders in developing school-wide behaviour plans (for example, Benda, 2000; Leithwood et al., 2004). A broader body of evidence indicates: that 'the principal is the most potent factor in determining school climate', and 'a direct relationship between visionary leadership and school climate and culture is imperative to support teacher efforts that lead to the success of the instructional [and disciplinary] program' (Rencherler, 1991).

A small number of studies have also identified leadership practices likely to increase a school's academic press (for example, Alig-Mielcarek, 2003; Jacob, 2004, Jurewicz, 2004) including:

- promoting school-wide professional development
- monitoring and providing feedback on the teaching and learning processes
- developing and communicating shared goals
- being open, supportive, and friendly
- establishing high expectations
- not burdening teachers with bureaucratic tasks and busy work
- helping to clarify shared goals about academic achievement
- grouping students using methods that convey academic expectations
- protecting instructional time

- providing an orderly environment
- establishing clear homework policies
- monitoring student performance in relation to instructional objectives
- basing remediation efforts on the common instructional framework
- requiring student progress reports to be sent to the parents
- making promotion dependent on student mastery of basic grade level skills.

The emotional path

The rational and emotional paths are much more tightly connected than many leaders believe. Considerable evidence indicates, for example, that emotions direct cognition: they structure perception, direct attention, give preferential access to certain memories, and bias judgement in ways that help individuals respond productively to their environments (Oatley et al., 2006).

A review of more than 90 empirical studies of teacher emotions and their consequences for classroom practice and student learning (Leithwood, 2006; Leithwood and Beatty, 2007) unambiguously recommends leaders' attention to variables on the emotional path as a means of improving student learning. Exercising influence on variables located along the emotional path depends fundamentally on leaders' social appraisal skills (Zaccaro et al., 2004) or emotional intelligence (Goleman, 1995).

Selecting variables to influence

Our recent review pointed to a large handful of teacher emotions with significant effects on teaching and learning. These included both individual and collective teacher efficacy, job satisfaction, organisational commitment, morale, stress/burnout, engagement in the school or profession, and teacher trust in colleagues, parents and students. Let us consider what we know about just two of these emotions, by way of illustration.

Collective teacher efficacy (CTE)

This emotion is conceptualised as the level of confidence a group of teachers feels about its ability to organise and implement whatever educational initiatives are required for students to reach high standards of achievement. The effect of efficacy (or collective confidence) on performance is indirect through the persistence it engenders in the face of initial failure and the opportunities it creates for a confident group to learn its way forward (rather than giving up).

In highly efficacious schools, evidence suggests that teachers accept responsibility for their students' learning. Learning difficulties are not assumed to be an inevitable by-product of low socio-economic status, lack of ability, or family background. Collective teacher efficacy creates high expectations for students as well as the collectively confident teachers. Evidence suggests that high levels of CTE encourage teachers to set challenging benchmarks for themselves, engage in high levels of planning and organisation, and devote more classroom time to academic learning. High CTE teachers are more likely to engage in activity-based learning, student-centred learning and interactive instruction. Among other exemplary practices, high CTE is associated with teachers adopting a humanistic approach to student management, testing new instructional methods to meet the learning needs of their students and providing extra help to students who have difficulty, displaying persistence and resiliency in such cases, rewarding students for their achievements; believing their students can reach high academic goals; displaying more enthusiasm for teaching; committing to community partnerships; and having more ownership in school decisions.

While the total number of well-designed studies enquiring about CTE effects on students is still modest (about eight studies), their results are both consistent and impressive. This relatively recent evidence demonstrates a significant positive relationship between CTE and achievement by students in such areas of the curriculum as reading, mathematics and writing. Furthermore, and perhaps more surprising, several of these studies have found that the effects on achievement of CTE exceed the effects of students' socio-economic status (for example, Goddard et al., 2000), a variable that typically explains by far the bulk of achievement variation across schools, usually in excess of 50 per cent. High CTE schools also are associated with lower suspension and dropout rates as well as greater school orderliness (Tschannen-Moran and Barr, 2004).

Trust in colleagues, students and parents

This form of relational trust includes a belief or expectation, in this case on the part of most teachers, that their colleagues, students and parents support the schools' goals for student learning, and will reliably work toward achieving those goals. Transparency, competence, benevolence and reliability are among the qualities persuading others that a person is trustworthy. Teacher trust is critical to the success of schools, and nurturing trusting relationships with students and parents is a key element in improving student learning (for example, Bryk and Schneider, 2003; Lee and Croninger, 1994).

Trust remains a strong predictor of student achievement even after the effects of student background, prior achievement, race and gender have been taken into account in some recent studies of trust in schools. Goddard (2003) argues that, when teacher–parent and teacher–student relationships are characterised by trust, academically supportive norms and social relations have the potential to move students toward academic success. Results of a second study by Goddard and his colleagues (2001) provide one of the largest estimates of trust effects on student learning. In this study, trust explained 81 per cent of the variation between schools in students' mathematics and reading achievement.

Influencing selected variables

Collective teacher efficacy

There are two sources of insight about how leaders might improve the collective efficacy of their teaching colleagues, the theoretical work of Bandura (for example, 1993) and a small number of studies of principals' transformational leadership (for example, Leithwood and Jantzi, 2008). In combination, these two sources indicate that teachers' CTE will increase when leaders:

- clarify goals by, for example, identifying new opportunities for the school, developing (often collaboratively), articulating and inspiring others with a vision of the future, promoting cooperation and collaboration among staff towards common goals
- encourage their staffs to network with others facing similar challenges in order to learn from their experiences
- structure their schools to allow for collaborative work among staff
- offer individualised support by, for example, showing respect for individual members of the staff, demonstrating concern about their personal feelings and needs, maintaining an open-door policy and valuing staff opinions
- sponsor meaningful professional development
- provide appropriate models of both desired practices and appropriate values.

Trust

Principal leadership has been highlighted in recent evidence as a critical contributor to trust among teachers, parents and students (for example, Bryk and Schneider, 2003). This evidence suggests that principals engender trust with and among staff and with both parents and students when they:

- recognise and acknowledge the vulnerabilities of their staff
- listen to the personal needs of staff members and assist as much as possible to reconcile those needs with a clear vision for the school
- create a space for parents in the school and demonstrate to parents that they (principal) are reliable, open, and scrupulously honest in their interactions
- buffer teachers from unreasonable demands from the policy environment or from the parents and the wider community
- behave toward teachers in a friendly, supportive, and open manner
- set high standards for students and then follow through with support for teachers.

The organisational path

Structures, culture, policies, and standard operation procedures are the types of variables to be influenced on the organisational path. Collectively, they constitute teachers' working conditions which, in turn, have a powerful influence on teachers' emotions (Leithwood and Beatty, 2007). These variables constitute both the school's infrastructure and a large proportion of its collective memory.

Like the electrical, water and road systems making up the infrastructure of a neighbourhood, variables on the organisational path are often not given much thought about until they malfunction. At a minimum, a school's infrastructure should not prevent staff and students from making best use of their capacities. At best, school infrastructures should magnify those capacities and make it much easier to engage in productive rather than unproductive practices. Ensuring that variables on the organisational path are working for, rather than against, the school's improvement efforts is vital to a school's ability to sustain its gains. A new instructional practice, for example, will not be sustained if it requires unusual amounts of effort for an indefinite period of time.

Sustaining gains also depends on transforming individual into collective learning. Learning first occurs in a school at the level of the individual. The challenge for organisations attempting to get smarter is how to take collective advantage of what its individual members are learning (Cohen, 1996). Modifying variables on the organisational path to reflect what individual members learn, creates the potential for that learning to shape the behaviour of many others in the organisation. This is often how promising practices move beyond initial implementation by a few people to longer-term institutionalisation by many.

Selecting variables to influence

Hattie's (2009) synthesis of evidence identifies more than a dozen variables located on the organisational path. Some can be found in the classroom (for example, class size, ability groupings), some are school-wide (for example, school size, multi-grade/age classes, retention policies); many are typically controlled by agencies outside the school (for example, school funding, summer school). One of the more powerful and fully researched variables on the organisational path is instructional time. A brief review of evidence about this variable helps illustrate why it would be a good choice for leadership attention.

Early research on time for learning introduced four distinct ways in which it could be conceptualised and measured. The *total amount of time* potentially available for learning, is a simple function of the number of days of schooling per year and the number of hours of instruction per day. *Time actually devoted to instruction* is the potential time left for learning once unplanned events, recesses, transitions, interruptions and the like are subtracted from the total potential time. *Opportunity to learn (OTL)* is a targeted version of time actually devoted to instruction which acknowledges that the content or focus of instructional time has significant effects on the nature of student learning. This measure of time was first introduced by Carroll (1963) in his model of school learning. Finally, *academically engaged time* is the time students actually spend on their own learning within the time devoted to instruction.

Research about the extent to which these different ways of conceptualising and measuring instructional time influence student learning (for example, Marburger, 2006; Roby, 2004; Tornroos, 2005; Wang, 1998) indicates that:

- the *total amount of time* potentially available for instruction, typically measured as student attendance rates, has been reported to have effects on student learning varying from weakly significant to quite strong

- the total amount of *time actually devoted to instruction* has moderate effects on student learning
- the content of the curriculum which students spend time studying, *opportunity to learn*, has quite strong effects on the nature of their learning
- students' total amount of *academically engaged time* is strongly associated with student learning.

Influencing selected variables

There has been little direct evidence reported about leadership practices for optimising instructional time in schools, with the major exception of research on leadership 'buffering'. A venerable leadership practice, the value of buffering as a contribution to organisational goals is justified by evidence collected both in schools and many other types of organisations (Yukl, 1994). In schools, buffering aims to protect the efforts of teachers from the many distractions they face from both inside and outside their organisations. Such protection allows teachers to spend their time and energies on teaching and learning. In the case of principals, 'outside' buffering entails behaviours such as running interference with unreasonable parents, supporting teachers in the discipline of students, and aligning government and district policy initiatives with the school's improvement.

In schools which recognise the importance of how students spend their time, school schedules, timetables, structures, administrative behaviours, instructional practices and the like, are all designed to ensure that students are engaged in meaningful learning for as much of their time in school as possible. Distractions from meaningful learning are minimised. The key to successful leadership, in the case of instructional time, is to help ensure that the day-to-day functioning of the school conspires to focus everyone's efforts on desirable student learning. Indeed, optimising instructional time, increasing academic press and improving the school's disciplinary climate are interdependent leadership initiatives.

The family path

It is often claimed that improving student learning is all about improving 'instruction' (Nelson and Sassi, 2005; Stein and Nelson, 2003). While improving instruction is both important and necessary work in many schools, this claim, by itself, ignores all of the powerful variables found on both the emotional and organisational paths described in two of the earlier sections of the chapter. Even more critically, this claim seems to dismiss factors accounting for as much as 50 per cent of the variation in student achievement across schools (for example, Kyriakides and Creemers, 2008). These are variables located on the family path. Since best estimates suggest that everything schools do within their walls accounts for about 20 per cent of the variation in students' achievement (for example, Creemers and Reetzigt, 1996), influencing variables on the family path is a 'high leverage' option for school leaders.

Selecting the most promising variables

Treating as many variables as possible on the family path as alterable rather than given was considered to be the new work of leaders more than 15 years ago (Goldring and Rallis, 1993). By now, there is considerable evidence about what these variables might be. For example, Hattie's (2009) synthesis of evidence points to seven family-related variables with widely varying effect sizes. At least four of these variables are open to influence from the school, including home environment (d = 0.57), parent involvement in school (d = 0.51), time spent watching television (d = −0.18) and visits to the home by school personnel (d = 0.29).

Leithwood and Jantzi's (2006) synthesis of 40 studies points to the important influence on children's academic success of family work habits, academic guidance and support provided to children, stimulation to think about issues in the larger environment, provision of adequate health and nutritional conditions, and physical settings in the home conducive to academic work. Perhaps most important are the academic and occupational aspirations and expectations for children (for example, Hong and Ho, 2005) of parents, guardians and other significant members of their immediate community; Hattie reports an effect size of 0.58 for parent expectations which, as he notes, 'was far greater than parental involvement at the school (d = 0.21)' (2009: 69).

Influencing selected variables

Although parent involvement in school has far less impact on student learning than parent influence in the home, children benefit from their parents' engagement in their learning in both locations (Epstein, 1995). Evidence from Leithwood and Jantzi's (2006) review indicates that parent engagement in school is nurtured when parents come to understand that such involvement is a key part of what it means to be a responsible parent, when parents believe they have the skills and know-how to make meaningful contributions to the school's efforts and when they believe that school staffs, as well as their own children, value their participation in the school. School leaders and their staffs contribute to such beliefs by, for example:

- issuing invitations for parent participation that are personal and specific rather than general
- matching parent skills to the activities in which they will participate
- providing very specific information and feedback to parents about their child's progress
- creating opportunities for parents to interact with one another about school matters
- designing their classroom activities to include special projects which involve parents in direct support of instruction requiring skills well-matched to parents' capacities
- communicating effectively with parents, for example, by altering schedules to accommodate the schedules of parents, modifying the format of parent conferences to make them less intimidating and more meaningful for parents, providing a private environment in which to have parent–teacher conferences, soliciting parent views on key matters concerning their children's education and engaging in joint problem-solving with parents
- appointing a community liaison person as a link between the parents and the school in order to build both teacher and parent capacity to communicate with one another.

Parent involvement in their children's education at home can take many forms, as Hattie's (2009) synthesis suggests. But some families have far more resources than others to be involved in productive ways. Families facing poverty, linguistic and cultural diversity, unemployment and housing instability typically have considerable difficulty finding those resources.

One of the most common forms is engagement with young children in learning to read. A recent synthesis of evidence about alternative ways in which parents might help their children learn to read (Senechal and Young, 2008) found that approaches in which either parent or child were relatively passive were of little value. Children's reading improved when parents actively taught their children how to read using a variety of techniques well known to teachers of reading. Of course, many parents will not have opportunities to learn such active forms of reading instruction unless the school intervenes. This would also be something that in most schools would require principal initiative.

Alignment of leadership influence across paths

While variables associated with each of the four paths are distinct, they also interact with variables on the other paths; our previous account of variables on several paths pointed to several examples of such interaction. Typically, failure to take such interaction into account severely limits school leaders' influence. This means, for example, that if a school leader decides to improve the status of a school's academic press (a variable on the rational path), she will also need to consider what her teachers' feelings will be, in response. The leader will need to ensure that her teachers begin to feel, for example, efficacious about their role in fostering the school's academic press (a variable on the emotional path). Such nurturing of teacher efficacy may take the form of establishing a teacher work team with responsibility for planning how to improve the school's academic press (the organisational path). Participation on such a work team will provide teachers with opportunities to design strategies for improving academic press which they consider to be realistic. It may also provide them with the chance to think through their parents' reactions to this initiative (the family path) and how best to build parent support for it.

The need for alignment across paths initially seems to hugely complicate leaders' work. But, as our academic press example illustrates, picking only one or two powerful variables (such as academic press) on a path and planning for the most likely interactions makes the leadership task much more manageable. This way of thinking about the leadership task, however, does add weight to the argument that leaders' success will typically depends on devoting one's attention to a small number for priorities.

Aside from its surface reasonableness, the case for alignment of leadership influence across paths can be justified on both historical and theoretical grounds. From a historical perspective, at some point over the past six decades reformers have considered selected interventions on each of the four paths independently to be the solution to problems of student underachievement, and each has been found wanting. Post-Sputnik efforts to reform curriculum and instruction exemplified a preoccupation with the rational path but to little apparent effect. Disappointed reformers then began a journey along the emotional path, the most visible manifestation of which was the organisational development (OD) movement of the 1980s and its efforts to improve working relationships in schools and districts. With OD's failure to live up to expectations, reformers switched to the organisational path during the late 1980s and early 1990s, setting off a wave of school restructuring which appeared to make little difference to student learning. Previous examples of efforts to exercise influence on the family path include both the community school and full-service school movements.

Theoretical justification for the alignment of leadership influence across paths can be found in an explanation of human performance originating in industrial psychology (O'Day, 1996; Rowan, 1996). What teachers do, according to this theory, is a function of their motivations (addressed by the emotional path), abilities (found on the rational path) and the situations in which they work (the organisational and family paths). The relationships among these variables are considered to be interdependent. This means two things. It means that each variable has an effect on the remaining two (for example, aspects of teachers' work environments are significant influences on their motivations). It also means that changes in all three variables need to happen more or less in concert or performance will not change much. For example, neither high ability and low motivation, nor high motivation and low ability foster high levels of teacher performance; neither does high ability and high motivation in a dysfunctional work environment. Furthermore, a dysfunctional work setting will likely depress initially high levels of both ability and motivation.

Conclusion

This chapter has been firmly rooted in evidence about those features of classrooms, schools, and the wider environment, which make practically significant contributions to student learning. It has proposed a way for leaders to think about and plan their work so that the majority of their efforts have the consequences they wish for their students. On the assumption that leaders' effects on students are indirect, the chapter has identified a large sample of variables which do have a direct influence on what students learn. The chapter has explored the results of research about a sub-set of these variables and summarised what can be gleaned from relevant research about how successful leaders influence the status of these powerful variables.

Organised around 'four paths', the evidence reflected in this chapter implicitly rejects narrow conceptions of instructional leadership as far too simplistic a view of how school leaders in heads' or principals' positions can improve education in their organisations. Indeed, this evidence indicates quite clearly that improvements to many variables other than teachers' instructional practices stand at least as good a if not better, chance of improving student learning as do improvements to such practices.

This is not to dismiss efforts to improve teachers' instructional practices; such efforts will be very important in some schools for some purposes. It does acknowledge, however, that improvements at the margins of what already good teachers are doing cannot be expected to produce large gains in student achievement, and that principals or heads need to delegate much of the work of improving classroom instruction to others, since they are typically the only people in schools in a position to stimulate improvements to most of the other powerful variables on the four paths leading to improved student learning.

Principals' work has been described as hectic, fast paced and relentless. In response to the wide array of functions they must ensure their schools perform, along with the demands for attention from teachers, students, parents, governing bodies and governments, it is easy to lose track of what actually influences student learning. The four paths and the variables demonstrably influencing student learning on each path serve as reminders about what ought to be given priority if the main responsibility of principals is to be fulfilled.

Further reading

Goddard, R. (2003) 'Relational networks, social trust, and norms: a social capital perspective on students' chance of academic success', *Educational Evaluation and Policy Analysis*, 25(1): 59–74.

Leithwood, K. and Beatty, B. (2007) *Leading with Teacher Emotions in Mind*. Thousand Oaks, CA: Corwin.

Notes

1. Effect size (ES or d) is any of several measures of association or of the strength of a relation (for example, Pearson's *r* or eta) and is often thought of as a measure of practical significance (Vogt, 1999). Also see Cohen (1988).
2. In schools with strong academic press, administrators and teachers set high but achievable school goals and classroom academic standards. They believe in the capacity of their students to achieve and encourage their students to respect and pursue academic success. School administrators supply resources, provide structures and exert leadership influence. Teachers make appropriately challenging academic demands and provide quality instruction to attain these goals. Students value these goals, respond positively, and work hard to meet the challenge.

3. In the last couple of decades, there has been a shift in the focus of research on discipline from individual students to the school. Willms and Ma (2004) argue that the traditional way of dealing with discipline, mainly at the classroom level, seems insufficient and that the disciplinary climate of the classroom and school has important effects on students. This climate is shaped by features of schools and the larger community. For example, classroom disruption can be a direct reflection of the conflict or tension between teachers and students across the school as a whole.

References

Alig-Mielcarek, J.M. (2003) 'A model of school success: instructional leadership, academic press, and student achievement', unpublished doctoral dissertation. Ohio State University, Columbus, OH.

Bandura, A. (1993) 'Perceived self efficacy in cognitive development and functioning', *Educational Psychologist*, 28(2): 117–48.

Benda, S.M. (2000) 'The effect of leadership styles on the disciplinary climate and culture of elementary schools', unpublished doctoral dissertation. Widener University, PA.

Bryk, A.S. and Schneider, B. (2003) 'Trust in schools: a core resource for school reform', *Educational Leadership*, 60(6): 40–4.

Carroll, J. (1963) 'A model of school learning', *Teachers College Record*, 64: 723–33.

Cohen, J. (1988) *Statistical Power Analysis for the Behavioral Sciences*. 2nd edn. Hillsdale, NJ: Erlbaum.

Cohen, M.D. (1996) 'Individual learning and organizational routine', in M.D. Cohen and L.S. Sproull (eds), *Organizational Learning*. Thousand Oaks, CA: Sage. pp. 188–202.

Corbett, H.D. and Rossman, G.B. (1989) 'Three paths to implementing change: a research note', *Curriculum Inquiry*, 19(2): 163–90.

Creemers, B.P.M. and Reezigt, G.J. (1996) 'School level conditions affecting the effectiveness of instruction', *School Effectiveness and School Improvement*, (7): 197–228.

Epstein, J. (1995) 'School/family partnerships: caring for the children we share', *Phi Delta Kappan*, 76(9): 701–12.

Goddard, R. (2003) 'Relational networks, social trust, and norms: a social capital perspective on students' chance of academic success', *Educational Evaluation and Policy Analysis*, 25(1): 59–74.

Goddard, R., Hoy, W.K. and Woolfolk Hoy, A. (2000) 'Collective teacher efficacy: Its meaning, measure and impact on student achievement', *American Educational Research Journal*, 37(2): 479–507.

Goddard, R.D., Tschannen-Moran, M. and Hoy, W.K. (2001) 'A multi-level examination of the distribution and effects of teacher trust in students and parents in urban elementary schools', *Elementary School Journal*, 101(1): 3–19.

Goldring, E.B. and Rallis, S.F. (1993) *Principals of Dynamic Schools: Taking Charge of Change*. Newbury Park, CA: Corwin.

Goleman, D. (1995) *Emotional Intelligence*. New York: Bantam Books.

Hattie, J. (2009) *Visible Learning: A Synthesis of Over 800 Meta-analyses Relating to Achievement*. London: Routledge.

Hong, S. and Ho, H. (2005) 'Direct and indirect longitudinal effects of parental involvement on student achievement: Second-order latent growth modeling across ethnic groups', *Journal of Education Psychology*, 97(1): 32–42.

House, E. (1981) 'Three perspectives on innovation: technological, political, and cultural', in R. Lehming and M. Kane (eds), *Improving Schools: Using What We Know*. Beverly Hills, CA: Sage. pp. 17–41.

House, E. and McQuillan, P. (1998) 'Three perspectives on school reform', in A. Hargreaves, A. Lieberman, M. Fallan and B.W. Hepken (eds), *International Handbook of Educational Change*. Dordrecht: Kluwer. pp. 198–213.

Jacob, J.A. (2004) 'A study of school climate and enabling bureaucracy in select New York City public elementary schools', unpublished doctoral dissertation. University of Utah, Salt Lake City, UT.

Jurewicz, M.M. (2004) 'Organizational citizenship behaviors of middle school teachers: a study of their relationship to school climate and student achievement', unpublished doctoral dissertation. College of William and Mary, Williamsburg, VA.

Kyriakides, L. and Creemers, B.P.M. (2008) 'Using a multidimensional approach to measure the impact of classroom-level factors upon student achievement: a study testing the validity of the dynamic model', *School Effectiveness and School Improvement*, 19(2): 183–205.

Lee, V.E. and Croninger, R.G. (1994) 'The relative importance of home and school in the development of literacy skills for middle-grade students', *American Journal of Education*, 102(3): 286–329.

Leithwood, K. (2006) *Teacher Working Conditions that Matter: Evidence for Change*. Toronto: Elementary Teachers' Federation of Ontario.

Leithwood, K. and Beatty, B. (2007) *Leading with Teacher Emotions in Mind*. Thousand Oaks, CA: Corwin.

Leithwood, K. and Jantzi, D. (2006) *A Critical Review of the Parent Engagement Literature*. Toronto: Ontario Ministry of Education.

Leithwood, K. and Jantzi, D. (2008) 'Linking leadership to student learning: the role of collective efficacy', *Educational Administration Quarterly*, 44(4): 496–528.

Leithwood, K., Seashore Louis, K., Anderson, S. and Wahlstrom, K. (2004) *How Leadership Influences Student Learning: A Review of Research for the Learning from Leadership Project*. New York: Wallace Foundation.

Ma, X. and Klinger, D.A. (2000) 'Hierarchical linear modeling of student and school effects on academic achievement', *Canadian Journal of Education*, 25(1): 41–55.

Marburger, D.R. (2006) 'Does mandatory attendance improve student performance?', *Journal of Economic Education*, 37(2): 148–55.

Nelson, B. and Sassi, A. (2005) *The Effective Principal: Instructional Leadership for High Quality Learning*. New York: Teachers College Press.

O'Day, J. (1996) 'Incentives and student performance', in S. Fuhrman and J. O'Day (eds), *Rewards and Reform: Creating Educational Incentives that Work*. San Francisco, CA: Jossey-Bass.

Oatley, K., Keltner, D. and Jenkins, J.M. (2006) *Understanding Emotions*. 2nd edn. Malden, MA: Blackwell.

Robinson, V.M. (in press) 'From instructional leadership to leadership capabilities: Empirical findings and methodological challenges', *Leadership and Policy in Schools*.

Roby, D.E. (2004) 'Research on school attendance and student achievement: a study of Ohio schools', *Educational Research Quarterly*, 28(1): 3–14.

Rolheiser-Bennett, C. and Anderson, S. (1991–92) 'Administrative support of cooperative learning: converging paths to implementation', *Journal of Research for School Executives*, 1(Winter): 84–92.

Rowan, B. (1996) 'Standards as incentives for instructional reform', in S.H. Fuhrman and J.J. O'Day (eds), *Rewards and Reform: Creating Educational Incentives that Work*. San Francisco, CA: Jossey-Bass.

Senechal, M. and Young, L. (2008) 'The effects of family literacy interventions on children's acquisition of reading from kindergarten to grade 3: a meta-analytic review', *Review of Educational Research*, 78: 880–907.

Stein, M.K. and Nelson, B.S. (2003) 'Leadership content knowledge', *Educational Evaluation and Policy Analysis*, 25(4): 423–48.

Tornroos, J. (2005) 'Mathematics textbooks, opportunity to learn and student achievement studies', *Studies in Educational Evaluation*, 31: 315–27.

Tschannen-Moran, M. and Barr, M. (2004) 'Fostering student achievement: the relationship between collective teacher efficacy and student achievement', *Leadership and Policy in Schools*, 3(3): 189–209.

Vogt, W.P. (1999) *Dictionary of Statistics and Methodology: A Nontechnical Guide for the Social Sciences*. 2nd edn. Thousand Oaks, CA: Sage.

Wang, J. (1998) 'Opportunity to learn: the impacts and policy implications', *Educational Evaluation and Policy Analysis*, 20(3): 137–56.

Willms, J.D. and Ma, X. (2004) 'School disciplinary climate: Characteristics and effects on eighth grade achievement', *Alberta Journal of Educational Research*, 50(2): 169–88.

Yukl, G. (1994) *Leadership in Organizations*. 3rd edn. Englewood Cliffs, NJ: Prentice-Hall.

Zaccaro, S.J., Kemp, C. and Bader, P. (2004) 'Leader traits and attributes', in J. Antonakis, A.T. Cianciolo and R. J. Sternberg (eds), *The Nature of Leadership*. Thousand Oaks, CA: Sage. pp. 101–24.

CHAPTER 3

Leading with Moral Purpose: The Place of Ethics[1]

Paul T. Begley

In recent years there has been a dramatic increase in the amount of attention directed to the consideration of ethics as an influence on educational leadership and management, by both academics and educational practitioners. This trend appears to be driven by a number of forces, but most notably the increasing diversity of our communities. One of the most obvious outcomes of increasing cultural diversity in our communities is a broader range of social values, some of which are not compatible with each other, and a subsequent increase in the frequency of culturally based value conflicts that require attention. A second social condition that has highlighted the need to consider ethics is the revolutionising effects of several technological innovations. The Internet has radically changed our access to and use of information. For example, issues of copyright have become a very common problem. Bullying, a classic issue in schools, has now taken on new forms as cyber-bullying. Economic forces associated with globalisation have also become associated with a number of high-profile scandals occurring in several countries where significant lapses in professional ethics on the part of individuals and organisations have created huge hardships for the general population. The global market collapse that occurred in the latter part of 2008 is just the latest, if not grandest, example of persistent and troubling challenges to the well-being and survival of our society that can be at least partly explained as the outcomes of unethical actions.

Social circumstances such as those discussed above seem to have triggered a perceived need among educational administrators to reacquaint themselves with basic ethical principles and the purposes of education. Although it has become popular, especially in North America, to apply corporate values to educational processes, three broad and relatively transcending purposes have been traditionally associated with education. Although various terms may be used to describe these purposes, they generally focus on three areas – aesthetic purposes, economic purposes and ideological purposes (Hodgkinson, 1991). The basic premise of this chapter is that effective as well as moral school leaders need to keep the fundamental purposes of education at the forefront of their administrative practices. Whether articulated as leadership for moral literacy, ethical leadership practices or leadership with moral purpose, the common foundation is purpose-driven educational leadership.

Leading with moral purpose

School leaders in many countries currently confront as a normal condition of their work a veritable quagmire of reform initiatives, curricular innovations and policy dictates. This has become a defining characteristic of educational leadership in many sectors of the world. Given the dynamics of these multiple social and professional expectations for schools, it has become more necessary than ever for school administrators to fall back on basic principles and the fundamental purposes of education – as they exist traditionally and as they are currently interpreted in locally relevant contextual settings. Using these ethical postures as guidelines is probably the soundest way for school leaders to critically deconstruct the edu-babble they regularly encounter, respond effectively to trendy initiatives and perhaps even help to defuse those assaults on the teaching profession that have become so common to education.

Unfortunately, this clearly good advice for leaders is often ignored. When educational administrators carry out their roles without explicit reference to educational purposes, they run the risk of directing their energy to inappropriate or wasteful tasks, and become more vulnerable to manipulation and exploitation by individuals, organisations and special interest groups bent on pursuing their self-interests. Indeed, one of the most common failings observable among educational leaders today is a failure to adequately distinguish between means and ends. Are standardised test scores best thought of as a means or an end? When leaders manage the operation of educational programmes in their schools – a traditional notion of instructional leadership in many countries, is this attending to a means or an end? Even venerable and seemingly inviolate notions like child-centred or learner-centred education might be best thought of as a means to an educational end rather than some sort of absolute objective, particularly if the educational focus is on the individual child rather than children in the more global sense. Moreover, in the practitioner world it often seems that every educational innovation that comes along is touted as some sort of unquestioned end of education. Obviously, they cannot all be that important, and one of the best ways for educational leaders to navigate these perennial challenges is to keep their professional goals and purposes at the forefront of their administrative practices.

The purposes of education

Hodgkinson (1991) provides an insightful and comprehensive exploration of the special purposes of education. He does so by examining the historical roots of each category of educational purpose. He traces aesthetic purposes back to the humanistic traditions of Greece – a focus on the formation of character and the subsequent notions of a classic liberal education. Applied to modern education practices in many countries in recent decades, a concern with aesthetic purposes has become associated with progressive education and focused by notions like student self-esteem, personal fulfilment of the individual, and lifelong learning. There is also a curricular tradition that most clearly associates with aesthetic purposes. It is that of transformational learning with its emphasis on synthesis and reapplication of learning and personal transcendence (Miller and Seller, 1995).

The economic purposes of education, according to Hodgkinson (1991), can be traced back to the influence of the Romans. Learning to earn is a simple but accurate way to conceptualise the economic purposes in education. The Romans were apparently the first to promote the notion of professional accreditation in the sense that has become so common to our societies today. For example, a centurion might have been expected to successfully complete particular training to become qualified for that military role in the same way we do today with aircraft pilots, doctors, lawyers, yoga instructors and perhaps even kindergarten graduates. The curricular tradition that aligns best with the economic purposes of education is a transactional orientation to learning. If it is accurate to say that teachers have a bias towards the aesthetic purposes of education, then it is parents, the media and business leaders that tend to champion the primacy of economic purposes in education today. Yet economic purposes, as much as aesthetic purposes, remain an important priority for school leadership.

The ideological or socialisation functions of education represent perhaps the most basic of educational purposes. This third broad purpose is normally associated with notions of citizenship and social skills. During the early days of North American settlement, or any newly developing region of the world, it is not hard to imagine parents being highly motivated to quickly establish schools so their children can learn what they need to know to function in society, comply with the norms of society, and contribute to the well-being of their communities. Moreover, this is one of the most powerful ways for a society to pass on its norms and standards of conduct to succeeding generations of citizens. Other smaller-scale manifestations of ideological purposes in modern schooling might include an anti-racism curriculum, the promotion of tolerance for cultural diversity, and notions of environmental responsibility. The curricular tradition that most closely aligns with ideological purposes of education is the transmission mode of curriculum – the direct transfer of knowledge and skill to the learner, the filling of the empty vessel.

Examining the educational mission statements produced by many school districts typically reveals the implicit if not explicit presence of all three of these purposes of education, albeit with the usual culturally driven ebb and flow of emphasis from district to district and region to region across time. To this extent the purposes of educational leadership can become codified and made accessible to professional educators as a mandate. However, a balanced education can be defined in terms of how well all three purposes have been accommodated as part of the educational experience of each child. Too much emphasis on one purpose can compromise the overall educational experience of learners. For example, consider the current preoccupation in many countries, but especially the USA, with standardised testing. These circumstances are widely understood as having narrowed the curriculum to a transactional relationship between learner and educator. In particular, the arts have been discounted in favour of the sciences. This illustrates a disturbing trend in a diverse range of countries towards an overemphasis on economic purposes and transactional curriculum at the expense of the more transformational agendas of aesthetic learning, and the social interaction skills associated with ideological literacy. Nevertheless, even at the best of times, the purposes of education are somewhat fluid and dynamic, the emphasis and balance shifting with time and circumstances. Yet, they require a balanced presence.

Otherwise educational purposes can be skewed by loud, persistent or powerful voices as the emphasis among purposes cycles through alternating periods of conservatism and liberalism.

Sorting out terminology: morals, values and ethics

Before getting into a full-blown discussion of leadership with moral purpose, it is important to sort out a few terms. Depending on the country and scholarly context, terms like 'morals', 'values' and 'ethics' are often used interchangeably – to the chagrin of classically trained philosophers and the confusion of graduate students and practitioners. For the purposes of this chapter the terms will be defined and differentiated from each other.

The term 'values' can be thought of as the umbrella term within which other specialised forms of values can be subsumed. Values can be formally defined as conceptions of the desirable with motivating force characteristic of individuals, groups, organisations and societies that influence choices made from available resources and means (Hodgkinson, 1978). Begley (2006) describes the influence of values within individuals as the internal psychological reflections of more distilled levels of motivation (for example, a concern for personal interests, consequences or consensus) that become tangible to an observer in the form of attitudes, speech and actions. Thus, values in their various forms, including ethics, can be thought of as conscious or unconscious influences on attitudes, actions and speech. However, it is important to note that valuation processes can involve more than ethics. Values can take different forms and can be best categorised according to their motivational grounding.

Ethics, as a particular form of values, as opposed to the study of ethics as a scholarly discipline, are normative social ideals or codes of conduct usually grounded in the cultural experience of particular societies. In that sense they are a sort of *uber* form of social consensus. For example, many societies have core ethics equivalent to the American notions of democracy, freedom of speech and the priority of individual rights. Those of us steeped in the traditions of such classic Western philosophical thought can easily make the mistake of assuming that our most cherished ethical postures, such as democracy, are universal. However, they seldom are, especially as interpreted from culture to culture. Ethics in their purest forms tend to be expressed in a relatively context-stripped form that conveys only the essence of the normative behaviour. Indeed, in some forms and social applications they can be, and often are, treated as absolute values. This inclination to view ethics as some sort of absolute value is sometimes inappropriately enabled by evidence of consensus across cultures on certain ethical postures like respect for human rights, honesty and democracy. And, indeed, there are probably some ethics of the human condition that approach a condition of universal relevance. However, the devil is literally in the details when it comes to ethical postures. The interpretation of meaning associated with an ethic can vary greatly from society to society. Simply pondering the contrasting notions of what constitutes democracy in countries like Sweden, the USA and China illustrates this point. Except perhaps in the most culturally homogeneous of contexts, using ethical postures as a basis for making social choices requires the inclusion of a dialogic component. This is not to argue against the relevance and importance of ethics to leadership actions. It is more a caveat to their proper use.

There are other issues when it comes to ethics and their relevance to educational leadership processes. Human behaviour involves a range of motivational bases, only a few of which can be associated with ethical postures. These other motivational bases can range from self-interest to a concern for rationalised positions grounded in consensus or consequences, not just the transrational groundings of ethical postures (Begley, 2006; Hodgkinson, 1978). The point is that because ethical postures are usually associated with ideal states, they do not necessarily accommodate the full range of motivations for human behaviour. This circumstance is critically important to individuals in leadership positions seeking to understand their own motivational bases as well as those of others. It hardly needs to be said that not all individuals encountered in organisational settings act in ethical ways. Ethics-based postures are highly relevant for guiding appropriate responses to complex organisational situations, but they may not be sufficient in themselves for a comprehensive analysis and understanding of human motivations.

For the purposes of this chapter, the term 'ethics' is used to signify a specific category of values – those that are trans-rational in nature, usually normatively grounded in a particular cultural context and taking the form of statements of basic principle expressed in abstract and context-stripped forms. A final key term is 'moral'. This term is properly associated with a situated or context-specific form of values. Moral actions are values-justified actions. Moral actions usually occur in a specific context. Morals are values in an applied form. More discussion of motivational bases and value types follows in a later section addressing the valuation processes of leaders.

Scholarly perspectives on moral leadership

In an educational administration context, moral purposes are generally brought to bear as leaders make decisions, manage people or resources and generally provide leadership within their organisations. In contrast, scholars approach the study of valuation processes and ethics from a variety of distinct foundational perspectives. For example, Starratt's work (1994) is grounded in philosophy, whereas Shapiro and Stefkovich, (2001, 2005); Stefkovich, (2006); Stefkovich and Shapiro, (2003) are influenced by a legal perspective. Gross and Shapiro (2004) reflect a social justice orientation in their work. Langlois's (2004) orientations are applied ethics and moral theory. Begley's orientations (2004) are on the cognitive processes of administrators engaged in problem-solving. Other seminal sources on the subject, from which many of these more recent perspectives derive, include: Hodgkinson's (1978, 1991, 1996) extensive writings on the philosophy of administration; Evers's (Evers and Lakomski, 1991) Australian pragmatist discourse on brain theory, coherence and the formation of ethical knowledge; and Willower's (1994, 1999) Deweyian naturalistic notions of valuation processes and reflective practice.

Beyond the potentially confusing range of foundational perspectives evident among scholars, ethical postures and frameworks are typically presented as abstract concepts stripped of any of the contextual details that would give them relevance and specificity in particular settings and in support of particular roles. This can result in a number of problems in practice. The most obvious problem is that an ethic stripped of context requires interpretation as it is applied to a particular social or cultural context. This can become a serious challenge in culturally diverse societies where, for example, headgear (for example, a Sikh turban) is sometimes more than just a hat, or daggers are religious symbols and not as much a weapon. In application, these fundamental purposes, and indeed any ethical posture, can be thought of as context-stripped statements of principle. For this reason, in application, and especially by practitioners, ethical postures often take on more specific forms as they are interpreted for particular educational contexts. This is an important point that illustrates how application of any ethic occurs within a normative and cultural context. Consider how a 'focus on mission' as a professional ethical posture would mean radically different things to a school principal as compared to an infantry officer. For the school principal it is clearly a 'means', whereas for the army officer mission completion is the objective. Furthermore, human nature being what it is, individuals, groups and societies are often inclined to interpret ethics or principles in ways that are consistent with their preferences and traditions rather than any commitment to the social inclusion of minorities. These interpretations can often extend to preserving self-interests at the expense of the freedom of others. If the moral deliberation is being carried out by a person in a professional role, the process becomes even more complicated because professionals are also expected to be agents of society or of their profession. So, their pursuit of ethical practice or leadership with moral purpose must involve more than addressing their own belief systems.

Practitioners tend to be attracted to practicality and relevance. By their nature, philosophically based discussions about ethics and valuation processes may not be very appealing in terms of relevance because of the context-stripped manner in which they are usually portrayed. For example, the ethics of administration, as proposed by Strike et al. (1998), identify maximising benefits and respecting individual rights through protocols of due process as key notions associated with an ethic of justice perspective. However, the task of clarifying the inherent benefits associated with a situation, and the fair distribution of benefits among an a priori identified set of potential recipients sorted according to degree of entitlement and need, is something that requires contextual knowledge as well as skill. For these reasons, there is a lot of merit in speaking of ethical actions within a specific professional context or through the use of heuristic applications of ethical postures appropriate to a professional or personal context.

Several examples of these heuristic applications can be drawn from the literature as illustrations. Furman (2003) uses the 'ethic of community' as a focus point for ethical educational practice in North American schools. Stefkovich (2006; Stefkovich and Shapiro, 2003) adopts the notion of best interests of students as a focus for her professional ethics in education. Begley (2006) speaks of authentic leadership as an approach to presenting ethical leadership practices and moral literacy in a manner that has relevance for people working in school leadership situations. Authentic leadership, as Begley defines it, is the outcome of self-knowledge, sensitivity to the orientations of others, and a technical sophistication that leads to a synergy of leadership action (Begley, 2001, 2003, 2006). However, all of these context-grounded heuristic applications require definition and the establishment of consensus on meaning. Fortunately, there is literature that can be helpful in this regard. Stefkovich and Begley (2007) and Stefkovich and O'Brien (2004) have identified and explored the various meanings associated with the concept of 'best interests'.

Similarly, 'authentic leadership' is a perspective that has been explored in recent years by several other scholars beyond this author. Other scholars who have adopted this term include Taylor (1991), Duignan and Bhindi (1997) and Starratt (2004).

Alternate ethical paradigms: critique, care, justice, profession and community

The complexity of social and administrative situations makes it attractive for school leaders to employ processes to aid their inter-pretation and structuring of situations, but this must be done in socially and culturally sensitive ways. For example, Shapiro and Stefkovich (2005) espouse the application of a multi-ethical analytical approach to the interpretation of ethical dilemmas as a way to improve or ensure the quality of decision-making. The key ethical orientations suggested by these scholars include the ethic of justice, the ethic of critique, the ethic of care and a hybrid multi-dimensional model, the ethic of profession.

Although Shapiro and Stefkovich propose the use of multiple ethical lenses as a basis for responding to the dilemmas of school leadership, they stop short of proposing any particular sequence for applying those ethics. Their research suggests that individuals vary in their preferred ethical postures and are satisfied with espousing that administrators adopt a multi-ethical analysis of problems and situations. For example, a school principal respond-ing to an ethical dilemma might prefer, in the sense of a *personal* inclination that is the outcome of their social formation, to gravi-tate towards the application of an ethic of care. In contrast, Begley (2006) argues that in the *professional* context of school leadership, where the individual is essentially an agent of society, there is probably an implied sequence for the appropriate application of these classic Western ethical lenses. Begley argues that there is a professionally appropriate sequence for the application of these ethical lenses in a school leadership situation. Beginning with the ethic of critique is justified in order to name and understand as much as possible the alternate perspectives applicable to a situa-tion, especially those of minorities and individuals otherwise with-out voice or representation. To do otherwise is to risk gravitation to the preferred cultural orientations of the leader or the main-stream orientations of a given cultural group. The ethic of care can naturally follow in the sequence as a way to keep the focus of the process on people and their best interests rather than an overly quick gravitation towards organisational imperatives or policies. Using the ethic of care, one can assess the capacity and responsibility of stakeholders to a situation in a humane way. Finally, once the ethics of critique and care have been used to carefully interpret a situation, the ethic of justice can be applied as a basis for deciding on actions that will maximise benefits for all while respecting the rights of individuals. This is not to suggest a dogmatic adherence to a prescriptive sequence of application for these classic ethics of Western philosophy. In all cases, the sequencing and application of ethical perspectives needs to be very fluid and dynamic as an initial organiser, not a recipe, and as a stimulus for reflection or dialogue, not a prescription. However, the application of any lens to a situation, including ethics, begins the process of highlighting some information as relevant and diminishing or veiling the relevance of other information. School leaders accountable to their communities must take care to interpret situations in a sensitive way.

Leading with moral purpose as valuation

In order to understand the relationship between motivation and values, and between values and moral administrative action, it is helpful to conceptually situate values within the context of one person's being using a simple onion figure. Figure 3.1 (Begley, 2003) is an adaptation of a graphic originally proposed by Christopher Hodgkinson (1978, 1991, 1996).

Beginning from the outside, the first ring represents the observable actions and speech of the individual. Leaders working in professional settings, as well as people in general, intuitively rely on the clues provided by the actions and attitudes of others to derive predictive insights into the nature of the values others hold. This is a sound strategy, but it has the same limits to its reliability in day-to-day life as it does in a research context. Political leaders, principals, teachers, parents and children regularly demonstrate through their speech and actions that their observable actions may or may not be accurate indicators of their underlying values. Individuals often articulate or posture certain values while actually being committed to quite different values. In both the research and the leadership context, the implication is clear. Validity and reliability of interpretation is best enhanced by sustained periods of observation and multiple measures.

The next ring or layer of the figure represents attitudes. Attitudes can be thought of as the membrane between values and the observable

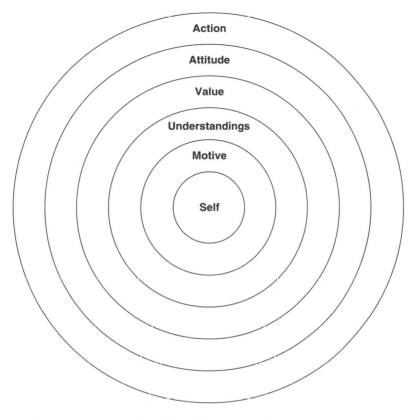

Action

Attitude

Value

Understandings

Motive

Self

Figure 3.1 Values syntax (Begley, 2004)

actions or speech of an individual, or the interface between the psychological and physical world. They are the predisposition to act specifically as a result of values or value systems acquired previously and elsewhere (Begley 2001). For example, educators' attitudes towards students encountered in their professional setting may change when they become parents with children of their own. Conversely, when we look across a career, we can see that the values of an individual in one role as a teacher, principal, or professor can readily spill over as attitudes into other social roles. Hodgkinson (1991) also tells us that attitudes can often be detected in the body language of posture, gait or unconscious muscular tensions. These are the outward and visible signs of inner and invisible inclinations.

The next layer represents the actual values held or manifested by an individual. For example, an individual might prefer a glass of beer to a glass of red wine. Another might prefer a chat with friends in the staff lounge to reading the newspaper. Someone may prefer working independently over working in a group. Others may favour a monarchial system of government over a republican system. In an educational context, a principal might gravitate towards relatively controlled approaches to delegating authority over more open styles of distributed leadership. A teacher might prefer computer-mediated instruction to workbook exercises, or instruction individualised to students' needs as opposed to a teacher-centred curriculum. The important thing to keep in mind is that identifying these values is one thing, while knowing why they are held is quite another. Making that latter judgement requires going deeper into the onion.

Between the values layer and motivational base layer of the figure is a category that can be labelled 'available knowledge' or 'understandings'. The kinds of knowledge referenced here are acquired through life experiences, professional training, and reflection, and provide a linkage and context between the motivational bases and the specific values adopted by the individual. An individual responds to basic motivations by adopting particular value positions that will support the fulfilment of that basic motivation in a specific way. These responses are manifested through actions or speech selected by the individual to achieve the valued objective. Of course, people vary in terms of the skills and sophistication they can bring to bear on achieving their objectives. This is generally applicable to all aspects of human enterprise. Consider how an experienced school administrator, motivated as a professional to achieve a complex set of educational objectives, might employ a carefully orchestrated collaborative school improvement project to achieve those educational objectives. By contrast, a less experienced administrator, with the same desire to build consensus among the faculty, but responding to different levels of knowledge or the absence thereof, might naively decide a memo is all that is required to achieve the same objective.

The motivational base layer of the onion figure provides the key to understanding the nature and function of values as influences on leadership. This is the motivating force dimension behind the adoption of a particular value which, working out through the layers of the figure, shapes attitudes and potentially influences subsequent actions. Hodgkinson (1978, 1991, 1996), proposes that there are four basic motivational bases. These are *personal preference* or self-interest; an inclination towards *consensus*; an inclination towards or concern for *consequences*; and an inclination towards trans-rational *ethics or principles*. These four motivational bases are relatively broad and arbitrary distinctions. In application, individuals can manifest a predisposition towards one motivational base over another, or adopt more than one motivational base when responding to a given situation.

The final layer at the centre of the figure is the *self* – the biological self as well as the existential or transcendent self. The following section addresses the formation of the self.

Arenas of leadership as sources of influence, conflicts and identity

In recent decades, school leaders have learned how important it is to lead and manage with proper reference to the broader environmental context of their community. The influences on leadership, decision-making, and education in general can be thought of as coming from multiple social sources. Some of these influences can take on the status of values when they are perceived as conceptions of the desirable with motivating force (Hodgkinson 1991). Unfortunately, our personal values as well of those of the profession, organisation, community and society are not necessarily consistent or compatible with each other. As a result, these influences and values derived from the various arenas of our environment can generate inconsistencies and conflicts. A second onion figure (see Figure 3.2) is used to illustrate these distinctions. These are the interactive environments within which valuation processes and administration occur. They are also the source of personal, professional and social values, as well as the source of many of the conflicts people encounter in life.

Within Figure 3.2, the individual is represented within the centre ring and extending through all the rings. His or her character is the outcome of many transient influences as well as relatively more enduring values acquired from multiple arenas.

The second ring from the centre represents the arena of groups, and other collective entities including family, peers, friends and acquaintances. The third ring, profession, represents a more formal arena of administration that is closely related to the second ring, but is given special emphasis here because of its relevance to the professional context that is the focus of this chapter.

The fourth ring represents the arena traditionally of most concern to academics and practitioners in the field of educational administration, the organisation. Much of the literature of educational administration and most of the corporate literature are grounded within the organisational perspective, adopting it as a primary reference point for administrative activity.

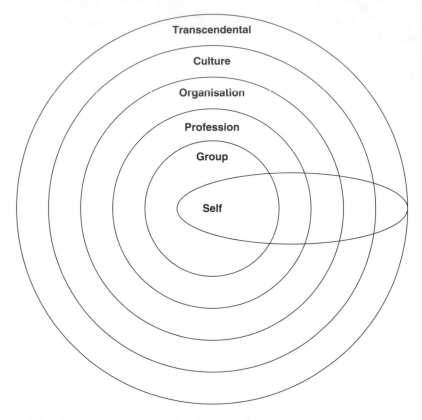

Figure 3.2   Arenas of influence (Begley, 2004)

Moving further outwards in the figure, one encounters the arenas representing the greater community, society, and culture. Within recent decades, school administrators have learned that it is necessary to pay a lot more attention to the community as a relevant administrative arena and source of influence on school leadership (Leithwood et al., 1992). The increasing diversity of our societies and a general trend towards globalisation has highlighted society and culture as relevant arenas of administrative activity.

A final, seventh ring is included to accommodate notions of the transcendental – God, faith, spirituality, even extra-sensory perception. Spirituality is of considerable importance to many individuals, and has begun to attract the attention of more scholars as an important influence on educational leadership. Even administrators who do not subscribe to a spiritual dimension as a source of influence in their own daily lives are well advised to keep this arena in mind, if only because at least some individuals associated with their professional role do. A leader who wants to understand the motivations of those they are supposed to lead will be sensitive to all potentially significant categories of influence.

Practitioner perspectives on leading with moral purpose

Values, ethics and valuation processes relate to moral leadership and educational decision-making processes in several important ways. Perhaps the most fundamental way in which morals, values and ethics relate to leadership is as an influence on the cognitive processes of individuals and groups of individuals. It is important, perhaps essential, for those in leadership roles to understand how values reflect underlying human motivations and shape the subsequent attitudes, speech, and actions of personnel (Begley, 2006; Hodgkinson, 1978; Kohlberg and Turiel, 1971). Begley's conception of authentic forms of leadership (2006) emphasises this capacity as something that begins with self-knowledge and then becomes extended to sensitivity to the perspectives of others. In that context it is argued that leaders should know their own values and ethical predispositions, as well as be sensitive to the value orientations of others. Branson (2006) has developed a very effective instructional strategy, called the deeply structured reflection process, that can be used as a support for developing this kind of knowledge and self-awareness. It involves the identification by individuals of critical incidents that have contributed to their personal or professional formation. Through deconstruction of, and reflection on, personal narratives of critical incidents, individuals develop an awareness of how their motivations, values and attitudes are derived and become predictive indicators of their actions in response to situations they will encounter in the future.

Consistent with this line of thinking, Begley (2006) proposes that genuine forms of leadership begin with the understanding and thoughtful interpretation of observed or experienced valuation processes by individuals. This implies the appropriateness of a focus on the perceptions of individuals in the context of school leadership situations. Although organisational theories, the policy arena and other macro perspectives are relevant as elements of the context in which a school leader works, they are not a primary locus of concern.

A second way in which valuation processes relate to moral leadership practices is as a guide to action, particularly as supports to making decisions and resolving ethical dilemmas. Ethics and valuation models are highly relevant to school leadership as rubrics, benchmarks, socially justified standards of practice and templates for moral action. These may be used by the individual leader or in more collective ways by groups of people. Langlois (2004), to name one scholar, has conducted much research on the ethical dilemma analysis processes of principals and superintendents. A typical application for ethics in this administrative context is as a personal guide to action, particularly as supports to resolving ethical dilemmas. A number of other scholars have also conducted research and published in this area. These include Begley and Johansson (1998), Stefkovich (2006) and Branson (2006). These scholars have each developed well documented processes for the analysis of dilemma situations and development of ethical responses. One of these processes is outlined and discussed in some detail at the conclusion of this chapter and presented as a resource in support of leading with moral purpose.

However, there is a third and more strategic and collective application for ethics in moral leadership processes. It is common in a school or school district setting for ethical postures to be adopted with a strategic organisational intent – for example, as a focus for building consensus around a shared social or organisational objective. To illustrate, a school district superintendent might choose 'ethic of community' (Furman 2003) as a rallying meta-value to focus the energies of personnel on collective action. Or, ethical notions such as 'due process' (Strike et al., 1998) or 'social justice' (Shapiro and Stefkovich, 2005) might be used as the objective for focusing the reform of school district processes in support of students with special needs. These more collective and strategic applications of ethics may very well be the more common manifestation of this value type in the administration of schools and school districts, at the government level, as well as in the corporate sector. In this sense leaders literally use ethics as leadership tools to support actions taken, model ideal practice, and/or promote particular kinds of organisational or societal activity. However, as will be argued, these strategic adoptions of ethical postures may or may not be ethical.

Using ethics versus being ethical

Research findings (for example, Begley and Johansson, 1998) confirm that the relevance of principles or ethics to administrative situations seems to be prompted in the minds of school administrators by particular circumstances. These circumstances include: situations where an ethical posture is socially appropriate (for example, the role of the arts); situations where consensus is perceived as difficult or impossible to achieve (for example, an issue involving ethnic bias); or situations when high stakes and urgency require decisive action (for example, student safety). There is also some evidence to suggest that school leaders use ethics in strategic applications as ways to develop group consensus, and a basis for promoting compliance with minimum need for justifying proof of effects (Langlois, 2004). These are all examples of *ethically sound* – meaning socially justifiable applications of ethics to situations.

One has only to survey the newspaper or work in an organisation or live in a community for a few years to readily detect situations where ethics-based postures can be unethical and socially unjust. Ethical postures may be *unethical* under a number of circumstances: for example, when a cultural ethic is imposed on others, when an ethic is used to justify otherwise reprehensible action, an ethical posture veils a less defensible value or when an ethic is used to trump a basic human right. The implication is that using ethical postures is not always *ethical* action. Such is the nature of ethics when they are adopted as guides to action. Trans-rational values (Hodgkinson, 1978, 1991, 1996) of any sort, and ethics and principles in particular, are rather vulnerable to multiple interpretations in application from one social context to another. When unexamined values are applied in arbitrary ways, they can be anything but ethical. The essential, and often absent, component that makes adherence to a value genuinely ethical is dialogue. For these reasons, unexamined ethics applied in instrumental ways, or values accepted at face value without prior deliberation of meaning, represent a particular category of action that may not be consistent with moral leadership processes. It should be apparent that in order to cultivate the ability to distinguish the difference between using ethics and being ethical, we need the capacity to discriminate actual intentions within ourselves and among others. This is not an argument for moral relativism, nor is it value absolutism, it is an argument for the critical thinking necessary for leading with moral purpose.

How leaders respond to moral dilemmas

Dilemma situations have become common to educational leadership processes in most countries, but especially those communities experiencing increased cultural diversity among their population. The achievement of consensus on educational issues among even traditional educational stakeholders within a single community has become more difficult in many sectors. School administrators increasingly encounter dilemmas or value conflict situations where consensus cannot be achieved, rendering obsolete the traditional rational notions of problem-*solving*. Administrators must now often be satisfied with *responding* to a situation since there may be no solution possible that will satisfy all. Such dilemmas can occur within a single arena of administration or among two or more arenas. The most difficult dilemmas occur when one ethic literally trumps another.

A pilot study conducted during 2004 examined principals' perceptions of, and responses to, the moral dilemmas encountered in the professional context of their roles (Begley, 2005). The data were collected from a sample of principals from Ontario, Canada and Pennsylvania, USA using a survey instrument and follow-up interviews. The data were interpreted through a values framework (Begley, 2006) that is the outcome of an interdisciplinary integration of administrative theory about valuation processes with information processing theory derived from the field of cognitive psychology. The findings from this research provides insights into how school leaders respond to the ethical dilemmas encountered in their professional work.

Theme or context of dilemmas

The dilemmas identified by the principals in this study could be readily grouped according to a number of themes or topics. A surprising number of the dilemmas focused on various forms of educational system policies that were alternately perceived as overly punitive, procedurally rigid, and/or negatively influencing a principal's professional autonomy or expertise and discretion. Another common theme was the principals' overarching desire to do what they perceived to be in the best interests of students. Other themes included conflicts with parents or other community members, dealing with abusive or incompetent professional staff, and risking career or job in the defence of personal moral beliefs.

Sources of dilemma

Begley's (2004) graphic portrayal of the arenas or domains (see Figure 3.2) of administration was employed as a guide to determining the source or sources of the dilemmas presented by the participants. Many of the dilemmas reported by the participants could be readily connected to organisational policies (for example, zero tolerance policies, required reporting of alleged abuse) that reduced the professional discretion of the administrator to make decisions in the best interest of students or the school. The most difficult of situations was perceived to be when the policies are seen as inappropriately punitive or when the student in question had no intention to break a rule or violate policy. Several school leaders also reported dilemmas that clearly revealed conflicts between personal moral positions and those of the profession, school district or community (that is, persistent racial discrimination by administrative colleagues).

Interpersonal versus intra-personal dilemmas

The notion of arenas as a guide for identifying the source of the dilemmas was also useful for assessing whether the dilemmas were interpersonal or intrapersonal; that is, whether the dilemma explicitly involved more than one person or was an essentially internal struggle experienced by one person. In a surprising number of cases, clear evidence suggests that the dilemmas were intrapersonal. School administrators seem much inclined to sort out professional dilemmas on their own, without seeking the opinions and support of others. For the school administrators participating in this study, the dilemmas of practice seem to be viewed as private and personal challenges. Only one principal made reference to actively involving other staff or colleagues in the moral deliberation of the dilemmas encountered in the school.

Guiding meta-values

Most educational leadership literature highlights accountability as a significant influence on school administrators' assessment and interpretation of situations. This apparently quite consistent pattern of response has also been associated with an inclination for school administrators to gravitate towards the rational motivational bases of consequences and consensus. This phenomenon has also been used to explain in part why school administrators often avoid ethics as an explicit guide to decision-making, in preference to more rationally defensible decision processes grounded in consequences or consensus.

The data collected in support of this study about administrative responses to dilemmas both confirm and challenge the pre-eminence of accountability as a meta-value for school principals. Many of the dilemmas cases submitted by the participants do indeed make explicit and/or implicit reference to accountability as an overriding concern. However, there is another equally strong and frequently articulated meta-value that becomes apparent, and that is 'doing what is best for kids' or 'the best interests of students'. As much as accountability may be a primary influence on the general decision-making processes of school administrators, when situations are perceived by administrators to be dilemmas, there appears to be an equally strong inclination to adopt 'students' best interests' as the meta-value of choice.

Strategies for interpretation

The strategies employed by the participants to interpret and respond to the dilemmas of practice they perceived conform fairly well to the findings of research conducted by Roche (1999) based on the practices of principals in Queensland, Australia. His inquiry focused on how school administrators actually respond to moral and ethical dilemmas. He identified four primary ways in which principals respond to moral dilemmas. Predictably, he found that the press for accountability appears to heavily influence such processes. Listed in order of frequency of use by the administrators in Roche's study, the strategies principals used in response to the professional dilemmas they encounter are avoidance, suspended morality, creative insubordination and taking a personal moral stand. Avoidance (reinterpreting the situation so it no longer involves an ethical dimension) is the most frequently employed response among the administrators in the Roche (1999) study. Suspended morality, the second most common strategy, illustrates the ability of administrators to set aside some of their personal value orientations, and consciously respond to situations from a professional or organisational perspective. The third category of response identified by Roche is creative insubordination. As a strategy it is an opposite response to suspended morality. In this case organisational dictates are set aside, or creative approaches to compliance are found, that favour more humane concerns. The taking of a personal moral stand was the least frequently employed response, usually adopted only when the administrator assessed a high likelihood of successfully challenging the competing demands of the profession, organisation or society.

There is evidence of all four of Roche's identified strategies also being used by the respondents in the Begley (2005) study. Appeals to policy as a basis for responding to a situation equate with the avoidance strategy. Many of the dilemmas submitted by the principals conveyed the angst encountered when they felt compelled to suspend their own morality in favour of a professional or organisational

---

Questions to Guide the Moral Analysis of a Situation, Problem or Decision

These questions may be helpful as guides, to be used by individuals or groups, interested in analysing and responding ethically to critical incidents or dilemmas of practice encountered in school leadership situations.

Step 1: Interpretation of the Problem (ethic of critique)

- Who are the **stakeholders?** Are any unrecognised or without voice?
- What **arenas of practice** (self, profession, organisation, community, culture) are relevant?
- Does the conflict exist **within an arena or between two or more**? (for example, personal vs organisational)
- Can the **values in conflict** be named?
- How much **turbulence** are the values in conflict creating? (Degree of risk for structural damage to people, organisations, or community.)

Step 2: Towards a Humane Response (ethic of care)

- What **motivations and degrees of commitment** are apparent among the stakeholders?

Four levels of motivation:

- concerned with self, personal preference, habitual, comfort (sub-rational values grounded in preference)
- concerned with desired outcomes, avoidance of undesirable (rational values grounded in consequences)
- concerned with perceptions of others, consultation, expert opinion (rational values grounded in consensus)
- concerned with ethical postures, first principles, will or faith (trans-rational, no need for rational justification)

- Is the conflict **interpersonal** (among individuals) or **intrapersonal** (within an individual)?
- What are the **human needs**, as opposed to organisational or philosophical standards?

Step 3: Ethical Action (ethic of justice)

- What actions or response would **maximise benefits** for all stakeholders?
- What actions or response would **respect individual rights**?
- Are desired **'ends'** or purposes interfering with the selection of a **'means'** or solution?
- If an **ethical dilemma** exists (a choice between equally unsatisfactory alternatives), how will you resolve it? (Avoidance, Suspended Morality, Creative Insubordination, Taking a Moral Stand)

Figure 3.3   Value audit guidelines (Begley, 2005)

position. A few of the reported dilemmas reveal the intent of the principal to take a public moral stand.

The value audit process: a resource for leading with moral purpose

In an effort to help school leaders develop their capacity to make ethically sound and professionally effective decisions, Begley has developed several versions of a value audit guide that can be used as a resource in support of leadership for moral purpose (see Figure 3.3).

Originally based on a series of value audit questions proposed by Hodgkinson (1991), this resource document has gone through several evolutions and refinements as a result of being used with a succession of groups of school leaders in several countries over several years.

An examination of the version included here will reveal that it incorporates many of the key concepts introduced and discussed in this chapter, including: a sequenced application of the ethics of critique, care and justice; a bias towards careful interpretation before moving to action; and the four motivational bases of valuation by individuals. Begley has used this activity with some success in several countries as a component of graduate-level courses and also as a workshop activity in support of the professional development of principals.

Conclusion: leadership with moral purpose

Complexity, human interaction, and the dynamics of continually evolving social expectations are characteristic of the educational leadership role. Leadership involves management, but management skills are not sufficient. The mediation of competing interests and the fair allocation of scarce resources in support of an increasingly complex educational process necessitates that educational leaders have a clear set of educational purposes and a strong sense of moral purpose. They need to be able to lead, to navigate through multiple and competing interests.

As argued in this chapter, there are historically clear purposes of education. They are multifaceted and therefore complex to manage, but they are nevertheless the socially justified objectives of education in our societies. The mandate is clear and it is an educational one, not a corporate agenda or an economic agenda. The challenge for educational leaders is to keep the aesthetic, economic and ideological purposes of education in the forefront as guides to decision-making and strategic planning. They are the meta-values of the profession. This is nothing less than a purpose-driven approach to morally defensible educational leadership.

Four other key points are made in this chapter. One is that the purposes of educational leadership are the dynamic outcome of influences from several arenas or social domains, not just educational organisations. Secondly, authentic forms of leadership are defined as the outcome of self-knowledge, sensitivity to the perspectives of others, and the technical skills of organisation management and personnel leadership. Thirdly, leading for moral purpose requires a focus on leadership intentions and a commitment to reflective practice, not just the description or emulation of the practices of others. Finally, the increased diversity of society makes necessary an increased awareness of intercultural variations in perceptions and interpretation of leadership purposes. Context makes a big difference. These are the specialised purposes and nature of leadership with moral purpose.

Notes

1. Portions of this chapter are based on material taken with the permission of the publishers from three previously published sources. These sources are: Begley, P.T. and Stefkovich, J. (2007) 'Integrating values and ethics into postsecondary teaching for leadership development: Principles, concepts, and strategies', *Journal of Educational Administration* 45(4): 398–412; Begley, P.T. (2006) 'Self-knowledge, capacity and sensitivity: prerequisites to authentic leadership by school principals', *Journal of Educational Administration*, 44(6): 570–89; and Begley, P.T. (ed.) (2008) *School Leadership in Canada*. 4th edn. Mt St Louis: Paul Begley and Associates.

References

Begley, P.T. (2001) 'In pursuit of authentic school leadership practices', *International Journal of Leadership in Education*, 4(4): 353–66.

Begley, P.T. (2003) 'In pursuit of authentic school leadership practices', in P.T. Begley and O. Johansson (eds), *The Ethical Dimensions of School Leadership*. Dordrecht: Kluwer Academic. pp. 1–12.

Begley, P.T. (2004) 'Understanding valuation processes: exploring the linkage between motivation and action', *International Studies in Educational Administration*, 32(2): 4–17.

Begley, P.T. (2005) 'The dilemmas of leadership: perspectives on the moral literacy of principals from Ontario and Pennsylvania', paper delivered at the Annual Meeting of the American Educational Research Association, Montreal, Quebec, April.

Begley, P.T. (2006) 'Self-knowledge, capacity and sensitivity: prerequisites to authentic leadership by school principals', *Journal of Educational Administration*, 44(6): 570–89.

Begley, P.T. and Johansson, O. (1998) 'The values of school administration: preferences, ethics and conflicts', *The Journal of School Leadership*, 8(4): 399–422.

Branson, C. (2006) 'Effects of structured self-reflection on the development of authentic leadership practices among Queensland primary school principals', *Educational Management Administration and Leadership*, 35(2): 227–48.

Duignan, P. and Bhindi, N. (1997) 'Authentic leadership: an emerging perspective', *Journal of Educational Administration*, 35(3): 195–209.

Evers, C.W. and Lakomski, G. (1991) *Knowing Educational Administration*. Toronto: Pergamon Press.

Furman, G. (2003) 'Moral leadership and the ethic of community', *Values and Ethics in Educational Administration*, 2(1): 1–8.

Gross, S. and Shapiro, J. (2004) 'Using multiple ethical paradigms and turbulence theory in response to administrative dilemmas', *International Studies in Educational Administration*, 32(2): 47–62.

Hodgkinson, C. (1978) *Towards a Philosophy of Administration*. Oxford: Basil Blackwell.

Hodgkinson, C. (1991) *Educational Leadership: The Moral Art*. Albany, NY: SUNY Press.

Hodgkinson, C. (1996) *Administrative Philosophy*. Oxford: Elsevier-Pergamon.

Kohlberg, L. and Turiel, E. (1971) 'Moral development and moral education', in G. Lesser (ed.), *Psychology and Educational Practice*. New York: Scott Foresman. pp. 530–50.

Langlois, L. (2004) 'Making the tough calls: complex decision-making in light of ethical considerations', *International Studies in Educational Administration*, 32(2): 78–93.

Leithwood, K.A., Begley, P.T. and Cousins, J.B. (1992) *Developing Expert Leadership for Future Schools*. London: Falmer Press.

Miller, J. and Seller, W. (1985) *Curriculum: Perspectives and Practice*. New York: Longman.

Roche, K. (1999) 'Moral and ethical dilemmas in Catholic school settings', in P.T. Begley (ed.), *Values and Educational Leadership*. Albany, NY: SUNY Press. pp. 255–72.

Shapiro, J. and Stefkovich, J.A. (2001) *Ethical Leadership and Decision Making in Education*. Mahwah, NJ: Lawrence Erlbaum Associates.

Shapiro, J. and Stefkovich, J.A. (2005) *Ethical Leadership and Decision Making in Education*. 2nd edn. Mahwah, NJ: Lawrence Erlbaum Associates.

Starratt, R.J. (1994) *Building an Ethical School*. London: Falmer Press.

Starratt, R.J. (2004) *Ethical Leadership*. San Francisco, CA: Jossey-Bass.

Stefkovich, J.A. (2006) *Best Interests of the Student: Applying Ethical Constructs to Legal Cases in Education*. Mahwah, NJ: Lawrence Erlbaum Associates.

Stefkovich, J. and Begley, P.T. (2007) 'Conceptualizing ethical school leadership and defining the best interests of students', special issue of *Educational Management and Leadership*, 35(2): 205–26.

Stefkovich, J.A. and O'Brien, G.M. (2004) 'Best interests of the student: an ethical model', *Journal of Educational Administration*, 42(2): 197–214.

Stefkovich, J. and Shapiro, J. (2003) 'Deconstructing communities: Educational leaders and their ethical decision-making processes', in P.T. Begley and O. Johansson (eds), *The Ethical Dimensions of School Leadership*. Dordrecht: Kluwer Academic Press. pp. 89–106.

Strike, K.A., Haller, E.J. and Soltis, J.F. (1998) *The Ethics of School Administration*. 2nd edn. NewYork: Teachers College Press.

Taylor, C. (1991) *The Ethics of Authenticity*. Cambridge, MA: Harvard University Press.

Willower, D.J. (1994) *Educational Administration: Inquiry, Values, Practice*. Lancaster, PA: Technomics.

Willower, D.J. (1999) 'Values and valuation: a naturalistic inquiry', in P.T. Begley (ed.), *Values and Educational Leadership*. Albany, NY: SUNY Press. pp. 121–138.

CHAPTER 4

Distributed Leadership: Evidence and Implications

Alma Harris

Introduction

Distributed leadership, or the expansion of leadership roles in schools, beyond those in formal leadership or administrative posts, represents one of the most influential ideas to emerge in the field of educational leadership (Hallinger and Heck, 2009). The idea of distributed leadership has found favour with researchers, policy-makers, practitioners and educational reformers around the globe (Harris, 2008; Leithwood et al., 2009; Spillane, 2006). Few ideas, it seems, have provoked as much attention, debate and controversy, in the school leadership field, than this particular concept.

It is important to note at the outset that distributed leadership is not an idea devoid of critique. Writes like Hatcher (2005); Fitzgerald and Gunter (2008) and Hargreaves and Fink (2009) have called into question the motivation of those espousing distributed leadership. In their view, distributed leadership is little more than a palatable way of encouraging teachers to do more work, a way of reinforcing standardisation practices. It is simply 'old managerialism' in a contemporary guise. Fitzgerald and Gunter (2008: 335) suggest that teacher leadership, which is closely associated with distributed leadership, 'merely, cements authority and hierarchy whereby leaders monitor teachers and their work to ensure set of predetermined standards are met. They argue that teacher leadership is deeply rooted in neo-liberal versions of the performing school and that it is a management strategy and not a radical alternative'. Those who write about teacher leadership tend not to view it this way and there is little empirical confirmation that distributed leadership is part of some new hegemony. However, it is important not to lose sight of such critical perspectives.

Distributed leadership might appear to be the leadership idea of the moment but its genesis can be traced back to the field of organisational theory in the mid-1960s (Barnard, 1968). While the idea of shared, collaborative or participative leadership is far from new, distributed leadership theory has provided a new lens on a familiar theme. The work of Spillane et al. (2001) has sparked renewed interest in leadership as *practice* focusing particularly on the interactions between leaders, followers and their situation. This work on distributed leadership theory reinforces that there are multiple sources of influence within any organisation and has refocused empirical attention on the 'leader plus' aspect of leadership work (Spillane, 2006: 3).

The current discourse about educational leadership has shifted decidedly towards a focus upon multiple sources of influence (Leithwood and Mascall, 2008). This shift, in part, reflects some disillusionment with individual conceptions of leadership often characterised as the 'great man' theory but it also represents an increasing understanding of the importance of informal sources of influence within organisations. This understanding has been greatly enhanced by distributed leadership theory, which offers a powerful analytical frame for exploring the various ways in which leadership interactions, both formal and informal, occur within a school (Spillane et al., 2001). Research using this theoretical framing has primarily addressed the question of 'who leads when the principal isn't leading' and has highlighted how those without formal roles of responsibilities can be powerful instructional and curriculum leaders (Spillane, 2006; Spillane and Camburn, 2006).

Distributed leadership in theory

Drawing upon social psychology, a distributed perspective on leadership concentrates on the interactions rather than the actions of leaders. Scribner et al. (2007) argue that the success of distributed leadership depends not only on individuals performing different leadership *functions* effectively, but also on new patterns of *interaction and influence* among staff in the school. They frame distributed leadership as social influence where interactions are at the core of leadership practice. How leaders interact is considered to be more important than the nature of their formal leadership roles, responsibilities or functions. While it is important to know what leaders actually do, and there is a great volume of literature on this particular subject, analysing and understanding patterns of influence from a distributed perspective, it is argued, gets closer to the actual practice of leadership.

Leadership is increasingly being seen as an organisational-wide phenomenon where collective or distributed leadership is a contributor to organisational growth and success. From this perspective, it is the nature and the effects of leadership practice that matter. Knowing if, how and in what way distributed leadership practice influences organisational outcomes is at the heart of recent empirical enquiry (Harris, 2009; Leithwood et al., 2009). Contemporary evidence would indicate a positive relationship between distributed leadership, organisational improvement and student achievement (Hallinger and Heck, 2009; Harris, 2008, 2009; Leithwood and Mascall, 2008; Louis et al., 2009). These studies have underlined the importance of distributed leadership as a potential contributor to positive organisational change and improvement. However, these researchers acknowledge that there is more work to be done and that any headlong rush to normative action is probably unwise.

Distributed leadership in practice

Despite the fact that the evidence base about distributed leadership is still emerging, distributed leadership has already been adopted as part of educational reforms in a number of countries including the UK, the USA, Australia, parts of Europe, and New Zealand. Implicitly all these reforms take a normative stance on leadership distribution and emphasise extended forms of leadership at school, district and system level. Most of these reforms endorse and reinforce, shared or collective leadership practices within and between schools.

In most cases, these policy reforms have been located in Western contexts but in 2000 Hong Kong became one of the first Asian societies to explicitly adopt distributed school leadership. This was part of a new system of educational management that established school decision-making councils and a new curriculum leadership role in all schools. In England, distributed leadership has featured heavily in workforce remodelling and reform along with the introduction of new models of schooling such as federations, partnerships, networks and multi-agency working. So despite words of caution from the research community, distributed leadership is already being advocated and endorsed in many countries around the world.

The good news is that there is evidence to suggest that certain forms of collective leadership or forms of distributed influence 'have a modest but significant indirect effect on student achievement' (Leithwood and Mascall, 2008: 546). However they key issue here is *how* rather than whether leadership is distributed. The evidence base on distributed school leadership highlights both positive and negative effects and outcomes of leadership distribution. Distributed leadership is not intrinsically a good or bad thing. It depends upon the school itself, the purpose of the distribution and most importantly, *how* leadership is distributed.

As Leithwood et al. (2009) have clearly shown in their empirical work, some patterns of distribution have a greater influence on organisational outcomes than others. The empirical evidence shows that 'purposeful or planned leadership' distribution is more likely to impact positively on school development and change. This finding is further confirmed by evidence from a large-scale study of the impact of leadership on student learning outcomes. This work shows that the formal leaders of schools that have sustained improvement (in terms of academic attainment in various contexts) exhibit certain key leadership practices. The evidence shows that they purposefully restructure, reformulate and redesign leadership practice to be more distributed. The important point here is that those in formal leadership positions actively create and support certain forms of distributed leadership and reject others. Distributed leadership within improving schools, it would seem, occurs by purposeful design rather than by default (Day et al., 2009). In summary, exactly how leadership is distributed explains its subsequent effect, for good or ill, on the organisation.

Therefore, we need to know much more about the patterns of distribution and understand which configurations are most likely to have a positive organisational impact. We need to know *how* distributed leadership makes a difference to organisational outcomes rather than continually seeking more confirmation that it does. But as a starting point we need to look at the existing empirical evidence about distributed leadership and organisational change. If distributed leadership is worth further research and empirical investigation we have to be assured that there is something worth pursuing. The school leadership field is very fond of producing new labels for leadership without any empirical verification or confirmation. So what do we know about distributed leadership and organisational outcomes?

This chapter draws upon the research base and explores the available empirical evidence to address two key questions:

1. What evidence do we have about the relationship between distributed leadership and classroom/school/system level change?
2. What are the implications for school leaders and leadership development?

The empirical test

In looking at the evidence, the first issue to address is that of definition. Distributed leadership can be an elusive concept. It can slide between descriptive, analytical and normative interpretations. It is often used to mean distinctively different things and such discrepancy in meaning allows researchers to *talk past each other* (Mayrowetz, 2008: 425). One common misuse of the term is as a convenient 'catch all' descriptor for any form of shared, collaborative or extended leadership practice. This interpretation is quite prevalent in the literature, blurring the meaning of the term even further. Despite recognition of the problem of definition, different conceptualisations and interpretations of the term persist and prevail (Harris, 2007).

A common misinterpretation is to position distributed leadership as the antithesis of top-down, hierarchical leadership. This is both unhelpful and misleading. While distributed leadership is certainly an alternative way of understanding leadership practice and can certainly be positioned in relation to 'top-down' models of leadership, it is not the opposite. Distributed leadership, essentially involves both the vertical and lateral dimensions of leadership practice. Distributed leadership encompasses both formal and the informal forms of leadership practice within its framing, analysis and interpretation. It is primarily concerned with the co-performance of leadership and the reciprocal interdependencies that shape that leadership practice (Spillane, 2006: 58). This co-leadership can involve both formal and informal leaders, it is not an 'either/or'. To construe it this way only serves to create and maintain an unhelpful dichotomy. It also fuels a rather futile debate about whether hierarchical or distributed leadership might be more desirable.

Mayrowetz (2008) argues that it is crucial to inventory the multiple usages of the term distributed leadership for two reasons. First, because of the variation in meaning and secondly, in order to make clearer connections between these usages and the goal of school improvement. If we are to look at the relationship between distributed leadership and school improvement, precision of definition is crucial. This has to be right but, as Mascall et al. (2009) have pointed out, there seems to be little to be gained in continuing to debate the rights and wrongs of different positions or perspectives on distributed leadership. The main challenge is to start thinking about measuring the degree and extent of any organisational impact and effect.

Although much has been written about distributed leadership, two pressing questions remain. First, what difference, if any, do certain patterns or configurations of distributed leadership make to classrooms, schools and school systems? Secondly, how do we know? The methodological challenges associated with research into these two questions are considerable. Part of the reason for the proliferation of accounts of single and often 'heroic' leaders, is partly explained by the methodological ease of data gathering. If leadership equates with role and position, then it is relatively straightforward to collect evidence about the actions and responsibilities of those occupying leadership positions. It is fairly easy to compile case studies based upon the actions, usually self-reported, of individual leaders. However, if leadership is construed as interaction, and the aggregate of a complex set of social processes, then the methodological challenges increase exponentially.

It is without question, more difficult to investigate distributed leadership because of the multiple sources of influence. But it is not impossible. Clearly, the data collection methods need to be more sophisticated and nuanced to capture distributed leadership practice. As the work of Jim Spillane and his colleagues has shown, it is possible to research distributed leadership practice and to provide an operationalisation of distributed leadership in schools. This rich empirical work has provided the basis for much of the contemporary evidence about distributed leadership practice (Spillane, 2006).

Work by Spillane et al. (2001) highlights how the practice of leadership moves between those in formal and informal leadership positions. It focuses on the nature of interdependencies and the co-performance of leadership practice. Implicit in the notion of 'co-performance' is the possibility that those performing the practice might be pursuing different or even contradictory goals. 'From a distributed perspective, leaders can interact in the co-performance of leadership routines even when they seek different or conflicting outcomes' (Spillane, 2006: 84). This does not mean that dissent or a breakdown in performance is inevitable. The distributed perspective simply recognises the possibility that people may be working with different goals or outcomes in mind.

The evidence

But what do we already know from the empirical evidence about distributed leadership? What, if anything, can we say are its impact and effects? First, we know that the empirical base about distributed leadership can be found in different research fields and traditions. Studies that offer research-informed insights into distributed leadership are located in the literatures pertaining to school improvement, organisational change, teacher leadership and school leadership. This research terrain is inevitably diverse and draws upon various traditions and methodological positions. However, despite the miscellaneous nature of the evidential base, there are consistent messages about distributed leadership and organisational change that are worth noting, most importantly that there is evidence of a positive relationship and beneficial effects to the organisation of wider leadership distribution (Harris, 2008; Leithwood and Mascall, 2008).

Secondly, there is a growing number of studies that have started to focus attention explicitly on the impact of distributed leadership on teachers and learning (Leithwood et al., 2009). These studies provide evidence about the nature, form and impact of distributed leadership practices in schools. Studies by Camburn and Han (2009), Hallinger and Heck (2009) and Mascall et al. (2009) highlight a positive relationship between distributed leadership and certain student learning outcomes, plus a positive impact on teachers' levels of self-efficacy and motivation. As Leithwood et al. (2009) conclude, the field is now much closer to developing impact studies of distributed leadership as a result of the theoretical, conceptual and empirical work undertaken to date. The next challenge is to design these studies.

Thirdly, a number of research studies have conceptualised distributed leadership as a form of work redesign and have deliberately looked at distributed leadership as a form of job redesign or work restructuring (Harris, 2008; Louis et al., 2009). Other researchers have paid close attention to the different patterns of leadership distribution in schools (Leithwood et al., 2009; Spillane and Camburn, 2006). In both cases, the main question being pursued is what patterns of distributed leadership exist in schools and whether, and in what way, if any, do they affect organisational outcomes? The findings show, as highlighted earlier, that the configuration of leadership distribution is important and that certain patterns of distribution have a more positive effect than others upon organisational development and change (Leithwood et al., 2007, 2009).

It is also clear from the evidence that there are different formations of leadership distribution in schools; some are random and some are carefully orchestrated. Leithwood et al. (2009) reinforce the importance of planned, aligned distributed leadership practice that is purposeful and focused. Other evidence reinforces the importance of co-ordinated approaches to distributed leadership, and the positive impact on organisational outcomes, from certain forms of leadership distribution (Day et al., 2009; Harris, 2008). The key message here is that some patterns of distributed leadership are more likely to result in positive organisational outcomes than others. We need to know much more about those patterns. Also we need to know much more about the type of structural and cultural conditions that make distributed leadership more rather than less likely to contribute to positive organisational change.

This takes us to the fourth clear finding that schools that are successful, have restructured and redesigned themselves deliberately so that leadership can be more widely shared and spread (Harris, 2008). They have remodelled roles and responsibilities. They have created new teams, flattened structures and essentially given individuals greater responsibility and accountability for their work. As highlighted earlier some writers propose that distributed leadership is in fact a form of work redesign (Mayrowetz et al., 2009). The implication here is that certain forms of work redesign create key critical psychological states where employees feel more responsible for their work, are given greater autonomy and are provided with adequate feedback on performance. Mayorwetz et al. (2009) propose an elaborated model for the study of distributed leadership based upon work redesign that explains how distributed leadership equates with redesigned work and how this connects to motivation and learning resulting, potentially, in improved organisational outcomes.

The emerging evidence reinforces that distributed leadership has a greater impact upon organisational development where certain structural and cultural barriers are in place (Louis et al., 2009). These findings are substantiated by the organisational development and improvement literature. Within this literature is the strongest indication yet that distributed leadership has the *potential* to positively influence organisational change and student learning outcomes (Iandoli and Zollo, 2008).

This takes us to the fifth area of evidence, distributed leadership and student learning outcomes. It is clear that this is the most important yet contested area. Positions on the relationship between distributed leadership and student learning outcomes vary. Some writers have argued that seeking to explore this relationship is a futile exercise. They suggest that the 'search for normative links between specific leadership distribution patterns and student achievement results is unlikely to yield clear guidelines for practice' (Anderson et al., 2009: 135). Others have argued that distributing leadership is only desirable if the quality of leadership activities contributes to 'assisting teachers to provide more effective instruction to their students' (Timperley, 2009: 220). But what does the evidence show?

Distributed leadership and student outcomes

There are a limited number of studies that have explicitly explored the relationship between distributed leadership and learning outcomes. Two studies, in particular, offer a useful starting point in highlighting what we know about distributed leadership and student learning outcomes. The first study by Leithwood and Jantzi (2000) suggests that distributing a larger proportion of leadership activity to teachers has a positive influence on teacher effectiveness and student engagement. They also note that teacher leadership has a significant effect on student engagement that far outweighs principal leadership effects after taking into account home family background. The second study, by Silins and Mulford (2002: 16), also provides confirmation of the key processes through which more distributed kinds of leadership influence student learning outcomes. Their work concluded that 'student outcomes are more likely to improve when leadership sources are distributed throughout the school community and when teachers are empowered in areas of importance to them'.

A study of teacher leadership conducted in England found positive relationships between the degree of teachers' involvement in decision making and student motivation and self-efficacy (Harris and Muijs, 2004). This study explored the relationship between teacher involvement in decision-making within the school and a range of student outcomes. These findings show a positive relationship between distributed leadership and student engagement. In addition, both teacher and student morale improved where teachers felt more included and involved in decision-making within the school.

Contemporary work that has focused upon distributed leadership and instructional change includes work by Camburn and Han (2009) that explored the outcomes of distributed leadership by drawing upon extensive evidence from an investigation into the America's Choice CSR programme. A core design feature of this programme is the requirement to distribute leadership responsibilities to teacher leaders in schools, and this distribution of leadership, in turn, is intended to act as a key lever for instructional change. Their research work outlined the impact of this programme in 30 urban elementary schools and investigated the association between the distribution of leadership to teachers and instructional change. This study concluded that distributing leadership to teachers can support positive instructional change.

In their research, Hallinger and Heck (2009) explored the impact of system policies on the development of distributed school leadership and school improvement. Their quantitative analysis and results support a relationship between distributed leadership and school capacity for improvement. They conclude that distributed leadership is an important co-effect of school improvement processes. Similarly, research by Day et al. (2009: 17) found that 'substantial leadership distribution was very important to a school's success in improving pupil outcomes'. The findings showed that distributed leadership was positively correlated to the conditions within the organisation, including staff morale, which in turn impacted positively upon student behaviour and student learning outcomes. Other studies that have focused, in part, on the relationship between leadership and learning (Mascall et al., 2009) have also highlighted the potentially positive influence of distributed leadership practices on student learning outcomes.

In summary, the empirical evidence about distributed leadership and organisational development is encouraging but more work is needed. We need to know much more about the barriers, unintended consequences and limitations of distributed leadership before offering any advice or prescription. We also need to know the limitations and pitfalls as well as the opportunities and potential of this 'new model' of leadership practice. The methodological challenges in addressing these questions are extensive (Timperley, 2005: 417). Yet, as Spillane et al. (2006) have shown, distributed leadership can be operationalised so that we can investigate further exactly how different patterns of distributed leadership practice affect organisational performance.

Implications

Contemporary attempts at large-scale reform are running into difficulty. Models of school transformation premised on standardisation, accountability and traditional models of leadership are showing diminishing returns on investment. Governments are seeking alternatives; different approaches and new strategies for transforming their schools and school systems (Fullan, 2008). In the struggle to transform educational systems, one thing is abundantly clear – we need new organisational forms and new approaches to leadership if we are to succeed. The promise of system transformation is unlikely to be fulfilled or realised if we remain wedded to models of leadership suited to a previous age. This is not to suggest that traditional, hierarchical models of leadership have not served us well, they have, but the world is changing, so must schools and so must our conceptions of school leadership. It is becoming increasingly apparent that 'in a world of global networks, we face issues for which "top down" leadership is inherently inadequate' (Senge et al., 2005: 12).

Writers like Lakomski (2005) have long questioned whether 'leadership' is the correct label or descriptor for the type of activity or influence that is considered to drive organisational change. She challenges the premise that leadership is a natural entity or essence within the organisation, proposing instead that leadership is a distraction from exploring the real workings of organisational practice. Her work calls into question whether our 'taken for granted understanding of leadership … squares with how leaders and organizations really work given what we know about human cognition and information processing' (Lakomski, 2005: 4). It has reiterated that leadership is a label that is applied to organisational behaviour which could just as easily be labelled as something else.

If we accept that leadership is the 'right label', then it is important to ask what exactly are we labelling. There is still a powerful association between leadership and certain behaviours, traits and characteristics (Fullan, 2006) The romantic notion of the 'hero leader' is still one that prevails and persists despite countless examples of organisational vulnerability and dependency from this form of leadership practice. While it may seem superficially attractive to policy-makers, it would seem short-sighted and indeed unwise to base system-wide reform upon this type of leadership alone. As Hargreaves and Fink (2006: 95) argue, 'in a complex, fast paced world, leadership cannot rest on the shoulders of the few'. It is their contention that 'sustainable leadership is distributed leadership that ultimately stays centred on learning' (ibid: 35).

Distributed leadership is characterised by two properties – interdependence and emergence. First, the joint performance of leadership is determined by the interactive influences of multiple members in the organisation. Second, these interdependent roles are constantly renegotiated and defined by the changing needs of the organisation. Together, the dynamic interactions form the basis for developing knowledge creating systems and the ability to secure organisational change. As highlighted earlier, there is evidence to suggest a correlation between multiple leadership functions and sustained school improvement (Day et al., 2007, 2009). The dynamic model outlined by Hallinger and Heck (2009) begins to validate the viability of a set of key leadership processes that can be linked to school and student improvement. More specifically, the findings support the active building of professional and leadership capacity in schools as a route to improved organisational outcomes.

So what are the implications for schools and school leaders? First, it is clear that the task of building professional capacity and distributed leadership requires principal support and the leadership of both principals and teachers in securing and sustaining school improvement (Day et al., 2009). Greater distribution of leadership outside the formal structure requires intervention 'on the part of those in formal leadership roles' (Mascall et al., 2009: 279). In short, distributed leadership necessitates some formal direction and orchestration.

Second, the evidence suggests that some patterns of distribution are more effective than others; so this has to be factored into any realignment of formal and informal leadership relationships in schools. How leadership is distributed is more important than whether it is distributed. Third, schools will need to move away from a 'leader–follower' relationship to a model where expertise is the driver of change, and this may require different leaders at different times. More fluid patterns of interaction will arise from new professional relationships based upon expert power and mutual agency rather than power or 'top-down' direction.

Finally, it is important not to fall into the trap of believing that any form of distributed leadership is inherently good. It depends. Distributed leadership is certainly not a panacea or a basis for reckless prescription. Those who write about it also highlight the limitations of the evidential base. They note that the main challenge is to enquire more deeply and critically into distributed leadership practice (Harris, 2009; Leithwood et al., 2009; Spillane, 2006).

Coda

The hope of transforming schools through the actions of individual leaders is quickly fading. Strong leaders with exceptional vision and action do exist but unfortunately they do not come in sufficient numbers to meet the demands and challenges of twenty-first century schooling. System transformation is unlikely to be achieved by leaders or schools acting alone. Much will depend upon the formation of new networks, partnerships, alliances or federations to share leadership knowledge, to collectively address problems and to share expertise. System transformation depends on successive generations of leaders who are adaptable enough to function within a rapidly changing and increasingly challenging context.

Meeting the needs of twenty-first century schooling will require greater leadership capability and capacity within the system than ever before. It will demand that principals concentrate their efforts on developing the leadership capability and capacity of others. But we do not simply need more leaders. Adding more leaders to organisations and systems is not the answer. Similarly, spreading leadership responsibilities too widely and thinly can be counterproductive. The steady accumulation of school leaders is not the same as distributing leadership. It is not an issue of numbers but rather one of enhancing leadership quality and improving leadership practice.

A decade ago it would have been unwise to develop leadership programmes based on the idea of distributed leadership. The operational and empirical platform was simply not robust enough. Now there is a clearer conceptualisation of distributed leadership practice. Empirical work has also started to map its direction and influence. There is now more research activity addressing the issue of the outcomes and effects of distributed leadership. Therefore, there is the real opportunity to draw upon what we know about distributed leadership and build this into leadership development programmes. The results of this integration may be imperfect but, in thinking about twenty-first century leadership, it offers one place to start.

Further reading

Harris, A. (2009) *Distributed Leadership: Different Perspectives*. Dordrecht: Springer.
Spillane, J. (2006) *Distributed Leadership*. San Francisco, CA: Jossey-Bass.

References

Anderson, S. Moore, S. and Sun, I. (2009) 'Positioning the principals in patterns of school leadership', in K. Leithwood, B. Mascall and T. Strauss (eds), *Distributed Leadership According to the Evidence*. London: Routledge.
Barnard, C. (1968) *Functions of the Executive*. Cambridge, MA: Harvard University Press.

Camburn, E. and Han, S.W. (2009) 'Investigating connections between distributed leadership and instructional change', in A. Harris (ed.), *Distributed Leadership: Different Perspectives*. Dordrecht: Springer Press.

Day, C., Leithwood, K., Sammons, P., Harris, A. and Hopkins, D. (2007) *Leadership and Student Outcomes*, London, DCSF Interim Report.

Day, C., Sammons, P., Leithwood, K., Harris, A. and Hopkins, D. (2009) *The Impact of Leadership on Pupil Outcomes, Final Report*. London: DCSF.

Fitzgerald, T. and Gunter, H. (2008) 'Contesting the orthodoxy of teacher leadership', *International Journal of Leadership in Education,* 11(4): 331–41.

Fullan, M. (2006) *Turnaround Leadership*. San Francisco, CA: Jossey-Bass.

Fullan, M. (2008) *The Six Secrets of Change*. Thousand Oaks, CA: Corwin Press.

Hallinger P. and Heck, R. (2009) 'Distributed leadership in schools: does system policy make a difference?', in A. Harris (ed.), *Distributed Leadership: Different Perspectives*. Dordrecht: Springer Press.

Hargreaves, A. and Fink, D. (2009) 'Distributed leadership: democracy or delivery?', in A. Harris (ed.), *Distributed Leadership: Different Perspectives*. Dordrecht: Springer Press.

Harris, A. (2007) 'Distributed leadership: conceptual confusion and empirical reticence', *International Journal of Leadership in Education,* 10(3): 1–11.

Harris, A. (2008) *Distributed Leadership: Developing Tomorrow's Leaders*. London: Routledge.

Harris, A. (2008) Distributed Leadership: What We Know? *Journal of Educational Administration,* 46(2) 172–88.

Harris, A. (ed.) (2009) *Distributed Leadership: Different Perspectives*. Dordrecht: Springer Press.

Harris, A. and Muijs, D. (2004) *Improving Schools through Teacher Leadership*. London: Oxford University Press.

Harris, A., Ghent, K. and Goodall, J. (2006) *Beyond Workforce Reform*. London: SSAT.

Hatcher, R. (2005) 'The distribution of leadership and power in schools', *British Journal of Sociology of Education,* 26(2): 253–67.

Lakomski, G. (2005) *Managing Without Leadership: Towards a Theory of Organizational Functioning*. London: Elsevier.

Iandoli, L. and Zollo, G. (2008) *Organisational Cognition and Learning*. New York: Idea Group.

Leithwood, K. and Jantzi, D. (2000) 'The effects of different sources of leadership on student engagement in school', in K. Riley and K. Louis (eds), *Leadership for Change and School Reform*. London: Routledge. pp. 50–66.

Leithwood, K. and Mascall, B. (2008) 'Collective leadership effects on student achievement', *Educational Administration Quarterly,* 44(4): 529–61.

Leithwood, K., Mascall, B. and Strauss, T. (2009) *Distributed Leadership According to the Evidence*. London: Routledge.

Leithwood, K., Mascall, B., Strauss, T., Sacks, R., Memon, N. and Yashkina, A. (2007) 'Distributing leadership to make schools smarter: taking the ego out of the system', *Leadership and Policy in Schools,* 6(1): 37–67.

Mascall, B., Leithwood, K., Strauss, T. and Sacks, R. (2009) 'The relationship between distributed leadership and teachers' academic optimism', in A. Harris (ed.), *Distributed School Leadership*. Dordrecht: Springer Press.

Mayrowetz, D. (2008) 'Making sense of distributed leadership: exploring the multiple usages of the concept in the field', *Educational Administration Quarterly,* 44(3): 424–35.

Mayrowetz, D., Murphy, J., Seashore Louis, K. and Smylie, M. (2009) 'Conceptualizing distributed leadership as school reform', in K. Leithwood, B. Mascall and T. Strauss (eds), *Distributed Leadership According to the Evidence*. London: Routledge.

Scribner, J., Paredes, J.R., Sawyer, K., Watson, S. and Myers, V. (2007) 'Teacher teams and distributed leadership: a study of group discourse and collaboration', *Educational Administration Quarterly*, 43(1): 67–100.

Seashore Louis, K., Meyrowetz, D., Smiley, M. and Murphy, J. (2009) 'The role of sensemaking and trust in developing distributed leadership', in A. Harris (ed.), *Distributed School Leadership*. Dordrecht: Springer Press.

Senge, P., Scharmer, C.O., Jawroski, J. and Flowers, B. (2005) *Presence – Exploring Profound Change in People, Organisations and Society*. London: Nicholas Brealey.

Silins, H. and Mulford, W. (2002) 'Leadership and school results', in K. Leithwood and P. Hallinger (eds), *Second International Handbook of Educational Leadership and Administration*. Dordrecht: Kluwer. pp. 561–612.

Spillane, J.P. (2006) *Distributed Leadership*. San Francisco, CA: Jossey-Bass.

Spillane, J.P. and Camburn, E. (2006) 'The practice of leading and managing: the distribution of responsibility for leadership and management in the schoolhouse', San Francisco, CA: American Educational Research Association.

Spillane, J., Halverson, R. and Diamond, J. (2001) 'Towards a theory of leadership practice: a distributed perspective', Northwestern University, Institute for Policy Research Working Article.

Timperley, H. (2005) 'Distributed leadership: developing theory from practice', *Journal of Curriculum Studies*, 37(4): 395–420.

Timperley, H. (2009) 'Distributed Leadership to improve Outcomes for Students', in K. Leithwood, B. Mascall and T. Strauss (eds), *Distributed Leadership According to the Evidence*. London: Routledge.

CHAPTER 5

Where to Next for Educational Leadership?

Peter Gronn

Introduction

For about a decade, although especially over the past five years or so, there has been an accelerating amount of scholarly and practitioner attention accorded the phenomenon of distributed leadership. As is generally the case with most newly popular ideas, there is an accumulating literature, indicators of which are two recent editions of the journals *Leadership and Policy in Schools* (vol 6, no. 1, 2007) and *Journal of Educational Administration* (vol 46, no. 2, 2008) entirely devoted to distributed leadership, and at least one edited collection of papers (Leithwood et al., 2009a). The idea of distributed leadership has also been show-cased in a number of publications of the National College for School Leadership in England and Her Majesty's Inspectorate of Education in Scotland. After a lengthy period during which solo or individual leadership understandings have dominated thinking in the field of educational leadership and beyond, this interest in distributed leadership is a sure sign that the search for 'post-heroic' conceptions of leadership is well under way. While the arrival of distributed leadership is to be welcomed, and while the present author has been instrumental in the recent past in promoting it as a timely idea, the purpose of this chapter is to articulate an alternative perspective to both heroic and distributed approaches. Essentially, the argument will be that heroic and distributed understandings may be, and indeed need to be, brought together and subsumed under the idea of 'hybrid' practice. That is, although scholars' preferred ways of representing leadership in organisations have been trending away recently from a near monopoly of solo-performed leadership to one of dispersal and sharing of influence, the reality of practice is such that individual leaders and plural performing leadership units operate side by side. Leadership practice, therefore, is most accurately conceptualised as an instance of hybridity.

I commence the chapter with a discussion of binary or dualistic thinking in leadership. This provides me with a departure point for the following section in which I introduce the idea of hybridity and its wider uptake in the social sciences. Next, I consider the idea of patterns of leadership practice which I refer to as configurations, and how and why these are likely to manifest a hybrid, rather than a binary, format or pattern. Then, in the following section, with regard to educational leadership configurations, I highlight two pressing research priorities: first, the imperative to try to map the various ways in which leadership is typically configured; second, the need to begin assessing the effectiveness of the impact of these leadership configurations on student learning. Finally, I foreshadow a third priority which arises from the concern with effectiveness: that is, the importance of developing and articulating the idea of leadership capability and what it means for leaders to be capable in fostering effective links between leadership and learning.

Binaries

In respect of the classification of phenomena generally, hybridity provides a contrast to binarism. Binary categories tend to be mutually exclusive, so that (in effect) one negates the other, or each category captures two opposed sets of attributes that are distinguished by tightly and precisely drawn boundaries and lines. In this sense, binaries (or dualisms) convey rigidification and inflexibility. Binaries are distinguishable from polarities which are end points of continua that allow for a range of inter-mediate positions between the two extremities. Whereas continua accommodate variations and differences of degree, binaries repre-sent dichotomous differences in kind. The field of leadership has proven particularly susceptible to binarism, with its two most well-known distinctions being leader–follower(s), and leadership–followership. This terminology contrasts with convention in the closely conceptually allied field of power, in which the binary of powerful–powerless tends to be used much more sparingly, and in which (for definitional purposes) the custom tends to be to express relations conceptually between two hypothetical parties labelled 'A' and 'B'. Other binaries have also become accepted in the leadership field. With the resurgence of interest in leadership in the 1980s and 1990s, for example, there is now also a leadership–management and a leader–manager binary. Another common split, which originated in the management studies field, is superior–subordinate (or occasionally superordinate–subordinate). Sometimes, as if to complicate matters, this distinction gets mapped onto leader–follower, with the detrimental effect that the category of leader is made the equivalent of superior and subordinate of follower. An unfortunate consequence of this kind of conceptual conflation is that it conveys the idea of a leadership as equivalent to incumbency of a formal position. That is, the possibility of any person other than an office-holder being a leader is precluded.

While hard and fast binaries need not automatically result from the drawing of distinctions between two entities, objects, states of affairs, phenomena or types, there is always a strong likelihood that this will occur, particularly where one category is defined in avowed reaction to the other. Such is the case with focused and distributed leadership. Thus, when Gibb (1968: 215) initially raised the possibility of leadership distribution occurring in small groups, for example, the wording of his chapter sub-heading was 'Focused versus distributed leadership'. In articulating this distinction, Gibb (1968: 272) went on to say that there may be a single leader in the group, or many 'may share the responsibilities and contributions that characterize leading'. Fast-forwarding more than five decades from when Gibb originally drew this distinction (that is, 1954), a problem arises with the potential binary which he created. Until the current revival of distributed leadership, the vast bulk of recent normatively popular leader types and models articulated by scholars have been framed with individual embodiment and action in mind (for example, the or a charismatic leader, the or a transformational leader). That is, such conceptions can be characterised as 'focused'. With the adoption and increased diffusion among scholars of what has come to be known as a distributed analytical 'lens', however, there is a genuine risk that focused–distributed becomes an additional hard-and-fast, either-or distinction that will stalk leadership studies. The effect, then, is simply to substitute one dominant convergent point of thinking in the field (that is, focused individualism) with another (that is, de-monopolised and de-leader-centred distribution). This would be an unfortunate development as focused–distributed is really a false dichotomy.

The reason it is false, as I shall indicate shortly, is that, empirically, single and shared leadership can be shown to coexist. The idea of convergence on one type flies in the face of a reality that consists of a configuration of hybrid types. Where and when single and shared leadership do coexist (that is, where key individuals continue to exercise influence in conjunction with other individuals alongside various 'small number' membership units within which leadership is shared), then the reality of leadership practice is one of heterogeneity, diversity and variation rather than homogeneity. In fact, this observation about hybridity is a more accurate way of describing a number of the recently published studies that purport to be distributed analyses of practice – including some of those in the publications highlighted in the introduction to this chapter.

Hybridity

The notion of hybridity is probably most commonly associated with the world of flora and fauna, and the cross-breeding of species. It has also been a strong focus of attention in post-colonial studies and cultural studies. In regard to the latter two fields, due to its complicity in the articulation and diffusion of nineteenth- and twentieth-century racial, cultural and imperial theories of identity and difference (for example, eugenics), hybridity has carried with it strong negative historical overtones. For many people it may have a shadowy past, because cultural hybridity, from the perspective of post-colonial theory, represents a distinctly impure or marginal status. There is a positive side to hybridity, however, as part of which it tends to be viewed as a third, liminal or in-between space and is understood as 'an energy field of different forces' (Papastergiadis, 1996: 258). Empirical work on a range of examples of hybrid third spaces has appeared in a rather disparate literature, along with studies of emerging hybrid professional role-holders, for example, who inhabit such third space workplaces in higher education (Whitchurch, 2008) and in health care (Kitchener, 2000).

To the best of my knowledge, leadership has not been a field in which, at least until now, hybridity has found application. But the fact of its absence from educational leadership in the face of its uptake elsewhere is an insubstantial basis for its adoption; indeed, simply to follow suit, as it were, risks accusations of responding, lemming-like, in order to 'get with the strength'. Instead, there are two reasons why I am making the connection. First, to the extent that I may have conveyed the impression in what I have previously written about distributed leadership (for example, Gronn, 2002) that it was the sole form of leadership of significance in schools, then I now regard this as inaccurate. Data on the ways in which co-leading arrangements become established, both in education and beyond it – such as pairings and couplings of leaders (Gronn, 1999; Krantz, 1989), even extending as far back in time as the dual kingship of Sparta (Mann, 1986: 197–205), and trio-like constellations (Hodgson et al., 1965) – have been documented for a good while. There are plenty of them available, yet for some reason these tend to be eschewed in favour of solo understandings. At the same time, however, the existence of such formations does not mean that, default-like, these supplant somehow or make redundant the significant ongoing impact of individuals. Indeed, the coexistence of a range of sources of influence is evidence of a much more nuanced picture of leadership practice, as I was to discover for myself (Gronn, 2009a).

And this leads me to my second point, which is that a so-called distributed 'lens' is constricting, for it does less than full justice to the weight of the evidence. In Gronn (2008) and (2009b), for example, I showed how, in four recent research investigations of distributed leadership in schools (Firestone and Martinez, 2007; Leithwood et al., 2007; Spillane et al., 2007; Timperley, 2005), specific individual leaders, while they by no means monopolised the totality of the leadership of the schools documented in each case, nonetheless exercised disproportionate influence for at least some of the time compared to their individual peers. Such patterns, I suggested, sit rather uneasily beneath the descriptive rubric of 'distributed', in which case an alternative mode of representing reality seems to be required that acknowledges instances, for example, of pairings (evident throughout the discussion in Spillane et al., 2007), trios (for example, Stein and Nelson, 2003: 435–41) and teacher teams (Timperley, 2005), not to mention various forms of networks, that parallel and complement the work of those individuals. Moreover, despite the attention they accord such phenomena as followers, situation and artefacts, and notwithstanding their putative distributed status, the focus of six case studies in a recent analysis of leadership in schools by Spillane and Diamond (2007) is overwhelmingly on individual school principals 'rather than other leaders as the central figure', as noted by Timperley (2008: 826). To my mind, this kind of reasoning does not sit easily with a purportedly distributed analytical unit. It is because of the kinds of shortcoming documented in this section that I am now proposing a switch to the broader idea of a leadership configuration as the preferred unit of analysis.

Configurations

'Configuration' is one of a number of terms which commend themselves as descriptors of leadership practice. Other possible candidates are complex, constellation, conglomeration, gestalt, archetype, assemblage or ensemble. There may indeed be more. Whatever the terminology that is preferred, it has to be able to accommodate or pay due recognition to a changing division of labour. All of the work highlighted in the previous section is evidence of a shifting division of labour in schools and beyond. Workplace divisions of labour have a dynamic of their own which, over time, means that they may retain some features of continuity (as, for example, in the perpetuation of roles, rules and routines) while discarding others, under internally induced or externally induced pressures on organisation members to innovate or to alter the totality and deployment of their resources. Such changes are evidence of the operation of *differentiation*, the key dynamic inherent in a division of labour, which yields increased *specialisation* of performance (of roles, duties and tasks) and a consequent redesign of activities. Without dwelling on the reasons for my preference for the term configuration, what is also required is a concept which is able to capture a sense of coherence or *wholeness*, as distinct from a mere aggregation of separate elements or *parts*, although not necessarily to the extent of the integration that is implied by a word like 'system'. For this reason, constellation might also be an appropriate choice, except that this has already been spoken for: along with *complementarity*, role differentiation and specialisation were two of the defining attributes previously utilised by Hodgson et al. (1965: xii) to define a role constellation which, in my terms, is a particular formation that may comprise part of the overall landscape of leadership practice.

There is an extensive literature on configurations, for which available space precludes a definitive review. Briefly, configurations have been understood in three main ways. First, in discussions of comparative research methodology configuration has been deployed as a way of characterising case studies. Ragin (2000: 68), for example, insists that the logic of a case is configurational because 'different parts of the whole are understood in relation to one another and in terms of the total picture or package that they form'. That is, configurations comprise combinations of attributes, with particular case configurations highlighting the various (causal) ways in which 'things have come to be as they are' and in which 'they might be different' (Byrne, 2005: 101). Second, in his history of power, Mann (1986) has shown how four main network-based sources of power (ideological, military, economic and political) have crystallised in both intended and unintended ways during different historical eras to form configurations: that is, dynamic patterns or sets of institutional arrangements that have acquired structural dominance. Third, interest in configurations among firms arose in business management in the 1980s as part of a rethink of contingency theory. What, for example, were the factors and circumstances which governed the proliferation and variety of different types of organisations? And, to what extent was the range of types broad or narrow? With such questions in mind (including their implicit evolutionist assumptions about selection and the winnowing out of a range of options), Miller (1981: 3) believed that configurations were 'patterns of adaptation undertaken by firms in response to shifting environmental and internal organizational factors' or 'common, thematically driven alignments of elements or dimensions' (Miller, 1999: 28). Viewed from this perspective, Miller (1987: 686) claimed that configurations constituted the effects or outcomes, while a series of imperatives was their cause. He distinguished four main causal imperatives: environment, structure, strategy and executive personality. It was the interrelationship and complementarity of these elements which operated to restrict organisational variety to a taxonomy of four main configurations: bureaucracies (machine and professional), adhocracies, simple organic organisations and complex diversified, multi-divisional firms (Miller, 1986, 1990).

The usage of configuration adopted here is similar to that of Lichtenstein (2000) who, while tracking changes in three small entrepreneurial businesses, utilised configuration to denote overall patterns of realignment in the firms' work activity domains, except that I am proposing a focus on the patterns of aligned and realigned leadership practice. And if, as I argued and illustrated in the previous section, the reality of practice is most accurately interpreted as hybrid – that is, traditionally understood individual roles are complemented by a range of small-number membership groupings – then the configuration idea is a particularly advantageous means of accommodating these emergent patterns of influence. In schools, for example, a number of elements of practice are likely to continue to be top-down driven as in the traditional idea of delegation and the more recent notion of formally distributing leadership (on which see MacBeath, 2005), while other practices are equally likely to be spontaneously generated by task-driven needs (Timperley, 2008: 829) and to be more bottom-up in their source of inspiration. As a blanket description in these circumstances, then, 'distributed', which captures the idea of numerical spread, is simply too coarse a rubric to encompass such emergent forms and diverse small-number units of influence, and to make assessments about leadership continuity and discontinuity. Just as with focus, therefore, distribution is part of the overall configuration but by no means the entirety of it.

Hybrid educational leadership configurations

Thus far, in an effort to begin building cumulative knowledge of how leadership works, I have been proposing configuration as a way of trying to move forward the school leadership field's understanding of practice. Provided this configurational idea achieves broad acceptability, then as I see it there are two immediate priorities. The first is to map practice and the second is to assess the effectiveness and impact of such practice. After discussing each, there is a brief statement about the significance of configurations.

Mapping

To ascertain the ways in which leadership is configured is to accord a higher priority to an evidence-based understanding of practice than to normative recommendations of preferred approaches to practice. (As was suggested at the outset of this chapter, the normative switch from heroics to distribution is already under way in educational leadership.) Leithwood et al. (2009b: 281) have referred to this initial priority as clarifying the 'anatomy' of leadership; that is, documenting how it works. For researchers this entails assembling evidence of hybridity. This strategy, as I have suggested elsewhere, amounts to leadership practice anatomised (Gronn, 2009b).

There are a number of ways in which the hybridising tendency that characterises the configurations for which I have been arguing manifests itself. Three illustrative examples are merger (or fusion), blending and coexistence. Whitchurch's (2008) example of role fusion is newly emerging third-space professional identities in higher education. These include people working in cross-boundary, unbounded and blended professional roles, rather than more conventionally structured professional jobs. Her examples are people combining traditionally distinct research and professional skills who work in such areas as student access and equity, study skills, transition, and community and regional partnerships (Whitchurch, 2008: 384). Collinson and Collinson's (2007) example of the blended expectations of followers is taken from seven case studies in the English further education (FE) sector. The significance of blended expectations is that FE managers are increasingly expected to respond to a mix of conflicting organisation member preferences for both hierarchical and laterally anchored forms of leadership with many interview respondents stating that 'they wanted to be consulted and listened to, but that they also valued clear and consistent guidance and direction from those in leadership positions' (Collinson and Collinson, 2007: 12). Such dissonant views demand versatile and flexible leadership. In a field study of leadership in a secondary school (Gronn, 2009a), forms of leadership usually thought of as conceptually distinct (for example, individuals, collectivities) coexisted or were overlaid on one another. Apart from the regular hierarchy of principal and deputy roles, and senior teacher portfolios of responsibilities, there were a number of informal groupings (for example, collaborating pairs of colleagues), teacher networks and teams. Decisions were made singly and jointly, there was considerable decision-making delegation and in some instances autonomy with subsequent reporting back up the authority spine.

As Miller's work on corporate organisational configurations illustrated, these are dynamic through time rather than static. Mapping practice, therefore, necessarily entails longitudinal data-gathering in order to capture developmental trajectories consequent upon anticipated changes in the division of labour, and the range of practitioner-led improvisations and adaptations: certainly there may be evidence of further differentiation, but equally probably of *de-* or *re-*differentiation (as with the merger and fusion processes just foreshadowed). This possibility opens up a clear role for ethnographically designed research. While Miller (1986, 1990) also indicated that the range of organisational configurations narrowed to just four – although for this restriction on variation he has been criticised severely by Donaldson (1996: 108–29), on the grounds that most organisational changes tend to be incremental rather than conforming to typologies – it would be equally important to try to ascertain the incidence and frequency of leadership configurations across a system or sector (for example, schooling). The reason is that if configurations typically group themselves into clusters, explanations for this tendency might provide a useful basis for evaluations of the effectiveness of particular ways of configuring leadership.

Effectiveness

That which gives educational leadership its distinctiveness as a form of leadership is its leadership of learning. The leading of learning is complex work. Moreover, to lead learning in global and national policy environments of high stakes accountability, and comparative student performance in competitively ranked student testing regimes (such as Programme for International Student Assessment – PISA) compounds this complexity. Ironically, however, the current state of knowledge of the links between leadership and learning is limited. Until recently, it has been unclear whether there are some task-related actions on the part of leaders which are more effective than others in influencing improved learning by students. This claim is true both of leaders acting singly, where evidence of leadership impact is known to be weak (statistically) and indirect, and in circumstances where leadership has been distributed.

Two recent studies, however, provide interesting evidence of leadership impact and suggest that the situation just described may be about to change. In the first, Robinson et al. (2008) re-analysed 27 empirical studies of leader effects for the period 1978–2006, for 22 of which it was possible to calculate a standard effect size on student learning. The effects measured were those of school leaders (mainly principals or headteachers, although half the studies measured the impact of other leaders) in a mix of elementary and secondary schools in studies utilising instructional and transformational leadership scale items. The majority of the research studies had been undertaken in the USA, with impact measures focused on mathematics, language and reading. The second of two analyses by Robinson et al. was of particular interest, for the authors disaggregated all 199 items from the various scales and re-grouped them into five categories of practice. This re-grouping revealed two statistically weak effects and two moderate effects, but one very large effect in the area of leaders promoting and participating in teacher learning and development (Robinson et al., 2008: 22). In the second piece of research, Timperley (2005) – in one of the few studies (at the time of writing) that has provided evidence of the impact of distributed leadership – showed how teachers learn from their teacher leaders in group situations. There was evidence of changed professional practice in her comparisons of literacy teacher dialogue taken from meetings in Years 2 and 3 of the project. During this time teachers' use of artefacts (for example, students' reading scores) had switched from non-specific discussions of generalised cohort-based student data to tightly focused talk about data designed to track the performance of specific students and teachers' pedagogical strategies needed to improve their learning (Timperley, 2005: 407, 415).

Significance

Who might benefit from configurations? And how might they benefit? Despite whatever normative understandings of leadership might recommend or prescribe, the reality of practice is that there is no right way to do leadership. Provided this premise finds acceptance then leaders will do whatever is required to get the job done, including improvising their actions, and adapting their routines and processes. Further, if the import of the points made earlier about role differentiation and complementarity is acknowledged, then the interdependent relations these imperatives imply will require a perspective on educational leadership that consists of more than a series of isolated proactive initiatives and influential undertakings. In this regard, configurational thinking commends itself because it provides leaders with a sense of how everything comes (or does not come) together, and demonstrates that there is a holistic totality of learning-directed activity that has to be thought about. If so, then examples of some of the key questions for leaders to ask might be: how well integrated are the various components of the school's structure? Is there a requisite balance to be struck between the tightness and looseness of the couplings? Given the pace and press of external demands that emerge in unpredictable ways, for example, what degree of flexibility to be able to respond rapidly is afforded us by our current structure? How well aligned are our sub-components of learning, such as curriculum structure, assessment and evaluation, monitoring and reporting? What about our collective skills-set: how well is the school maximising the use of its overall talent pool? Are the right people exercising the appropriate portfolios of responsibilities or do these appointments and the responsibilities themselves need to be thought through once again?

Towards educational leadership capabilities?

In the studies by Robinson et al. and Timperley, leadership was seen as embedded in the performance of tasks associated with teachers' and students' learning. This assumption, along with the studies' findings, has important implications for the future of educational leadership, for it suggests that a particular kind of knowledge may be required to lead learning. Taken at face value, it would appear that *domain-specific* task-focused understandings of leadership practice are more significant for educational leadership practice than is *generic* leadership knowledge. But there may be another way to conceive of that practice. An objection might be to say that 'instructional' connotes an unduly narrowly conceived view of learning, particularly that of students. After all, the increasing trend towards inter-agency engagement in schools and the lives of students, along with extended schools and the breaking down of agency 'silo-ing' as part of joined-up government, seems to require a more integrated role for front-line services for children and families. This development suggests, in turn, a broader knowledge of the circumstances impacting on learning. In relation to the leadership of learning, then, the question of what educational leaders might need to know if they are to enhance student outcomes remains open.

Stein and Nelson (2003: 424) have made an important contribution to answering this question with their idea of leadership content knowledge (LCK), which they define as 'the kind of knowledge that will equip administrators to be strong instructional leaders'. Leadership content knowledge comprises a nested or hierarchically layered view of knowledge anchored around the technical core of schooling, classroom teaching and learning. Moving outwards from the inner layer, and using secondary school mathematics as the illustrative case, the layered knowledge required of leaders (teachers, principals, superintendents, and so on) at each layer appears to be fivefold and entails a series of meta-level understandings: subject-matter knowledge of mathematics; knowledge of how children learn mathematics; knowledge of how teachers can assist children's learning; knowledge of how teachers learn to teach mathematics; and knowledge of how others (for example, district level specialists) can assist teachers' learning.

Clearly, such multilayered LCK will vary by school sector (for example, primary, secondary, special educational needs settings) and by subject domain. Given the impossibility of individual leaders having all the specialist knowledge that needs to be known about learning, they at least need to know how to identify and locate the necessary expertise, and to ensure it is deployed in a collective way. A significant part of LCK, then, especially for head-teachers and principals may entail knowledge of whether there are optimally effective and efficient ways of configuring leadership roles and responsibilities in schools. If effectiveness is to be school-wide then what might be needed is the co-ordination of multiple individual leaders, plural-member leadership units and networks, within and across domains of routines and activities. An important precondition for such co-ordination, as suggested by the findings of Bryk and Schneider (2002), is a well-developed basis of trust. Co-ordination for effectiveness means more than distributing leadership, either normatively in the sense that this is an inherently virtuous thing to do or pragmatically as a way of spreading the burdens of office because the job may be too big for one person or a handful of people. Rather, configuring leadership is likely to be about making specifically calculated, knowledge-informed decisions, based on feedback about aspects of practice, with the explicit intention of maximising beneficial learning (Timperley, 2008: 831–2).

While LCK is necessary, however, it may not be sufficient. Knowing what to do and having the capability to act on that knowledge are two different things (Robinson, 2009: 4). What it means for an individual to be capable of doing something has been articulated by Nussbaum (2006) as part of her comprehensive rebuttal of contractualism as the requisite philosophical basis for a theory of social justice. The 'central requirements of a life with dignity', she argues, comprise an open-ended list of 10 capability statements that encompass (sequentially) life; health; bodily integrity; senses, imagination and thought; emotions; practical reason; affiliation; other species; play and control over one's environment (Nussbaum, 2006: 75). While education does not constitute a separate capability, it forms part of two of Nussbaum's set: it is explicit in capability 3 (senses, imagination and thought) and implied in capability 6 (practical reason). Arguably, it is also an important precondition for the full realisation of the entire list of 10, all of which are claimed to apply universally (Nussbaum, 2006: 78). The key (and powerful) point about capabilities is that the wording of each (with one exception) is expressed as 'Being able to …'. That is, it is not sufficient for individuals to possess rights and entitlements, for they must be able to have, experience or realise the functioning expressed in each statement. Capability 2 (bodily health), for example, says 'Being able to have good health, including reproductive health; to be adequately nourished; to have adequate shelter'. Anything less is a life lived without dignity.

If the thrust of Nussbaum's claim is correct, then what might it mean for educational leaders to be capable of leading student learning? With the idea of leadership capabilities still being very much a work in progress, indicative suggestions are all that is possible. A key guiding principle in the specification of capabilities has to be demonstrated links between capabilities, types of leadership practice and student outcomes (Robinson, 2009: 5). In her recent review of evidence of capabilities, Robinson (2009: 27) has added complex problem-solving and (following Bryk and Schneider, 2002) the building of relational trust to LCK, and has noted the importance of interdependencies between different capability realms. Clearly, there is still much conceptual and empirical work to be done, in a terrain where the ground has already been staked out for some time by proponents of skills, dispositions and competences, not to mention traits (Zaccaro, 2007). At the end of the day a firm focus on what people attributed with leadership have to be able to do, singly or jointly, to assist colleagues to secure outcomes, offers a realistically grounded alternative to such dubious prescriptions as heroism and distributing the overall burden of work.

Conclusion

In this chapter I have endorsed the idea of leadership configurations as the preferred unit of analysis in educational (particularly school) leadership. The reason I have done so is that, while scholars have been increasingly persuaded of the shortcomings of leadership conceived as individually focused action, and have begun substituting a distributed or shared approach, they may have adopted a template which does not accurately accord with the realities of practice. Both a reinterpretation of data in accounts of distributed leadership, and evidence from a handful of new studies, points in the direction of leadership configurations that are mixed or hybrid in texture. On this basis I have outlined a potential future trajectory of research into the practice of educational leadership, one pay-off for which is likely to be a grounded understanding of the dynamism of leadership configurations, along with the extent of their variation or narrowing around a handful of types. The second potential pay-off for educational leaders is evidence that some configurations may be more reliably associated with student learning than others. In the final section of the chapter I argued that to be able to configure leadership in knowledge-based ways may be a leadership capability, and that a capability focus offers scholars and practitioners a viable, learning-informed and non-heroic alternative way of thinking about and practising educational leadership.

Further reading

Leithwood, K., Mascall, B. and Strauss, T. (eds) (2009) *Distributed Leadership According to the Evidence*. New York: Routledge.
Robinson, V.M.J., Lloyd, C.A. and Rowe, K. (2008) 'The impact of leadership on student outcomes: an analysis of the differential effects of leadership types', *Educational Administration Quarterly*, 44(5): 635–74.

Stein, M.K. and Nelson, B.S. (2003) 'Leadership content knowledge', *Educational Evaluation and Policy Analysis*, 25(4): 423–48.

References

Bryk, A.S. and Schneider, B. (2002) *Trust in Schools: A Core Resource for Improvement.* New York: Russell Sage Foundation.

Byrne, D. (2005) 'Complexity, configurations and cases', *Theory, Culture & Society*, 22(5): 95–111.

Collinson, D. and Collinson, M. (2007) *'Blended Leadership': Employee Perspectives on Effective Leadership in the U.K. FE sector.* Working Paper, Centre for Excellence in Leadership, Lancaster University Management School.

Donaldson, L. (1996) *For Positivist Organization Theory: Proving the Hard Core.* London: Sage.

Firestone, W.A. and Martinez, M.C. (2007) 'Districts, teacher leaders, and distributed leadership: changing instructional practice', *Leadership and Policy in Schools*, 6(1): 3–35.

Gibb, C.A. (1968) 'Leadership', in G. Lindzey and E. Aronson (eds), *The Handbook of Social Psychology*, 2nd edn, vol. 4. Reading, MA: Addison-Wesley. pp. 205–83.

Gronn, P. (1999) 'Substituting for leadership: the neglected role of the leadership couple', *Leadership Quarterly*, 10(1): 41–62.

Gronn, P. (2002) 'Distributed leadership as a unit of analysis', *Leadership Quarterly*, 13(4): 423–51.

Gronn, P. (2008) 'The future of distributed leadership', *Journal of Educational Administration*, 46(2): 141–58.

Gronn, P. (2009a) 'Hybrid leadership', in K. Leithwood, B. Mascall and T. Strauss (eds), *Distributed Leadership According to the Evidence*. Mahwah, NJ: Erlbaum. pp. 17–40.

Gronn, P. (2009b) 'Leadership configurations', *Leadership*, 5(3): 381–94.

Hodgson, R.C., Levinson, D.J. and Zaleznik, A. (1965) *The Executive Role Constellation: An Analysis of Personality and Role Relations in Management.* Boston, MA: Graduate School of Business Administration, Harvard University.

Kitchener, M. (2000) 'The "bureaucratization" of professional roles: the case of clinical directors in UK hospitals', *Organization*, 7(1): 129–54.

Krantz, J. (1989) 'The managerial couple: superior–subordinate relationships as a unit of analysis', *Human Resource Management*, 28: 161–75.

Leithwood, K., Mascall, B. and Strauss, T. (eds) (2009a) *Distributed Leadership According to the Evidence*. New York: Routledge.

Leithwood, K., Mascall, B. and Strauss, T. (2009b) 'What we have learned and where we go from here', in K. Leithwood, B. Mascall and T. Strauss (eds), *Distributed Leadership According to the Evidence*. New York: Routledge. pp. 269–81.

Leithwood, K., Mascall, B., Strauss, T., Sacks, R., Memon, N. and Yashkina, A. (2007) 'Distributing leadership to make schools smarter: taking the ego out of the system', *Leadership and Policy in Schools*, 6(1): 37–67.

Lichtenstein, B.B. (2000) 'Self-organised transitions: a pattern amid the chaos of transformative change', *Academy of Management Executive*, 14(4): 128–41.

MacBeath, J. (2005) 'Leadership as distributed: a matter of practice', *School Leadership and Management*, 25(4): 349–66.

Mann, M. (1986) *The Sources of Social Power, Vol 1: A History of Power from the Beginning to A.D. 1760.* Cambridge: Cambridge University Press.

Miller, D. (1981) 'Toward a new contingency approach: the search for organizational gestalts', *Journal of Management Studies*, 18(1): 1–26.

Miller, D. (1986) 'Configurations of strategy and structure: towards a synthesis', *Strategic Management Journal*, 7: 233–49.

Miller, D. (1987) 'The genesis of configuration', *Academy of Management Review*, 12(4): 686–701.

Miller, D. (1990) 'Organizational configurations: cohesion, change, prediction', *Human Relations*, 43(8): 771–89.

Miller, D. (1999) 'Notes on the study of configurations', *Management International Review*, special Issue, 39(2): 27–39.

Nussbaum, M.C. (2006) *Frontiers of Justice: Disability, Nationality, Species Membership*. Cambridge, MA: Belknap.

Papastergiadis, N. (1996) 'Tracing hybridity in theory', in P. Werbner and T. Modood (eds), *Debating Cultural Hybridity: Multi-Cultural Identities and the Politics of Anti-Racism*. London: Zed Books. pp. 257–81.

Ragin, C.C. (2000) *Fuzzy-Set Social Science*. Chicago, IL: University of Chicago Press.

Robinson, V.M.J. (2009) 'From instructional leadership to leadership capabilities: empirical findings and methodological challenges', *Leadership and Policy in Schools* (under review).

Robinson, V.M.J., Lloyd, C.A. and Rowe, K. (2008) 'The impact of leadership on student outcomes: an analysis of the differential effects of leadership types', *Educational Administration Quarterly*, 44(5): 635–74.

Spillane, J.P., Camburn, E.M. and Pareja, A.S. (2007) 'Taking a distributed perspective to the school principal's workday', *Leadership and Policy in Schools*, 6(1): 103–25.

Stein, M.K. and Nelson, B.S. (2003) 'Leadership content knowledge', *Educational Evaluation and Policy Analysis*, 25(4): 423–48.

Timperley, H.S. (2005) 'Distributed leadership: developing theory from practice', *Journal of Curriculum Studies*, 37(4): 395–420.

Timperley, H.S. (2008) 'A distributed perspective on leadership and enhancing valued outcomes for students', *Journal of Curriculum Studies*, 40(6): 821–33.

Whitchurch, C. (2008) 'Shifting identities and blurring boundaries: the emergence of *third space* professionals in UK higher education', *Higher Education Quarterly*, 62(4): 377–96.

Zaccaro, S.J. (2007) 'Trait-based perspectives of leadership', *American Psychologist*, 62(1): 6–16.

Section II

Developing Leaders

Teacher Professionalism and Continuing Professional Development: Contested Concepts and Their Implications for School Leaders

Les Bell and Ray Bolam

Introduction

The aim of this chapter is to explore the ways in which contested notions of professionalism in a number of different countries influence the content and provision of continuing professional development (CPD) and to consider the implications of these conceptualisations of professionalism and CPD for school leaders. The debate about the nature of teacher professionalism is a long-standing one. As part of that debate professionalism, both as a concept and as a workplace practice, is constantly being redefined. In Australia the last decade has seen extensive debates about the nature of teacher professionalism and concerns have been expressed about the extent to which current conceptualisations of professionalism contain any understanding that teachers have professional responsibilities beyond the classroom (Kennedy, 2005). In countries such as Canada and the USA teachers have, until recently, been regarded as at least semi-autonomous, able to take decisions within broad parameters about the content and delivery of what was taught and largely in control of their own career progression and development. However, Sachs (2003) expresses concerns about how far teacher professionalism should be grounded in a restrictive approach to education based on basic skills and testing at the expense of a more expansive and transformative professionalism.

If, for some societies, the main concern about the conceptualisation of teacher professionalism is whether or not it should be concerned with more than teaching and learning, in other systems, China, Malaysia and Singapore for example, teachers have long been state employees with restricted powers of decision-making and limited control over development and progression. Here the notion of teacher professionalism is a less overt concept as teachers are subsumed within various government agencies. In countries such as Ghana and South Africa, professionalism denotes not an extension of the responsibilities of teachers, but a standard of behaviour and practice to which all aspire but which some do not achieve (Adegoke, 2003; Harber, 2005). Moloi (2007) argues that achieving greater levels of professional competence is trapped by a form of social meliorism 'where the commitment to a vision of *what should be* clouds the ability to consider seriously *what is*, so that … good intentions … have more influence on policy than social and school realities' (Moloi, 2007: 464).

In South Africa, as elsewhere, perhaps the most powerful recent influences on teacher professionalism and the management of professional development have been those generated by the extensive national reforms introduced in many countries since the 1980s (Heystek, 2007). School leaders in many countries increasingly work in a political context in which external 'restructuring' changes, initiated by national, state or local authorities to raise standards of achievement, exert priority over their own vision of desirable improvements. Their dilemma is, therefore, how to manage the implementation of an onerous external change agenda while simultaneously acknowledging the role of teachers as professionals and trying to promote school-initiated improvement and the associated professional development.

The nature and extent of this dilemma necessarily varies according to the situation within each school and with the content and scope of the plethora of national reforms initiated since the 1980s. For example, while many countries decentralised school management tasks to the local or school level, in England and Wales the redistribution of power was more complex. Schools gained some powers but local authorities lost many functions that were centralised to national level (Karstanje, 1999). This was accompanied by a form of neo-liberal deregulation, notably the promotion of increased competition between schools, in the belief that quasi-market mechanisms would promote quality improvement (Whitty, 1997). A similar trend was also observed in other countries such as Hungary (Balazs, 1999), where, for example, schools were encouraged to sublet parts of their buildings to small businesses in order to generate income. Other countries such as Norway and Spain adopted a different, less overtly market-driven and centralist policy stance (Bolam et al., 2000). Nevertheless, many countries adopted the same broad steering strategies, often based on dedicated or categorical funding, which tightly coupled CPD to the implementation of their reform policies. Indeed, this approach has probably become the dominant paradigm for systemic change in OECD (Organisation for Economic Co-operation and Development) member countries (Halasz, 2000).

After May 1997, the incoming Labour government in the UK continued with much of the reform thrust of its predecessors but its policy emphasis shifted away from marketisation to focus on the control of inputs, processes and outputs. Its main initiatives included the introduction of literacy and numeracy strategies in which teaching time, content and pedagogy were specified. These reforms resulted in extensive and radical changes in the roles and responsibilities of headteachers, other senior staff and teachers in general in what was, in effect, a cultural shift in schools and the teaching profession. Consequently, a new emphasis emerged on the involvement of a wider range of stakeholders, raising questions about who has the right to be involved in educational decisions.

In many countries a range of similar key trends is affecting both professional development and teacher professionalism. These often take the form of a 'modernisation' or 're-structuring' strategy and can be far-reaching in their effects. Many analysts have located these trends within a broader theoretical framework – that of managerialism or new public management, a concept adapted from the private sector (Ferlie et al., 1996; Levačić, 1999). In education, its features include reduced collegial involvement in national policy-making, an increased emphasis on managerial control of teachers' work in the interests of efficiency and accountability, the weakening of teacher autonomy, the creation of new managerial roles, skills and responsibilities and the emergence of a more distinct managerial layer in schools. In Norway, for example, a 'New Employment Agreement' was introduced in the mid-1990s. Although a new pay structure was at its heart, its main aim was to facilitate the introduction of new school policies by promoting the development of teaching competencies (Jordet, 2000). Similar approaches have been adopted by other countries in Europe and North America and by Australia and New Zealand (Moos and Dempster, 1998). This trend towards managerialism has significant implications for notions of teacher professionalism.

The contested nature of teacher professionalism

Until recently, teacher professionalism was identified by a number of key elements such as the exercise of discretionary judgement; collaboration; moral engagement; care; managing complexity; and continuous learning (Hargreaves and Goodson, 1996). Following the widespread changes that began in the 1980s, a series of attempts have been made by education policy-makers to redefine teacher professionalism. For example, a number of countries have introduced national standards of professional practice for teachers. One of the first examples was in the USA where the National Board of Professional Teacher Standards (NBPTS) developed standards and assessment procedures for 30 subject areas based on five principles:

- Teachers are committed to students and their learning.
- Teachers know the subject they teach and how to teach those subjects to students.
- Teachers are responsible for managing and monitoring students' learning.
- Teachers think systematically about their practice and learn from experience.
- Teachers are members of learning communities (NBPTS, 1993).

More recently the Council of Chief State School Officers (CCSSO) in the USA has produced a revised set of educational leadership policy standards (CCSSO, 2008) based on six standards for educational leadership:

- Visionary leadership – developing, articulating and implementing a shared vision of learning.
- Instructional leadership – sustaining an instructional program conducive to student learning.
- Organisational leadership – managing the organisation to produce a safe, efficient and effective learning environment.
- Collaborative leadership – responding to diverse community needs and interests and mobilizing community resources.
- Ethical leadership – acting with integrity and fairness.

- Political leadership – understand, influencing and responding to the political, social, economic, legal and cultural context (after CCSSO, 2008: 18).

These standards replace the Interstate School Leaders Licensure Consortium (ISLLC) Standards (CCSSO, 1996) and form the basis for school principal training programmes in many states in the USA. Questions have been raised, however, about the degree to which programmes based on either set of standards are sufficiently well matched to the contemporary world of schooling and are too focused on the principal at the expense of other members of the school community (Hess and Kelly, 2007; Pitre and Smith, 2004). Anderson et al. (2002) argue that the ISLLC Standards are more influenced by the language of business and engineering than that of education. They suggest that the standards lack empirical demonstration and verification and are, therefore, merely a matter of faith. They go on to point out that the standards produce a single predetermined approach adopted to school leadership, termed 'designer-leadership', which appears to deny the possibility of school leaders espousing different patterns of beliefs, values and actions: 'It is one thing to identify standards that represent the norm of the profession ... and quite another to normalize all prospective leaders' (Anderson et al., 2002: 2).

In South Africa, standards for the professionalisation of school leaders have also emerged through a complex series of policy documents (van der Westhuizen and van Vuuren, 2007). The South African Standard for Principalship (SASP) defines 'the role and key aspects of professionalism and expertise required for principalship in South Africa' (van der Westhuizen and van Vuuren, 2007: 439). Here, however, the challenges are very different from those in the USA. The appointment of principals with poor management and leadership skills has created an array of problems that make schools much more difficult to lead (Mestry and Singh, 2007). Hence, although the SASP promises to be a centralised programme intended to facilitate the implementation of government policy, this is welcomed because it is a move towards addressing the growing concerns about the need for professional development for school principals, which, it is argued, can only be effective through a national formal qualification (van der Westhuizen and van Vuuren, 2007).

In England and Wales, a similar set of centralised provisions have also emerged. The formalised definition of teacher professionalism was revised twice in a decade, as standards for trainee teachers were implemented and then extended to cover qualified teachers. In 1998 the Teacher Training Agency (TTA) introduced a competency based framework for initial teacher training (TTA, 1998). Tightly coupled to the strategies of successive governments for raising pupil attainment and school improvement, this framework was then used again to define the professional requirements for qualified teachers. The framework proved to be largely unworkable. In 2007 it was replaced by 33 standards to be achieved by all teacher trainees (DfES, 2007). These standards in turn formed the basis of the *Revised Framework of Professional Standards for Teachers* (TDA, 2008), developed by the Training and Development Agency (TDA) for schools in the expectation that it would enable teachers to review their professional practice, manage their own performance and identify their professional development needs.

Although this appears to reflect a fairly traditional model of professionalism, in fact the new framework links professionalism to the delivery of a centrally determined national curriculum; to national literacy and numeracy strategies in which the pedagogy is prescribed; to predetermined modes of assessment; and to participation in performance management, closely linked to continuing professional development. Furthermore, since the *Every Child Matters* agenda (DfES, 2004a) teachers have been required to work with providers of other children's services and to collaborate with staff from other professional backgrounds. The administration of education services at both national and local levels has been restructured to reflect this requirement, such that the responsibility for children in schools no longer rests solely with education services, and teachers are no longer the only professional group with an interest in and influence over the education of children. Traditional notions of teacher professionalism based on autonomy within the school and the classroom are being challenged. As Sachs (2003) notes, teacher professionalism now means working efficiently to meet standardised criteria and outcomes for student attainment.

A further feature of the 'modernisation' strategy in several countries is performance management and performance-related pay, to which a requirement to undertake specific forms of CPD is often linked. This topic will be dealt with fully in Chapter 8. Suffice it to say here that for some, performance management is seen as undermining teacher professionalism (Bell, 2007) while for others performance management strategies are a necessity in a changing educational climate. In the USA various types of schemes are being tried, based both on bonus payments linked to student results and a range of other strategies (Heneman and Milanowski, 2007). In England, Tranter and Percival (2006) note that the traditional model of teacher professionalism is no longer appropriate; schools are now very different organisations in which teachers work as members of extended teams which might include classroom assistants, technicians, administrators, governors and social workers. They argue that 'For many years teachers have overemphasized the idea of "professionalism", ... The ... spirit of teacher professionalism does cast a long shadow over attempts to raise standards in schools' (Tranter and Percival, 2006: 3).

They present performance management as an alternative to the traditional model of teacher professionalism to be pursued in the interests of school improvement. How far this is the case remains to be seen but the overall strategy is likely to continue to exercise a considerable influence on education and, more specifically, on the content and delivery of continuing professional development and conceptualisations of professionalism.

In England and Wales, the development of standards for teachers, performance management and other policy thrusts have been presented by government as workforce remodelling, with the argument that by these means it is introducing a new form of teacher professionalism. Central to this remodelling is the increased use of non-qualified staff to work in a range of teaching and non-teaching support roles with the explicit objectives of reducing teachers' workloads and driving up standards by the more effective deployment of staff (Stevenson, 2007). The remodelling of teachers' work includes the allocation of leadership, management and planning time and limits on time spent covering for colleagues (TDA, 2003). It is claimed that workforce remodelling will 'usher in a new professionalism for teachers, in which career progression and financial rewards will go to those who are continually developing their own expertise' (DfES, 2004b: 66).

This is what Barber (2000), based on his analysis of the developments in teaching over four decades, has consistently termed 'informed professionalism', an analysis which has been called, 'as distorted and politically partisan account of recent education history as one is likely to find' (Alexander, 2004: 13). What this remodelling has done in fact is to shift the focus of teacher professionalism from autonomy and informed decision-making towards compliance and competition within a tight contractual framework.

Thus, the price teachers have paid for this liberation from routine tasks has been to tie them more closely to explicit measures of performance, to the technical delivery of subject content and the achievement of pre-specified learning outcomes (MacBeath et al.,

2007). What appears to have happened is that: 'A complex, and professionally rewarding feature of teaching is ... being eclipsed from the role as teachers are compelled to focus on a much more narrow conception of teaching ... with increased emphasis on narrow academic outcomes, facilitated by the increased use of support staff' (Stevenson, 2007: 236).

It can be argued, then, that remodelling has led to the reconfiguration of the core tasks of teaching and learning in such a way as to constrain and diminish the nature of pedagogy and to transfer the delivery of these core tasks to unqualified staff (MacBeath et al., 2007). Some have further argued that this reconfiguring of teachers' work has created a new division of labour based on the increasing deployment of non-qualified staff to work alongside teachers:

> Teachers' work is being fractured both horizontally (with the removal of lower order teaching activities) and vertically (as academic and pastoral roles are artificially divided and the latter are annexed from teachers' work) ... Moreover, as the focus of teachers' work is concentrated even more narrowly on ... subject delivery, the pressure to demonstrate performance through student achievement in standardised tests increases correspondingly. (Stevenson, 2007: 239)

Others point to a similar trend because of a polarisation between teachers and school and college leaders, claiming that deprofessionalisation is a direct result of government policy which creates tensions between staff and managers, as teachers: 'continue to fight to maintain control over their labour process to counter both deskilling and the degradation of work ... Together these can be seen to represent the deprofessionalisation ... of this occupational group' (Randle and Brady, 1997: 136).

If this is true of schools and colleges in many countries, the same issues have their parallel in higher education. In the UK, for example, an instrumental and managerial discourse can be identified as part of a pattern of uneasy compromises between market forces, state control and professional interests. These are based on recognition and reward, quality and standards systems, competition and economic efficiency and mediated through government agencies such as the Higher Education Academy (HEA). This body sets both professional standards for competence in the *Professional Standards Framework for Teaching and Support Learning in Higher Education* (HEA, 2006) and a variety of institutional audits which locate continuing professional development in the sphere of accredited courses and training events (Crawford, 2009). The rhetoric of professionalism appears to focus on individual autonomy but, in practice, is increasingly shaped by strategic objectives and managerial agendas (Clegg, 2003). Furthermore, the increasing emphasis on consumerism and competition has an adverse effect on the notion of professionalism that has sustained higher education in many countries and has led to a growing emphasis on:

> A managerial and marketing ethic which stresses income genera-tion and reconceptualizes students primarily as potential income generation units and as consumers to be satisfied. The potential undercutting of professional knowledge and virtues by consumer demand and satisfaction may, perversely … have the effect of undermining, rather than enhancing, pedagogical relationships. (Naidoo and Jamieson, 2006: 880)

Professionalism, therefore, seems to have been reduced to a form of rule-following performance where what counts as professional practice rests upon meeting externally imposed, fixed criteria (Ball, 2005).

This is a reinterpretation of professionalism in which the modern professional is one who works towards meeting standardised criteria identified externally both for teachers and students, based on a concern for delivery rather than development; for efficiency rather than effectiveness; and for executive decision-making rather than consultation (MacBeath et al., 2007). It is a form of profes-sionalism in which key educational decisions about what to teach, how to teach it and how and when to assess are made elsewhere. The Association of Teachers and Lecturers rejected this 'concept of new professionalism which is limited to teachers being required to undertake development which relates to short-term aims directed by the school or, less still, by the government' (Association of Teachers and Lecturers, 2005: 4).

Although issues surrounding teacher professionalism are firmly on the agenda of the General Teaching Council for England (GTC, 2001) the position of the GTC is somewhat ambiguous. In spite of expressing the aspiration that teachers as professionals should be celebrated and trusted, the Chief Executive of the GTC still felt the need to tell teachers that CPD is about acquiring: 'those skills, knowledge and attributes we need to develop in the particular public service context in which we are working. That … must be at the heart of what it is to be a professional … What we are talking about is innovation with rigour, an informed and disciplined creativity' (Bartley, 2008: 2–3). Again, the concept of professionalism being developed here is narrow and instrumental. In this new discourse of professionalism, competences are given priority over knowledge and understanding, compliance has priority over judgement, and continued professional development for most teachers is largely limited to acquiring a tightly defined range of curriculum-specific skills.

Professionalism and continuing professional development

Continuing professional development is widely accepted as fundamental to the improvement of organisational performance and, therefore, as a core task of management and leadership. Strategies for CPD, especially in the context of leadership development, will be considered more extensively by Bush in Chapter 7. For the purposes of this chapter, suffice it to say that the continuing professional development of teachers implies a series of processes by which teachers seek to become more professional although, because the meaning of the concept is contested, the precise nature of those processes will depend on the position taken on the nature of teacher professionalism. Approaches to CPD have varied considerably between countries over the past 20 years and continue to do so (OECD, 1982, 1998). The dominant paradigm in England and Wales from the 1960s through to the early 1980s gave primacy to the needs of individual professionals and reflected the then dominant notion of teacher professionalism. As Bolam has argued:

> [P]rofessional development is the process by which teachers and headteachers learn, enhance and use appropriate knowledge, skills and values. The notion of appropriateness must itself be based on shared and public value judgements about the needs and best interests of their clients. Thus, although this perspective certainly includes staff, management and human resource development directed at raising standards and the improvement of teaching and learning, it recognizes that, because these are essentially employer- and organisation-oriented concepts, they should be seen as only a part of professional development, albeit a fundamentally important part. The essence of professional development for educators must surely involve the learning of an independent, evidence-informed and constructively critical approach

to practice within a public framework of professional values and accountability, which are also open to critical scrutiny. (Bolam, 2000: 272)

Bush and Middlewood (2005) take a similar view, arguing that it is the availability of career-long professional development that enables teaching to be seen as a career rather than just a job. Developments in national policy and in the financing of professional development in the mid-1980s changed this situation dramatically as a new but contested conceptualisation of professionalism emerged (Bolam, 1993). Bush and Middlewood (2005) note, however, that in England an instrumentalist position on continuing professional development predominates within which professional development seems only to be about making sure that teachers have the finest and most up-to-date tools for their job as defined by national standards and government policy.

Heystek (2007) recognises the extent to which a similar perspective can be found in South Africa and agrees with Thrupp and Willmott (2003), that developing extended professional skills is not the primary function of CPD, especially for headteachers, but rather it is intended to equip headteachers 'with tools and techniques to manage a certain situation better in order to achieve the aims determined by policy more efficiently, within the financial constraints determined by national budgets' (Heystek 2007: 500). In the South African context, Heystek (2007) argues that the recently introduced Advanced Certificate in Education in Education Management serves just such a purpose since content and outcomes of the programme are government controlled. Consequently it is argued that the term 'moulding' rather than 'development' or 'training' may be more appropriate for this type of CPD (Heystek, 2007).

This view is supported by a recent report on the continuing professional development of primary school teachers in the UK (McNamara et al., 2008) which argues that the educational climate has been characterised by increasing levels of centralisation, monitoring and accountability. A common framework of professional expectations has been established which is particularly apparent across the highly structured portfolio of programmes and qualifications in leadership. The degree of bureaucratisation and accountability involved, however, has engendered a 'technical rationalist' approach to educational outcomes and processes that has tended to restrict the nature of professional engagement and create a culture of compliance (McNamara et al., 2008).

McNamara et al. (2008) go on to argue that because current government policy emphasises the importance of new professionalism its predominant purpose seems to be to encourage teachers to participate in tightly prescribed continuing professional development that is largely restricted to equipping teachers to implement government reforms. Such highly directed activity contrasts with professional development which allows teachers to engage and be engaged as reflective practitioners, continually refreshing and renewing their knowledge and understandings of education, developing their own identities and enabling them to make informed professional judgements (Gray, 2005).

Thus, definitions of and involvement in CPD are far from unproblematic, especially in the many education systems worldwide which tend to focus on pupil performance identified by measurable outcomes as the main criteria for evaluating teacher effectiveness. The outcomes of teaching are often determined by what can be measured and the focus of training becomes that of improving performance in the testing process. As a consequence of this, educational and professional values are marginalised and the management of education becomes a technical issue divorced from critical reflections about the nature of education itself and the role of teachers as professionals within that context. Such an instrumental view of education reduces the role of teachers to that of technicians rather than reflective, self-motivated professionals with a direct interest in their own professional development. As Bottery (2004) argues, this has the effect of reducing professional activity merely to the level of compliance with external requirements rather than encouraging a flexible, reflective deployment of pedagogical and subject expertise. Thus any approach to CPD raises issues about the distinctive characteristics of professional development and professionalism and, accordingly, about the values and principles which should inform them.

Strategies for continuing professional development

In England and Wales there have been a number of significant changes in the strategies adopted to deliver continuing professional development for teachers. These largely reflect the shift from the traditional model of teacher professionalism to new professionalism and include the introduction of five compulsory training days for all teachers; the creation of a regulated market in which schools receive annual funding to provide and buy training and consultancy services; a framework of national priority topic areas linked to the national reforms; a substantial reduction in the capacity of local authorities to deliver training; the creation of the National College for School Leadership; a substantial increase in the number of professional associations and unions, private trainers and consultants, and other commercial agencies offering training; more flexible, market-driven, university-based, Master's-level provision (for example modularisation, credit transfer and accumulation, accreditation of prior learning and experience, professional development profiles, distance and open learning programmes); and a substantial increase in the number of taught doctorates, especially the education doctorate.

With the increasing instrumental focus on school improvement identified through pupil performance and what Ball (2008) terms zero tolerance of underperformance, there are a growing number of private providers of in-service programmes offering schools:

> ways to accommodate themselves to the demands of performativity and producing new organisational identities and 'turn-around' services to those schools and colleges which are struggling to respond to the requirements of performativity ... making policy manageable and sensible to schools ... they disseminate the discourses of reform, improvement and competition ... Concentra offers futureproofing; Tribal will make you into 'Pupils' Champions'. Mouchell Parkman deals in 'enabling improvement' and 'collaborative development' ... Prospects offer Performance Life Coaching; and CEA can provide 'Leading School Improvement Solutions'. (Ball, 2008: 195)

The websites that promote these in-service products promise immediate solutions to complex problems with no room for considerations of professional reflection or the wider possibilities that might be beneficial to teachers and pupils alike. Simple training solutions appear to be offered to complex professional problems. Continuing professional development appears to be concerned with pedagogy but is bereft of time for reflection or discussion about what and how children learn. Chapman (1995) in highlighting the difficulties encountered by teachers in implementing such strategies, concluded that rather than attempting to adopt simplistic solutions, a professionally-based collaborative approach was more likely to be effective and that it is the headteacher's job to create the conditions for this to take place.

It can be argued that a collaborative professional culture is a *sine qua non* for a learning organisation engaged in ongoing improvement. To some extent this culture is rooted in earlier ideas on school-focused in-service training as a mechanism for promoting school improvement (Fullan, 2001; OECD, 1982). Moreover, it finds support from more specific theories like experiential learning (Kolb, 1975), reflective practice, (Schön, 1987), process knowledge (Eraut, 1994), cognitive and problem-based professional learning (Leithwood et al., 1995) and professional socialisation. The nature of learning organisations, however, offers a significant challenge to both the conventional notion and the emerging concepts of professionalism. Such organisations are predicated on a broad view of education, shared learning, wide-ranging continuing professional development and the involvement of all stakeholders in the educative process. For example, Redmond et al. (2008) note that in higher education professional learning can develop based on collaboration:

> Close collaboration between ... academics, practitioners, administrators, funding agencies, students, employers and society at large ... is necessary if a quality education system is to be provided and maintained ... Collaborative working ... has a number of elements: co-operation, assertiveness, responsibility/accountability, communication, co-ordination, mutual trust and respect. (Redmond et al., 2008: 438)

In schools a similar form of professionalism is emerging in which teachers work more closely and collaboratively with colleagues, students and parents, linking teacher and school development (Hargreaves, 1994). As Liebermann and Friedrich (2007) report in the American context, professional collaboration can enable teachers to develop a wide range of strategies for building community, for drawing expertise from participation in professional development, for sharing knowledge and leadership with others. It encourages them to go public with both their successes and their questions.

Such a concept of a professional learning community is informed by what it is to be a professional in control of one's own learning and by the meaning of community. Thus, King and Newmann (2001) argue that teacher learning is most likely to occur when teachers:

- can concentrate on instruction and student outcomes in the specific contexts in which they teach
- have sustained opportunities to study, to experiment with and to receive helpful feedback on specific innovations

- have opportunities to collaborate with professional peers, both within and outside their schools, along with access to the expertise of researchers (King and Newmann, 2001).

If schools are to emerge as professional learning communities the tension between traditional and new conceptualisations of professionalism need to be addressed within the context of continuing professional development that is challenging, reflective and broadly based (Bates, 2005).

Some implications for school leaders

What, then, are the implications for headteachers and other school leaders with teacher management responsibilities? From a practical perspective, such leaders are confronted with a series of paradoxical expectations: think long term but deliver results now; innovate but avoid mistakes; be flexible but follow rules; collaborate but compete; delegate but retain control; share leadership but retain responsibility; encourage teamwork but assess individual performance; build capacity but focus on narrow instrumental outcomes (after MacBeath et al., 2007: 42–3). These paradoxes reflect the dilemma that faces school leaders when trying to come to terms with issues of teacher professionalism and continuing professional development – how to reconcile the need to cope with both externally initiated change and the demands of school improvement while recognising the needs of teachers as professionals who want more than instrumental development opportunities.

Furthermore, it is evident from international research and experience that teachers' work and professional development are central to the management tasks of headteachers. For example, approximately 700 new primary and secondary headteachers in five European countries were asked about the extent to which certain tasks or issues were a problem for them. The following were rated as a serious or very serious problem: 'ineffective teachers' by 40 per cent of respondents; 'getting teachers to accept new ideas' by 33 per cent; 'promoting professional development' by 25 per cent; and 'regular formal appraisal of teachers' by 20 per cent (Bolam et al., 2000: 28). The links between continuing professional development and the changing notions of professionalism were also apparent. Thus, in the Netherlands, 'promoting professional development' posed particular problems, apparently because of:

the tradition of teachers' professional freedom in determining whether or not they take part in such activities. With the introduction of greater autonomy for schools and school level control of funding for professional development, there has been a greater need for consistent school policies in this area. Teachers' traditional autonomy has posed problems for Dutch headteachers wishing to introduce a policy on professional development. (Karstanje, 2000: 30)

More generally, continuing professional development is also accepted as being: 'central to the way principals manage schools, in at least two respects: first, as instructional leaders, principals may be expected to coordinate professional progression of their staff; second, they need to manage the learning community as a whole, using development as part of school change' (OECD, 2001: 27). However, research evidence from England and Wales indicates that the actual impact on professional development and professionalism was somewhat different from the implied model. McMahon (1999) in a study of teachers in 66 English secondary schools found that in-service training provision was substantially influenced by both geographical location and the size of individual CPD budgets. Rural schools had poorer access to provision than their urban counterparts and some schools had three times as much money as others. Only 28 per cent of schools allocated any of the five standard training days to individual professional development needs. McMahon (1999) concluded that the professional development agenda was determined largely by the needs of centrally imposed reforms and by the needs of the schools and departments to implement them. This left little scope, given their limited resources and access to provision, for schools to meet the professional development needs of individual teachers, with obvious implications for teacher professionalism. The concept of new professionalism, therefore, can be seen here to have shaped much of the CPD provision at the expense of more individually focused learning.

If this is not to have a detrimental effect on the professional development of teachers school leaders must recognise, as Collinson (2008) argues, that they have a responsibility to develop capacity by creating an environment that promotes innovation, inquiry, dissemination and shared understandings, arguing that:

Individual learning is not enough ... Organisational learning requires all members to learn and contribute ... and understand how their own thinking and behaviors influence their environment ... Working to establish integrity and trust is critical ... Given ... the importance of social infrastructure to the organisation's capacity … leaders in school systems have to pay particular attention to how they and members influence the social environment. (Collinson, 2008: 448–51)

Similarly, Smylie (1995) drew upon a range of adult learning theories to identify conditions for effective workplace learning, including opportunities for teachers to learn from peer colleagues in collaborative group work settings, with open communication, experimentation and feedback. The community focus emphasises mutually supportive relationships and the development of shared norms and values, whereas the focus in the literature about professionals and professionalism is towards the acquisition of knowledge and skills, orientation to clients and professional autonomy (Louis and Kruse, 1995). Earley and Bubb (2004) argue that the six key features of a learning organisation are pupil learning; adult learning; leadership for learning; school-wide learning; school-to-school learning; and network to network learning, taking the notion of the learning organisation beyond the school boundaries.

Collinson (2008) notes, however, that teachers have tended to choose continuing professional development opportunities in a relatively haphazard way, although this might be seen as exercising professional judgement and choice. She suggests that for all members of the school community CPD within a learning organisation must move beyond individual learning but not be confined within a narrow instrumental framework of provision. School leaders must ensure that CPD provision enables all members of a school community to share their learning collectively, to engage in collaborative enquiry and to contribute towards the improvement of the system. Bush and Middlewood (2005) identify six key steps that school leaders can take if they are successfully to enable teachers in their schools to benefit from a less instrumental and mechanistic approach to continuing professional development, which acknowledges the nature of wider nature of teacher professionalism. These are to:

- be a role model learner personally committed to their own learning
- support all employees as learners, recognising that staff have different personal and professional aspirations
- encourage the sharing of learning
- build an emphasis on learning into all management processes
- develop a culture of enquiry and reflection
- assess the effectiveness of staff learning.

In addition, Bottery (2004) argues that if school leaders are effectively to support appropriate forms of CPD they must develop an ecological and political awareness of factors beyond the boundaries of their own institutions; espouse and articulate a more fully developed notion of the public good as a foundation for professional practice; and develop a much greater capacity for professional self-reflection. Thus school leaders must locate continuing professional development activities for themselves and their staff within a wider professional and political context, based on a model of professionalism that encourages self-development, reflection and is aimed at meeting an appropriate balance of national, school and individual teachers' needs and priorities.

It can be argued, therefore that in order to counteract a narrow, technicist, compliance-driven CPD agenda, school leaders need to move towards a form of continuing professional development that is 'professional in the sense that it is informed and actively engaged rather than passively "professional" through a timid but prescriptive and coercive technology of teaching and learning' (Bates, 2005: 2).

As Sachs (2003) argues, teacher professionalism should be collaborative, activist and knowledge creating. Hoyle and Wallace (2007) go further and argue that the typical notion of professionalism, involving a combination of expertise, autonomy and service, is inadequate to deal with the realities of the teacher's professional world. It must be supplemented by a recognition of personal, professional and contextual limitations and of the provisional nature of current professional knowledge and expertise. Successful professional practice in the current educational climate requires school leaders to adopt a professional stance based on scepticism towards declared legislative intentions, a pragmatic and piecemeal approach to implementation and the need to mediate between legislation and the context within which it has to be implemented. School leaders need to recognise the ambiguities, dilemmas and ironies generated by legislation and the nature of schools as organisations.

There is no simple response that school leaders can adopt to the dilemma that the contested nature of teacher professionalism presents. A strategy based loosely on a reconsideration of new professionalism and a recognition of the reality of schools as organisations must suffice. As Walker and Shuangye (2008) argue, writing about recent developments in Hong Kong, school leaders must:

> Connect to … realities. Within such a reality, schools are not always smooth, happy places, and leadership is not always easy … To be

worthwhile programs must face reality openly, building spaces where people feel able to express themselves and have their perceptions challenged. The people involved in running the program must set and model ethical beliefs. (Walker and Shuangye, 2008: 23)

Essentially it must be recognised that there is no single or 'correct' way either to lead or structure an organisation; the 'leaders', the 'led' and the organisation itself each have distinctive, even unique, characteristics, as do the tasks of leadership and management in what is invariably a changing, turbulent environment. Given the unavoidably contingent and unpredictable nature of their work, effective leaders and managers should adopt strategies and methods appropriate to their particular organisations, tasks, staff and contexts – local and national. It follows that they should learn and use a repertoire of styles and techniques and exercise informed professional judgement to operate effectively within the constraints and opportunities of their unique situation. If education in its widest sense is to move forward such a repertoire should be focused on sustaining an enhanced model of teacher professionalism and the CPD provision that this requires, rather than seeking refuge in a narrow and instrumental interpretation of the status of teachers and the mechanistic CPD that this implies.

Further reading

Bolam, R. and Weindling, D. (2006) *Synthesis of Research and Evaluation Projects Concerned with Capacity-building through Teachers' Professional Development.* Birmingham: General Teaching Council for England.

Hargreaves, A. (2006) 'Four ages of professionalism and professional learning', in H. Lauder, P. Brown, J. Dillabough and A.H. Halsey (eds), *Education, Globalization and Social Change.* Oxford: Oxford University Press.

Hextall, I., Gewirtz, S., Cribb, A. and Mahony, P. (2007) *Changing Teacher Roles, Identities and Professionalism: An Annotated Bibliography.* http://www.kcl.ac.uk/content/1/c6/01/41/56/bibliography.pdf

References

Adegoke, K.A. (2003) *Capacity Building of Lead Teacher Training Institutions in Sub-Saharan Africa.* Ghana: UNESCO Sponsored Project – 4500007474.

Alexander, R. (2004) 'Excellence, enjoyment and personalised learning', keynote address to National Union of Teachers' National Education Conference, 3 July. http://www.robinalexander.org.uk/downloads.htm (retrieved 21 November 2008).

Anderson, G., Creighton, T., Dartley, M., English, F., Furman, G., Gronn, P. and Marshall, C. (2002) 'Invited commentary. Problematizing the ISLLC Standards', *American Educational Research Association Division A – Educational Administration Newsletter*, University of Maryland.

Association of Teachers and Lecturers (2005) *Policy Statement on New Professionalism.* London: ATL.

Balazs, E. (1999) 'Institution-level educational management in Hungarian public education', in R. Bolam and F. van Wieringen (eds), *Research on Educational Management in Europe.* Munster/New York: Waxmann.

Ball, S. (2005) 'Educational reform as social Barberism: economism and the end of authenticity', *Scottish Educational Review*, 37(1): 4–16.

Ball, S. (2008) 'The legacy of ERA, privatization and the policy ratchet', *Educational Management Administration and Leadership*, 36(2): 185–200.

Barber, M. (2000) 'Large-scale educational reform in England: a work in progress', paper presented to the Managing Educational Reform Conference, Moscow, 29–30 October.

Bartley, K. (2008) 'Why teacher professionalism matters', address to Childhood, Well-being and Primary Education Conference, Westminster, 17 March.

Bates, R. (2005) Untitled paper presented to the Teacher Training Agency Teaching 2020 Colloquium, London, 2 March.

Bell, L. (2007) *Perspectives on Educational Management and Leadership.* London: Continuum Books.

Bolam, R. (1993) 'Recent developments and emerging issues', in GTC Trust (ed.), *The Continuing Professional Development of Teachers.* London: GTC Trust.

Bolam, R. (2000) 'Emerging policy trends: some implications for continuing professional development', *Journal of In-service Education*, 26(2): 267–79.

Bolam, R., Dunning, G. and Karstanje, P. (eds) (2000) *New Heads in the New Europe.* Munster/New York: Waxmann.

Bottery, M. (2004) *The Challenges of Educational Leadership.* London: Paul Chapman Publishing.

Bush, T. and Middlewood, D. (2005) *Leading and Managing People in Education.* London: Sage.

CCSSO (1996) *ISLLC Standards for School Leaders.* Washington, DC: Council of Chief State School Officers.

CCSSO (2008) *Educational Leadership Policy Standards ISLLC 2008: As Adopted by the National Policy Board for Educational Administration.* Washington, DC: Council of Chief State School Officers.

Chapman, N. (1995) 'Developing a sense of mission at Whitefields School: the tension between action research and school management', *Educational Management and Administration*, 23(3): 206–11.

Clegg, S. (2003) 'Problematising ourselves: continuing professional development in higher education', *International Journal of Academic Development*, 8(1/2): 37–50.

Collinson, V. (2008) 'Leading by learning: new directions in the twenty-first century', *Journal of Educational Administration,* 46(4): 443–60.

Crawford, C. (2009) 'Continuing professional development in higher education – tensions and debates in a changing environment', in L. Bell, M. Neary and H. Stevenson (eds), *The Future of Higher Education: Policy, Practice and the Student Experience.* London: Continuum.

DfES (2004a) *Every Child Matters.* London: Stationery Office.

DfES (2004b) *Five Year Strategy for Children and Learners.* London: Stationery Office.

DfES (2007) *The Revised Standards for Qualified Teacher Status*. London: Stationery Office.

Earley, P. and Bubb, S. (2004) *Leading and Managing Continuing Professional Development*. London: Paul Chapman Publishing.

Eraut, M. (1994) *Developing Professional Knowledge and Competence*. London: Falmer Press.

Ferlie, E., Ashburner, L. and Pettigrew, A. (1996) *The New Public Management in Action*. Oxford: Oxford University Press.

Fullan, M. (2001) *The New Meaning of Educational Change*. 3rd edn. London: Routledge/Falmer.

GTC (General Teaching Council) (2001) *Professional Learning Framework: A Draft for Discussion and Development*. London: GTC.

Gray, S. (2005) *An Enquiry into Continuing Professional Development for Teachers*. Cambridge: Esmée Fairbairn Foundation and Villiers Park Educational Trust.

Halasz, G. (2000) 'System regulation changes in education and their implications for management development', unpublished keynote paper for the Annual Conference of the European Network for the Improvement of Research and Development in Educational Management (ENIRDEM), 23 September, Tilburg University, Netherlands.

Harber, C. (2005) 'Roles, identities and professionalism: lessons from the comparative study of Africa', paper presented to the Conference on Changing Teacher Roles, Identities and Professionalism. London: King's College.

Hargreaves, A. (1994) *Changing Teachers, Changing Times: Teachers' Work and Culture in the Post-modern Age*. London: Cassell.

Hargreaves, A. and Goodson, I. (1996) 'Teachers' professional lives: aspirations and actualities', in A. Hargreaves and I. Goodson (eds), *Teachers' Professional Lives*. London: Falmer.

HEA (Higher Education Academy) (2006) *Professional Standards Framework for teaching and support learning in higher education*. http://www.heacademy.ac.uk/ourwork/policy/framework (retrieved 4 December 2008).

Heneman, H. and Milanowski, T. (2007) *New Approaches to Teacher Compensation: Research Results and Policy Applications*. Madison, WI: University of Wisconsin-Madison, Consortium for Policy Research in Education.

Hess, F. and Kelly, A (2007) 'Learning to lead: what gets taught in principal preparation programs', Teachers' College Record. http://www.tcrecord.org/print content.asp?contentid12742 (retrieved 30 April 2009).

Heystek, J. (2007) 'Reflecting on principals as managers or moulded leaders in a managerialist school system', *South African Journal of Education*, 27(3): 491–505.

Hoyle, E. and Wallace, M. (2007) 'Education reform: an ironic perspective', *Educational Management, Administration and Leadership*, 35(1): 9–25.

Jordet, C. (2000) 'New heads in Norway', in R. Bolam, G. Dunning and P. Karstanje (eds), *New Heads in the New Europe*. Munster/New York: Waxmann.

Karstanje, P. (1999) 'Developments in school management from a European perspective', in R. Bolam and F. van Wieringen (eds), *Research on Educational Management in Europe*. Munster/New York: Waxmann.

Karstanje, P. (2000) 'New heads in five countries', in R. Bolam, G. Dunning and P. Karstanje (eds), *New Heads in the New Europe*. Munster/New York: Waxmann.

Kennedy, K. (2005) 'Rethinking teachers' professional responsibilities: towards a civic professionalism', *International Journal of Citizenship and Teacher Education*, 1(1): 3–15.

King, M.B. and Newmann, F.M. (2001) 'Building school capacity through professional development: conceptual and empirical considerations', *International Journal of Educational Management*, 15(2): 86–93.

Kolb, D.A. (1975) *Experiential Learning*. Englewood Cliffs, NJ: Prentice-Hall.

Leithwood, K., Jantzi, D. and Steinbach, R. (1995) 'An organisational learning perspective on school responses to central policy initiatives', *School Organisation*, 15(3): 2–20.

Levačić, R. (1999) 'Managing resources for school effectiveness in England and Wales: institutionalising a rational approach', in R. Bolam and F. van Wieringen (eds), *Research on Educational Management in Europe*. Munster/New York: Waxmann.

Liebermann, A. and Friedrich, L. (2007) 'Changing teachers from within: teachers as leaders', in J. MacBeath and Y.C. Cheng (eds), *Leadership for Learning: International Perspectives*. Amsterdam: Sense.

Louis, K.S., and Kruse, S.D. (1995) *Professionalism and Community: Perspectives on Reforming Urban Schools*. Thousand Oaks, CA: Corwin Press.

MacBeath, J., Galton, M., Steward, S. and Page, C. (2007) 'Pressure and professionalism: the impact of recent and present government policies on the working lives of teachers', report commissioned by the National Union of Teachers, University of Cambridge, Faculty of Education.

McMahon, A. (1999) 'Promoting continuing professional development for teachers: an achievable target for school leaders?', in T. Bush, L. Bell, R. Bolam, R. Glatter and P. Ribbins (eds), *Re-defining Educational Management*. London: Paul Chapman Publishing.

McNamara, O., Brundrett, M. and Webb, R. (2008) *Primary Teachers: Initial Teacher Education, Continuing Professional Development and School Leadership Development. Primary Review Research Survey 6/3*. primaryreview.org.uk (retrieved 18 November 2008).

Mestry, R. and Singh, P. (2007) 'Continuing professional development for principals: a South African Perspective', *South African Journal of Education*, 27(3): 477–90.

Moloi, K. (2007) 'An overview of educational management in South Africa', *South African Journal of Education*, 27(3): 463–76.

Moos, L. and Dempster, N. (1998) 'Some comparative learnings from the study', in J. MacBeath (ed.), *Effective School Leadership: Responding to Change*. London: Paul Chapman Publishing.

Naidoo, R. and Jamieson, I. (2006) 'Empowering participants or corroding learning? Towards a research agenda on the impact of student consumerism in Higher Education', in H. Lauder, P. Brown, J. Dillabough and A.H. Halsey (eds), *Education, Globalization and Social Change*. Oxford: Oxford University Press.

NBPTS (National Board for Professional Teaching Standards) (1993) *What Should Teachers Know and Be Able to Do?* Detroit: NBPTS.

OECD (Organisation for Economic Co-operation and Development) (1982) *In-service Education and Training for Teachers: A Condition for Educational Change*. Paris: OECD.

OECD (Organisation for Economic Co-operation and Development) (1998) *Staying Ahead: In-service Training and Teacher Professional Development*. Paris: OECD.

OECD (Organisation for Economic Co-operation and Development) (2001) *New School Management Approaches*. Paris: OECD.

Pitre, P. and Smith, W. (2004) 'ISLLC standards and school leadership; who's leading this band?' http://www.tcrecord.org/printcontent.asp?contentid111382 (retrieved 30 April 2009).

Randle, K. and Brady, N. (1997) 'Managerialism and professionalism in the Cinderella service', *Journal of Vocational Education and Training*, 49(1): 121–39.

Redmond, R., Curtis, E., Noone, T. and Keenan, P. (2008) 'Quality in higher education: the contribution of Edward Deming's principles', *International Journal of Educational Management*, 22(5): 432–41.

Sachs, J. (2003) *The Activist Teaching Profession*. Buckingham: Open University Press.

Schön, D.A. (1987) *The Reflective Practitioner: How Professionals Think in Action*. New York: Basic Books.

Smylie, M.A. (1995) 'Teacher learning in the workplace: implications for school reform', in T.R. Guskey and M. Huberman (eds), *Professional Development in Education: New Paradigms and Practices*. New York: Teachers College Press.

Stevenson, H. (2007) 'Restructuring teachers' work and trade union responses in England: bargaining for change?', *American Educational Research Journal*, 44(2): 224–51.

TDA (Training and Development Agency) (2003) *Raising Standards and Tackling Workload*. London: Stationery Office.

TDA (Training and Development Agency) (2008) *The Revised Framework of Professional Standards for Teachers*. http://www.cfbt.com/lincolnshire/docs/TDA%20Professional%20Standards%20Presentation.ppt (retrieved 19 November 2008).

Thrupp, M. and Willmott, R. (2003) *Education Management in Managerialist Times: Beyond Textual Apologists*. Maidenhead: Open University Press.

Tranter, S. and Percival. A. (2006) *Performance Management in Schools*. London: Longman.

TTA (Teacher Training Agency) (1998) *National Standards for Qualified Teacher Status*. London: TTA.

Van der Westhuizen, P. and van Vuuren, H. (2007) 'Professionalising principalship in South Africa', *South African Journal of Education*, 27(3): 431–45.

Walker, A and Shuangye, C. (2008) 'Innovative programs: flexibility within structure: leader development in Hong Kong', *UCEA Review*, University Council for Educational Administration. 49(3): 22–3.

Whitty, G. (1997) 'Marketisation and the teaching profession', in A.H. Halsey, H. Lauder, P. Brown and A. Stuart Wells (eds), *Education: Culture, Economy and Society*. Oxford: Oxford University Press.

CHAPTER 7

Leadership Development

Tony Bush

Introduction: why is leadership development important?

There is great interest in educational leadership in the early part of the twenty-first century. This is because of the widespread belief that the quality of leadership makes a significant difference to school and student outcomes. In many parts of the world, including both developed and developing countries, there is increasing recognition that schools require effective leaders and managers if they are to provide the best possible education for their students and learners. Pashiardis (2001) argues that educational leaders should be 'torchbearers' for educational change but Crow et al. (2008) caution that leaders do not have control over all the elements which contribute to school improvement. However, Leithwood et al. (2006: 4) show that 'school leadership is second only to classroom teaching as an influence on pupil learning'. They conclude that: 'There is not a single documented case of a school successfully turning around its pupil achievement trajectory in the absence of talented leadership' (Leithwood et al., 2006: 5).

While the argument that leadership *does* make a difference is increasingly, if not universally, accepted, there is ongoing debate about what preparation is required to develop appropriate leadership behaviours. This relates to conceptions of the principal's role, 'preparation for what?' (Crow et al., 2008: 3). In many countries, school leaders begin their professional careers as teachers and progress to headship via a range of leadership tasks and roles, often described as 'middle management'. Principals may continue to teach following their appointment, particularly in small primary schools. This leads to a widespread view that teaching is their main activity (Roeder and Schkutek, 2003: 105).

This focus on principals as head*teachers* underpins the view that a teaching qualification and teaching experience are the only necessary requirements for school leadership. Bush (2008) notes that principals in Africa and much of Europe are often appointed on the basis of a successful record as teachers with the implicit assumption that this provides a sufficient starting point for school leadership. However, the increasing literature on leadership development in the twenty-first century (for example, Bush, 2008; Hallinger, 2003; Huber, 2004; Lumby et al., 2008a; Watson, 2003) portends a sea change in attitudes accompanied by a more limited but still tangible shift in policy and practice. These authors and editors point to a growing realisation that headship is a specialist occupation that requires specific preparation. Bush (2008) identifies four factors underpinning this change:

- The *expansion of the role of school principal*, arising from enhanced accountability requirements and, in many countries, the devolution of additional powers to the school level.

- The *increasing complexity of school contexts*, arising from globalisation, technological and demographic changes, and the demands of enhanced site-based responsibilities.

- *Recognition that preparation is a moral obligation*, because principals have onerous responsibilities that differ from those facing teachers, and leaders should have an 'entitlement' (Watson, 2003) to specialised preparation.

- *Recognition that effective preparation and development make a difference.* Many new principals 'flounder' (Sackney and Walker, 2006: 344) and leadership is not 'fixed at birth' (Avolio, 2005: 2), leading to a view that systematic preparation, rather than inadvertent experience, is more likely to produce effective leaders (Bush, 2008).

Who should be developed?

Bush and Jackson's (2002) review of school leadership programmes in seven countries showed that leadership development is usually targeted at current or aspiring principals. There was much less provision for leaders at other levels, although Singapore has a full-time course for middle managers and most states and provinces in North America require their assistant principals to be qualified. The English National College for School Leadership (NCSL) has the most comprehensive provision. Its Leadership Development Framework provides programmes at five levels from middle leaders to consultant headteachers. It also provides development opportunities for senior leadership teams (Bush, 2006, 2008).

The journey from classroom teacher to school principal usually involves the gradual accumulation of leadership responsibilities, linked to a reduction in the teaching role. Middle leaders, for example, typically receive some 'non-contact' time to compensate them for their work outside the classroom. Although the extra time is widely regarded as inadequate (Bush, 2002; Bush and Glover, 2008), it provides a modest recognition that leadership is a different role, with discrete demands.

Many second-tier leaders (variously described as deputy or vice-principals, assistant, associate or deputy heads) often have substantial non-contact time, which may be 50 per cent or more, depending on school size and the availability of financial and human resources. Most principals are either full-time leaders, or have only a limited classroom teaching role, suggesting a substantial shift over time from teacher to leader (see Figure 7.1). Ideally, each of these stages should be accompanied by specific preparation and development but, in practice, the main or exclusive focus in most countries is on preparing principals. This links to what Gronn (2002) describes as the 'heroic' model of leadership where the principal is held accountable for school outcomes, neglecting the reality that effective schools require many successful leaders, not just a competent principal. The increasing interest in distributed leadership (Harris, 2004) attests to discomfort with a singular model linked to the formal management position of the principal but, with a few isolated exceptions, this has not resulted in significant changes in the target audience for formal programmes of leadership development.

The imminent retirement of the 'baby boom' generation of principals, born in the years after the Second World War, threatens a leadership crisis in many nations, particularly in Europe and North America. This has led to an emphasis on succession planning in some countries, notably in England where the NCSL has introduced a programme designed to 'fast track' leaders into senior positions, and to encourage schools and local authorities to 'grow their own' leaders (Bush et al., 2009). While the evaluation of the programme shows a variable response to this initiative, there is some evidence that it has energised leadership development and encouraged many more teachers to seek careers as senior leaders (Bush et al., 2009).

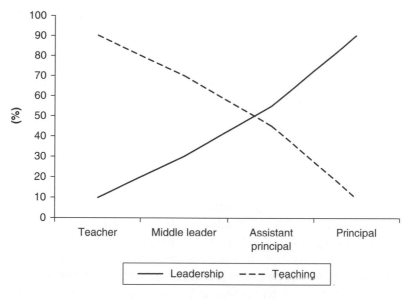

Figure 7.1 Career path from teaching to leadership

Culture, context and leadership development

The literature on leadership is dominated by Western perspectives, leading some writers to advocate a unitary, or 'one size fits all', model of leadership development. However, there is also increasing recognition of the importance of culture and context in designing leadership development programmes. Referring to leadership in the Middle East, MacPherson and Tofighian (2008: 406) caution against cultural homogeneity in theory building: 'The normal patterns of Western knowledge production regarding educational leadership have limited proven technical capacity to accommodate diversity as a norm in pluralistic societies.' Similar reservations are expressed in respect of Africa (Bush and Oduro, 2006), Chinese societies (Walker et al., 2008) and Small-Island states (Bush et al., 2008). These manifestations of the centrality of societal culture prompt Lumby et al. (2008b: 467) to comment that 'the dominance of Anglophone theory and practice is subject to a rising tide of objection'.

In some countries, the need for customised leadership preparation is becoming evident. What may be presented as 'generic' components of leadership have been dismissed by Leithwood et al. (1999: 4) as 'never more than the "basic skills" of leadership' because 'outstanding leadership is exquisitely sensitive to the context in which it is exercised'. Southworth (2005: 77) adds that 'where you are affects what you do as a leader'.

It is a small step from acknowledging context-specific leadership to advocating the desirability of customised development opportunities for school leaders. Heck (2003) uses the twin concepts of professional and organisational socialisation as a lens to examine the impact of preparation. Professional socialisation includes formal preparation, where it occurs, and the early phases of professional practice. Organisational socialisation involves the process of becoming familiar with the specific context where leadership is practised. This distinction is helpful in thinking about how leadership preparation and development should be planned. Where leaders are preparing to take a more senior position, such as principal, they are engaged in a process of professional socialisation. Because future leaders rarely know where they will be appointed, context-specific preparation is not possible, although developing skills of situational analysis is both possible and desirable. In-service leadership development, however, needs to include a significant element of school-specific learning. This leads to a consideration of the nature of leadership preparation and development.

The curriculum for leadership development

Bolam (1999: 196) argues that leadership development can be grouped into four modes:

- Knowledge for understanding.
- Knowledge for action.
- Improvement of practice.
- Development of a reflexive mode.

Content-led programmes, particularly those provided by universities, may be regarded as predominantly aiming at 'knowledge for understanding'. Each programme has a 'curriculum' that gives an indication of the topics to be included. Bush and Jackson (2002: 421) conclude that there is an 'international curriculum' for school principal preparation:

> Most courses focus on leadership, including vision, mission and transformational leadership, give prominence to issues of learning and teaching, often described as instructional leadership, and

incorporate consideration of the main task areas of administration or management, such as human resources and professional development, finance, curriculum and external relations.

In the United States, the content is linked to the Standards for School Leaders, developed by the Interstate School Leaders Licensure Consortium (ISLLC). Bjork and Murphy (2005: 14) claim that such programmes 'tend to place greater emphasis on the application of knowledge to improve practice than on theoretical issues'. In Singapore, there has been a national programme for school principals since 1984. The most recent version of this course, Leaders in Education, introduced in 2001, stresses 'delivery' rather than curriculum content (Chong et al., 2003: 170). This example illustrates a widespread shift in emphasis in the twenty-first century, from content to process, from 'what' is included in development programmes to 'how' they are designed and delivered.

Leadership development processes

Bolam's (1999) categories of 'knowledge for action', and 'improvement for practice' (see above) suggest a focus on process rather than content. Instead of the adoption of a prescribed curriculum, leaders are developed through a range of action modes and support mechanisms, often customised to the specific needs of leaders through what is increasingly referred to as 'personalised' learning. Such individualisation is justified because school leaders are adults, and senior professionals, who expect to be involved in determining their own leadership learning.

Personalised learning

Burgoyne et al. (2004: 3) conclude that there is no single way in which management and leadership development creates leadership capability. Rather, there are many different forms of development that can generate capacity. Personalised provision recognises the need for leadership learning to be tailored to the specific needs of individual leaders through devices such as facilitation, mentoring and coaching.

The redesigned National Professional Qualification for Headship (NPQH) is described as a 'personalised programme based on individual development needs' (NCSL NPQH website). 'Trainee heads' design their own personalised pathway, including a placement in another context, peer learning with other trainee heads, work-based learning in their current school, attending development events, and one-to-one coaching (ibid). According to the NCSL (ibid), trainee heads will be competent and confident to apply for headship, immediately on graduation. It is too early to judge if such claims are justified but they do show the college's confidence in the efficacy of personalised leadership learning.

Personalised learning often involves the support of a facilitator, mentor or coach.

Facilitation

Rigg and Richards (2005) argue that support for leaders needs to be multifaceted: mentor, coach, facilitator. While these approaches can be distinguished conceptually, there is considerable overlap in the ways they are practised. The facilitator may be seen as a source of expertise and as a mentor to participants (Rigg and Richards, 2005). Facilitation is used extensively in programmes provided by the English NCSL and is often one of the widely applauded dimensions of such programmes. It is particularly effective where the facilitators have specific knowledge of the contexts in which participants work, for example, small primary schools (Bush et al., 2007a).

Mentoring

Barnett and O'Mahony (2008: 222) refer to 'the growing recognition [of the need] to provide support for aspiring and practicing leaders' and point to mentoring (and coaching) as key support processes. Mentoring refers to a process where one person provides individual support and challenge to another professional. The mentor may be a more experienced leader or the process may be one of peer mentoring. Barnett and O'Mahony (2008: 238) describe it as 'one of the prominent fads to sweep the education scene' and 'a panacea for many problems that beset educators'. They add that mentoring is 'intended to encourage formal and informal career development [and] reciprocal learning between mentors and mentees' (2008: 238).

Bush et al. (2007a) note that mentoring is becoming more person-centred with an increased awareness of the need to match mentor and mentee, to ensure that mentors are properly trained and that there is time, support and understanding of the reflective process. Pocklington and Weindling (1996: 189) argue that 'mentoring offers a way of speeding up the process of transition to headship'.

Hobson and Sharp's (2005) systematic review of the literature found that all major studies of formal mentoring programmes for new heads reported that such programmes have been effective, and that the mentoring of new heads can result in a range of perceived benefits for both mentees and mentors. However, mentoring is only likely to succeed if there is careful selection of mentors, specific training linked to the needs of the programme, and purposive matching of mentors and mentees.

Coaching

Coaching is in the ascendancy as a mode of development in NCSL programmes (Bush et al., 2007a). Coaching differs from mentoring in being short-term (Barnett and O'Mahony 2008) and being focused on developing specific skills (Bassett 2001), but such distinctions are not applied consistently and coaching and mentoring practices often seem quite similar. Robertson's (2005) statement that coaching involves two people setting and achieving professional goals, being open to new learning, and engaging in dialogue for the purpose of improving leadership practice, for example, could just as easily apply to mentoring.

Simkins et al. (2006), looking at NCSL approaches, conclude that three important issues affect the coaching experience: coach skills and commitment, the time devoted to the process, and the place of coaching within broader school leadership development strategies. The NPQH is one major programme to include coaching. Trainee heads are entitled to one-to-one coaching for up to seven hours (NCSL NPQH website). Bush et al. (2007a) conclude that coaching appears to work best when training is thorough and specific, when there is careful matching of coach and coachee, and when it is integral to the wider learning process.

Group learning

Despite the tendency to emphasise individual leadership learning, group activities play a significant part in many development programmes. While this may sometimes be an opportunity for an essentially didactic approach, delivering a 'body of knowledge', there are several other group learning strategies that may be employed to promote participants' learning. Rusch (2008: 225) notes significant changes in the pedagogy of leadership development, worldwide, from lectures and examinations to 'more sophisticated knowledge about adult learning and recognition that the complex work of school leadership requires not only hands-on practice, but extensive critique of and reflection on that practice'. Three examples of this 'new' approach to leadership development are action learning, networking and portfolios.

Action learning
An enhanced focus on action learning arises, in part, because of an increased recognition that leadership and management are practical activities. While knowledge and understanding serve to underpin managerial performance, they provide an inadequate guide to practice. Hallinger and Bridges (2007: 2) argue that leadership development should aim at 'preparing managers for action'.

McGill and Beaty (1995) state that action learning provides for continuous learning and reflection by a 'set' of people, using an 'experiential learning cycle'. They show how action learning can contribute to management development through the development of the individual manager and the organisation as a whole (1995: 209). Action learning is an important part of the 'delivery architecture' in Singapore's 'Leaders in Education' programme (Chong et al., 2003) and in NCSL's New Visions programme, for new first-time heads. Bush and Glover (2005: 232) note that 'this approach is perceived to be highly effective'.

Networking
Bush and Glover (2004) advocate networking as one of four main leadership development approaches. Bush et al.'s (2007a) overview of NCSL evaluations shows that networking is the most favoured mode of leadership learning. It is likely to be more effective when it is structured and has a clear purpose. Its main advantage is that it is 'live learning' and provides strong potential for ideas transfer. Visits with a clear purpose may also lead to powerful leadership learning. Visiting similar contexts (for example, other small primary schools) appears to be particularly valuable. The new national qualification for principals in South Africa, the Advanced Certificate in Education (School Leadership), includes provision for 'cluster learning', where participants are arranged in geographical groups to facilitate networking and collaborative learning. However, the evaluation evidence suggests only limited benefits from this approach, with some groups meeting rarely or not all, while others meet to discuss their assignments rather than to share ideas about school leadership practice (Bush et al., 2009).

Internships can be seen as a specific form of networking and Crow (2001) argues that this may help with professional socialisation. Huber (2008: 171) claims that school-based internships may be regarded as 'the authentic workplace' to assure 'adequate complexity and authenticity leading to the learning processes required'. He notes that interns often shadow leaders, then partially take over leadership tasks and carry out projects independently. As noted above, the redesigned NPQH includes a placement in another school context, for between five and 20 days (NCSL NPQH website). Rusch (2008: 228) comments that internships have replaced the traditional requirement for school leaders to demonstrate mastery of leadership knowledge. Heck (2003: 247) adds that internships helped aspiring principals to develop 'a clear understanding of their roles and responsibilities'.

Portfolios

Portfolios are becoming significant elements of the assessment process in several leadership development programmes. Wolf and Gearheart (1997: 195) define it as: 'The structured documentary history of a carefully selected set of coached or mentored accomplishments, substantiated by samples of student work, and fully realised only through reflective writing, deliberation, and serious conversation.' Johnston and Thomas (2005) write that their US participants reported benefits, including a 'reciprocal process' between their portfolio work and their development as leaders. Pashiardis and Brauckmann (2008: 269) conclude that the real value of portfolios lies in 'serving the formative purposes of evaluation'. In contrast, Peterson and Kelley (2001) express reservations about teacher portfolios:

1. They are difficult to use for judgements because of a lack of uniformity.
2. Teachers may not be objective when portfolios are used for summative purposes, particularly those related to career development.

Despite these reservations, portfolios have the potential to make an important contribution to leadership learning, partly because programme assessment can be linked firmly to participants' schools, the context where leadership is practised.

Linking content and process?

As we have seen, leaders may be developed through content-focused programmes or process-rich activities. However, much less is known about the best ways to combine these approaches to provide a holistic learning experience to meet the needs of leaders at different career stages, and in different contexts. Bush et al. (2007a) identify four dimensions that should underpin the design of leadership development programmes:

- The learning environment – the most successful learning experiences occur when there is a bridge between the work situation and the learning situation and where participants have the opportunity to reflect on their own practice, and then to share their response with others.

- Learning styles – the most successful adult learning appears to grow from the identification of personalised learning needs.

- Learning approaches – the literature shows that there is only limited value in didactic approaches and considerable gain from active learning.

- Learning support – to ensure effective support, there is a need for careful matching, and ongoing evaluation of relationships, and the quality of support.

These four dimensions are normative constructs, the authors' views on how leadership learning can be enhanced through these four processes. However, in practice, much leadership and management development remains content-led, with a knowledge-based curriculum. Bjork and Murphy (2005: 15), drawing on experience in the USA, comment that 'most courses are delivered using a lecture format that is viewed as being isolated, passive and sterile knowledge acquisition'. Finding an appropriate balance between content and process remains a real challenge for those who design, and those who experience, leadership and management development programmes.

The impact of leadership and management development

There is widespread belief in the efficacy of development programmes, leading to the introduction and growth of such interventions in many countries (Bush, 2008; Hallinger, 2003; Huber, 2004; Watson, 2003). Governments are investing substantial sums in leadership and management development because they believe that it will produce better leaders and more effective schools systems. Individuals are also contributing their time, and often their own resources, to their own professional development because they think that it will enhance their career prospects and make them better leaders. However, the empirical evidence for such assumptions is modest:

> Foundations, governments, international agencies and professional associations have turned their attention to the quality of

formal leadership development and have raised central questions about the impact of existing efforts including the question of how one would assess this impact. But the empirical basis for answering these questions remains quite small' (Leithwood and Levin, 2008: 281).

In simple terms, the purpose of leadership and management development is to produce more effective leaders. An everyday definition of effectiveness is that the intended outcomes of an activity are achieved. Programmes and activities need to be judged against this criterion. Bush (2008: 108) asks whether such processes produce better leaders and, critically, are certain approaches likely to be more successful than others in achieving positive outcomes?

The challenges involved in designing, and evaluating, preparation and development initiatives may be expressed through a series of questions:

1. Is the main purpose of the activity to develop individual leaders or to promote wider leadership development?
2. Should leadership development be underpinned by succession planning, or be targeted at the needs and aspirations of individual leaders?
3. Should leadership development be standards-based, or promote a more holistic approach?
4. Should leadership development be content-led or based around processes?
5. Should leadership development programmes aim at inculcating a specific repertoire of leadership practices?
6. Should leadership learning be predominantly campus-based or field-based?
7. Should leadership learning address issues of equity and diversity? (Bush, 2008: 108–9).

There is insufficient space to address these issues but a full discussion may be found in Bush (2008).

Evaluation and impact: models and evidence

Leadership development programmes are often subject to evaluation but the approaches usually employed are subject to two main limitations:

1. They rely mainly or exclusively on *self-reported evidence*. Participants are asked about their experience of the activity and, more rarely, about its impact on their schools. This is a weak approach because it is not subject to corroboration, for example, by colleagues, and because it is inevitably subjective.

2. The evaluation is usually *short term*. Participants' views are often sought during and/or at the end of the development activity. It is widely recognised that the impact of interventions, such as a leadership programme, takes time. It is unlikely that significant changes in leadership practice will have occurred during the training period. (Bush, 2008: 114)

Even where these two pitfalls are avoided, there is still the problem of attributing beneficial effects to the development activity when there are likely to be many other contemporaneous events that could also contribute to change. However, addressing the two limitations set out above would produce more credible, if not totally reliable, findings.

In England, there is increasing concern about whether and how leadership impacts on school outcomes:

> Greater understanding is needed of the linkages and mediators between leadership and educational attainment and social outcomes … [there is a] lack of consensus about the contribution of different elements to the linkages, indirect effects and mediating factors for improving school leadership. (DfES, 2004: para. 22)

Leithwood and Levin (2004: 2) note that 'linking leadership to student outcomes in a direct way is very difficult to do'. They conclude that 'a study that seeks to assess the impact that school leadership can have on school outcomes faces some formidable challenges' (Leithwood and Levin, 2004: 25). This is partly because of the problems in attributing outcomes to a specific development initiative and partly because leadership is a mediated variable, impacting on student outcomes through influencing teachers' classroom practice.

Self-reported data

As noted above, many evaluations of leadership development activities rely wholly, or mainly, on self-reported data. Two such examples are the initial study of the impact of the NCSL programme, 'Leading from the Middle', (Naylor et al., 2006) and the evaluations of the

Scottish Qualification for Headship (Reeves et al., 2001). Both projects report beneficial effects on participants, including enhanced confidence, improved teamwork, and more reflective leadership. Naylor et al. (2006: 14) acknowledge that these findings may represent 'post-programme euphoria' (a potential problem with all short-term impact studies) and also note the limitations of such self-reported data.

Heck's (2003) study of 150 assistant principals, and their supervising principals, goes beyond self-reporting to include the perspectives of their super-ordinates. He notes that those candidates who had progressed to the principalship 'had developed a clear understanding of their role and responsibilities' (2003: 247). Many attributed this to their internship and to the support provided by mentors. These new principals had also established strong support networks that sustained them during difficult periods.

Role set analysis

The weaknesses of self-reporting can be addressed through adopting role set analysis. The perceptions of programme participants can be triangulated (Bush, 2007) by seeking views from close colleagues at the school or workplace. This enables candidates' claims to be corroborated or challenged by the perceptions of those who should be aware of changes in practice. I adopted this approach in three impact studies, two for the NCSL (Bush et al., 2005; 2006) and one in South Africa (Bush et al., 2009).

Bush et al. (2006) examined the impact of the *NCSL's 'New Visions' programme* on school outcomes as part of a wider evaluation of this programme. The research included case study work in a purposive sample of 15 schools in three regions. Researchers interviewed four people in each school to achieve respondent triangulation, and to gauge school effects from four contrasting perspectives: the participant headteachers, leadership team members, classroom teachers and governing body chairs. The authors comment that the effects of the New Visions programme are filtered through many levels before they impact on student outcomes but they also report triangulated evidence of gains in confidence and three main changes in leadership practice:

- A greater emphasis on shared leadership.
- An enhanced focus on leadership for learning.
- Specific changes in school organisation.

Bush et al. (2005) adopted a similar approach in their evaluation of two NCSL team programmes: Developing Capacity for School Improvement (DCSI) and Working Together for Success (WTfS). The evaluation involved case studies of ten schools (five DCSI and five WTfS). Within each school, researchers conducted individual or focus-group interviews with a range of participants and stakeholders as well as scrutinising relevant documents. Bush et al. (2005) conclude that there were significant effects from the WTfS programme, with certain techniques becoming embedded in leadership practice, but more modest effects from the DCSI initiative.

Bush et al. (2009) conducted an evaluation of South Africa's pilot ACE: School Leadership programme, funded by the Zenex Foundation. The research provides a comprehensive evaluation of the programme in order to inform the development of the course and to provide advice to the Minister of Education on whether it should become mandatory for new principals. The emerging evidence is that the ACE produces a short-term *decline* in effectiveness, as leaders focus on preparing their assignments instead of managing their schools, a classic case of an unintended consequence.

Overview

The global interest in leadership development is predicated on the widespread assumption that it will lead to school improvement, and enhanced learning outcomes. The empirical evidence for this perspective is limited and assessing impact is difficult because of several conceptual and methodological problems. First, the purposes of education, and of educational leadership, are wide and varied. The efficacy of leadership activities needs to be tested against all these criteria if a comprehensive assessment of impact is to be made. In practice, however, impact studies tend to focus on the measurable outcomes sought by governments, notably student test scores. Secondly, even where improvements occur, it is very difficult to attribute them with confidence to a specific intervention, such as a leadership development programme, when there are many other contemporaneous changes. Thirdly, while leadership is widely regarded as the second most important factor affecting student outcomes, after classroom teaching, it is a mediated variable with leaders exercising their influence indirectly. This makes it difficult to assess the nature and extent of leaders' impact. Finally, funding bodies rarely support long-term impact studies that could provide more solid evidence of the value of leadership development interventions.

Conclusion: the future of leadership and management development

There is widespread interest in educational leadership and management. The generally accepted belief that effective leadership is vital for successful schooling is increasingly being supported by evidence of its beneficial effects (Hallinger, 2003; Leithwood and Levin, 2008; Leithwood et al., 2006). Where there is failure, inadequate leadership and management is often a major contributory factor.

Given the importance of educational leadership, Bush (2008: 125) argues that the development of effective leaders should not be left to chance. It should be a deliberate process designed to produce the best possible leadership and management for schools and colleges. As the NCSL (2007: 17) succinctly argues, 'leadership must grow by design not by default', an implicit recognition that school leadership is a different role from teaching and requires separate and specialised preparation. The trend towards systematic preparation and development of school and college leaders, while by no means universal, has advanced to the point where the argument is widely accepted. However, there is continuing and ongoing debate about the nature of such provision.

Bush et al. (2007a) say that the most successful learning experiences occur when there is a bridge between the work situation and the learning situation. The NCSL (2007: 17) claims that 'a large amount of ... leadership learning should take place in school', but they also acknowledge that such work-based learning can be 'narrow and conservative' (2007: 18). There is no 'off-the-peg' solution to such dilemmas and course designers need to find a judicious and appropriate balance for their specific client group(s).

The most successful adult learning appears to grow from the identification of personalised learning needs. However, individualised learning is difficult to organise and can be expensive to deliver. For statutory provision, in particular, it also compromises the standardisation required to justify the 'national programme' label.

In the past decade, there has been a global trend towards more systematic provision of leadership and management development, particularly for school principals. Hallinger (2003: 3) notes that, in 1980, 'no nation in the world had in place a clear system of national requirements, agreed upon frameworks of knowledge, and standards of preparation for school leaders'. In the twenty-first century, many countries are giving this a high priority, recognising its potential for school improvement.

This trend is encapsulated most powerfully by the English NCSL but it can also be seen in France, Singapore and South Africa. Candidates undertake 'centralised' training before becoming principals and receive national accreditation on successful completion of the activity. Much of the development work is work based, recognising that leadership practice takes place in schools. Increasingly, current or former principals are involved in designing, leading and delivering leadership programmes, showing that 'craft' knowledge is increasingly respected. The case for systematic, specialised training for principals is persuasive and increasingly accepted (Bush, 2008).

Further reading

Bush, T. (2008) *Leadership Development in Education*. London: Sage.
Lumby, J., Crow, G. and Pashiardis, P. (2008) *Preparation and Development of School Leaders*. New York: Routledge.

References

Avolio, B.J. (2005) *Leadership Development in Balance: Made/Born*. London: Lawrence Erlbaum Associates.
Barnett, B. and O'Mahony, G. (2008) 'Mentoring and coaching programs for the professional development of school leaders', in J. Lumby, G. Crow and P. Pashiardis (eds), *Preparation and Development of School Leaders*. New York: Routledge.
Bassett, S. (2001) 'The use of phenomenology in management research: an exploration of the learner's experience of coach-mentoring in the workplace', paper presented at the Qualitative Evidence-Based Practice Conference, Coventry, May.
Bjork, L. and Murphy, J. (2005) *School Management Training Country Report: The United States of America*. HEAD Country Report. Oslo: BI Norwegian School of Management.
Bolam, R. (1999) 'Educational administration, leadership and management: towards a research agenda', in T. Bush, L. Bell, R. Bolam, R. Glatter and P.M. Robbins (eds), *Educational Management: Redefining Theory, Policy and Practice*. London: Paul Chapman Publishing.
Burgoyne, J., Hirsh, W. and Williams, S.T. (2004), *The Development of Management and Leadership Capability and its Contribution to Performance: The Evidence, the Prospects and the Research Need*. DfES Research Report 560. London: Department for Education and Skills.
Bush, T. (2002) *Middle Level Leaders: a Think Piece*. Nottingham: NCSL.
Bush, T. (2006) 'The National College for School Leadership: A successful English innovation', *Phi Delta Kappan*, 87(7): 508–11.
Bush, T. (2007) 'Authenticity in research – reliability, validity and triangulation', in A. Briggs and M. Coleman (eds), *Research Methods in Educational Leadership and Management*. 2nd edn. London: Sage.

Bush, T. (2008) *Leadership and Management Development in Education*. London: Sage.

Bush, T. and Glover, D. (2004) *Leadership Development: Concepts and Beliefs*. Nottingham: National College for School Leadership.

Bush, T. and Glover, D. (2005) 'Leadership development for early headship: the New Visions experience', *School Leadership and Management*, 25(3): 217–39.

Bush, T. and Glover, D. (2008) *Managing Teaching and Learning: A Concept Paper*. Johannesburg: Matthew Goniwe School of Leadership and Governance.

Bush, T. and Jackson, D. (2002) 'Preparation for school leadership: international perspectives', *Educational Management and Administration*, 30(4): 417–29.

Bush, T. and Oduro, G. (2006) 'New principals in Africa: preparation, induction and practice', *Journal of Educational Administration*, 44(4): 359–75.

Bush, T., Allen, T., Glover, D., Middlewood, D., Parker, R. and Smith, R. (2009) *Succession Planning Programme Evaluation: Final Report*. Nottingham: NCSL.

Bush, T., Briggs, A.R.J. and Middlewood, D. (2006) 'The impact of school leadership development: evidence from the 'New Visions' programme for early headship', *Journal of In-Service Education*, 32(2): 185–200.

Bush, T., Duku, N., Kola, S., Msila, V. and Moorosi, P. (2009) *The Zenex ACE: School Leadership Research: Final Report*. Pretoria: Department of Education.

Bush, T., Glover, D. and Harris, A. (2007a) *Review of School Leadership Development*. Nottingham: NCSL.

Bush, T., Purvis, M.T. and Barallon, L. (2008) 'Leadership development in small-island states', in J. Lumby, G. Crow and P. Pashiardis (eds), *Preparation and Development of School Leaders*. New York: Routledge.

Bush, T., Middlewood, D., Morrison, M. and Scott, D. (2005) *How Teams Make a Difference: The Impact of Team Working*. Nottingham: NCSL.

Chong, K.C., Stott, K. and Low, G.T. (2003) 'Developing Singapore school leaders for a learning nation', in P. Hallinger (ed.), *Reshaping the Landscape of School Leadership Development: A Global Perspective*. Lisse: Swets and Zeitlinger.

Crow, G.M. (2001) 'School leader preparation: a short review of the knowledge base'. NCSL Research Archive.

Crow, G., Lumby, J. and Pashiardis, P. (2008) 'Introduction: why a handbook on the preparation and development of school leaders?', in J. Lumby, G. Crow and P. Pashiardis (eds), *Preparation and Development of School Leaders*. New York: Routledge.

Department for Education and Skills (DfES) (2004) *School Leadership: End to End Review of School Leadership Policy and Delivery*. London: DfES.

Gronn, P. (2002) 'Distributed leadership as a unit of analysis', *The Leadership Quarterly*, 73(2): 1–10.

Hallinger, P. (2003) *Reshaping the Landscape of School Leadership Development: A Global Perspective*. Lisse: Swets and Zeitlinger.

Hallinger, P. and Bridges, E. (2007) *Preparing Managers for Action: A Problem-based Approach*. Dordrecht: Springer.

Harris, A. (2004) 'Distributed leadership and school improvement: leading or misleading?', *Educational Management, Administration and Leadership*, 32(1): 11–24.

Heck, R. (2003) 'Examining the impact of professional preparation on beginning school administrators', in P. Hallinger (ed.), *Reshaping the Landscape of School Leadership Development: A Global Perspective*. Lisse: Swets and Zeitlinger.

Hobson, A. and Sharp, C. (2005) 'Head to head: a systematic review of the research evidence on mentoring new head teachers', *School Leadership and Management*, 25(1): 25–42.

Huber, S. (2004) 'Context of research', in S. Huber (ed.), *Preparing School Leaders for the 21st Century: An International Comparison of Development Programs in 15 Countries*. London: RoutledgeFalmer.

Huber, S. (2008) 'School development and school leader development: New learning opportunities for school leaders and their schools', in J. Lumby, G. Crow and P. Pashiardis (eds), *Preparation and Development of School Leaders*. New York: Routledge.

Johnston, M. and Thomas, M. (2005) 'Riding the wave of administrator accountability: a portfolio approach', *Journal of Educational Administration*, 43(4): 368–86.

Leithwood, K. and Levin, B. (2004) *Assessing School Leader and Leadership Programme Effects on Pupil Learning: Conceptual and Methodological Challenges*. London: Department for Education and Skills.

Leithwood, K. and Levin, B. (2008) 'Understanding and assessing the impact of leadership development', in J. Lumby, G. Crow, and P. Pashiardis (eds), *Preparation and Development of School Leaders*. New York: Routledge.

Leithwood, K., Day, C., Sammons, P., Harris, A. and Hopkins, D. (2006) *Seven Strong Claims about Successful School Leadership*. London: Department for Education and Skills.

Leithwood, K., Jantzi, D. and Steinbach, R. (1999) *Changing Leadership for Changing Times*. Buckingham: Open University Press.

Lumby, J., Crow, G. and Pashiardis, P. (2008a) *Preparation and Development of School Leaders*. New York: Routledge.

Lumby, J., Pashiardis, P. and Crow, G. (2008b) 'Epilogue', in J. Lumby, G. Crow and P. Pashiardis (eds), *Preparation and Development of School Leaders*. New York: Routledge.

MacPherson, R. and Tofighian, O. (2008) 'Preparing and developing school leaders in the Middle East: towards mediating Westernisation with indigenous and evidence-based practice and theories of educative leadership', in J. Lumby, G. Crow and P. Pashiardis (eds), *Preparation and Development of School Leaders*. New York: Routledge.

McGill, I. and Beatty, L. (1995) *Action Learning: A Practitioner's Guide*. London: Kogan Page.

National College for School Leadership (NCSL) (2007) *What We Know about School Leadership*. Nottingham: NCSL. www.ncsl.org.uk

National College for School Leadership (NCSL) NPQH website. www ncsl.org.uk/npqh.

Naylor, P., Gkolia, C. and Brundrett, M. (2006) 'Leading from the middle: an initial study of impact', *Management in Education*, 20(1): 11–16.

Pashiardis, P. (2001) 'Secondary principals in Cyprus: the views of the principal versus the views of the teachers – a case study', *International Studies in Educational Administration*, 29(3): 11–23.

Pashiardis, P. and Brauckmann, S. (2008) 'Evaluation of school principals', in J. Lumby, G. Crow and P. Pashiardis (eds), *Preparation and Development of School Leaders*, New York: Routledge.

Peterson, K. and Kelley, C. (2001) 'Transforming school leadership', *Leadership*, 30(3): 8–11.

Pocklington, K. and Weindling, D. (1996) 'Promoting reflection on headship through the mentoring mirror', *Educational Management and Administration*, 24(2): 175–91.

Reeves, J., Casteel, V., Morris, B. and Barry, P. (2001) 'Testing a standard for headship: outcomes from the initial evaluation of the Scottish Qualification for Headship programme', *International Studies in Educational Administration*, 29(2): 38–49.

Rigg, C. and Richards, C. (2005) *Action Learning, Leadership and Organisational Development in Public Services*. London: Routledge.

Robertson, J. (2005) *Coaching Leadership*. Wellington: NSCER Press.

Roeder, W. and Schkutek, H. (2003) 'The selection, training and further education of headteachers in Germany', in L. Watson (ed.), *Selecting and Developing Heads of Schools: 23 European Perspectives*. Sheffield: European Forum on Educational Administration.

Rusch, E. (2008) 'Curriculum and pedagogy', in J. Lumby, G. Crow and P. Pashiardis (eds), *Preparation and Development of School Leaders*. New York: Routledge.

Sackney, L. and Walker, K. (2006) 'Canadian perspectives on beginning principals: their role in building capacity for learning communities', *Journal of Educational Administration*, 44(4): 341–58.

Simkins, T., Coldwell, M., Caillau, I., Finlayson, H. and Morgan, A. (2006) 'Coaching as an in-school leadership development strategy: experiences from Leading from the Middle', *Journal of In-Service Education*, 32(3): 321–40.

Southworth, G. (2005) 'Learning-centred leadership', in B. Davies (ed.), *The Essentials of School Leadership*. London: Paul Chapman Publishing.

Walker, A., Chen, S. and Qian, H. (2008) 'Leader development across three Chinese societies', in J. Lumby G. Crow and P. Pashiardis (eds), *Preparation and Development of School Leaders*. New York: Routledge.

Watson, L. (2003) *Selecting and Developing Heads of Schools: 23 European Perspectives*. Sheffield: European Forum on Educational Administration.

Wolf, S. and Gearheart, M. (1997) 'Issues in portfolio assessment: assessing writing processes from their products', *Educational Assessment*, 4(4): 265–96.

CHAPTER 8

Managing People and Performance

David Middlewood

Introduction

National governments, and politicians generally, continue to clamour for improved educational performance as a key to improving economic prosperity in their countries. Regularly published educational tables of comparative attainments, usually test results at certain ages, indicate clearly this emphasis – and thereby the pressure – placed on the educational institutions and their leaders to regularly raise the standards, that is, measurable attainment of pupils and students. Schools are often the institutions most stressed in these comparisons because, although in developed countries post-statutory education, including at university level, is also subject to comparison, there is no doubt that governments place most emphasis on performance during statutory school age because of the huge investments in this area. Public scrutiny is therefore greatest in this field.

Leadership and management of schools and of other institutions is seen by a growing number of countries as being a very significant factor in this improvement in their performance. 'There is recognition that schools require effective leaders and managers if they are to provide the best possible education for their students and learners' (Bush, 2008: 1). Research evidence has suggested that leadership can have an impact on student outcomes, although its *direct* influence is very difficult to ascertain (Leithwood and Levin, 2004). Hallinger and Heck (1996) suggested leadership could account for a 7 per cent difference in student achievement, but Leithwood et al. (2006) claimed the difference might be nearer 27 per cent if the impact of leadership at all levels were considered. This is important and underpins one of the three main 'core practices' of leaders as being 'developing people' (Leithwood and Riehl, 2005: 19–22). Studies in Australia (Gurr et al., 2005), Norway (Moller et al., 2005) and Shanghai (Wong, 2004) all demonstrated how leaders effectively engaging with their staff was clearly linked with school and student outcome improvement. In all this therefore is the recognition that those who engage *directly* with students are the key agents for improved performance, especially if they are effectively led and managed. This chapter examines some of the ways in which institutional leaders try to lead and manage these people (primarily teachers and to a lesser extent support staff) in order to improve their performance and consequently overall student and institutional performance.

The chapter's focus is restricted to three important elements of this aspect of leadership, namely:

- acquiring the highest quality staff
- supporting, guiding and developing them as necessary
- evaluating and giving feedback on their performance.

Recruiting and selecting high-quality staff

The ability of educational leaders to recruit and select the best possible staff for their individual institutions is considerably affected by the scope allowed to them according to the national system within which they operate. Broadly there are three which are relevant:

- highly centralised systems, such as China (Bush et al., 1998), Greece (Ifanti, 1995), Cyprus (Pashiardis, 2001)
- federal or state systems, such as Australia, Germany (Huber and Pashiardis, 2008)
- school-based management with decisions at institutional level (England and Wales, Denmark, New Zealand).

Some systems operate a mixture of centralised and federal, where some decisions are taken at provincial level but overseen by national bureaucracy. Each of the two main systems, centralist or institutional 'free market' has its advantages and disadvantages but the scope for the leaders' actions is significantly different. Figures 8.1 and 8.2 show the potential benefits and drawbacks of the two frameworks.

POSSIBLE ADVANTAGES	POSSIBLE DISADVANTAGES
• National policies can be closely adhered to • Records of staff applications maintained/monitored • Consistency of selection procedures more certain • Staff only have to apply once • Greater objectivity in selection process • Staff can be moved if situation requires it • Staff mobility guaranteed – less chance of stagnation	• Decisions made with little awareness of institutional context • Career progression not in applicant's control • National prejudices can be reinforced (for example, in gender, race) • Individuals may be placed in places which they dislike • Staff disruption – people moved if needed elsewhere • Disruption to personal circumstances may be ignored

Figure 8.1   Possible advantages and disadvantages of centralised systems

POSSIBLE ADVANTAGES	POSSIBLE DISADVANTAGES
• More of a genuine '2 way process', applicant can reject offer and apply elsewhere • Institutions know their own local requirements best • Selection process can involve local stakeholders • Individual organisational cultures can be considered • Applicants need only apply to places where they *want* to work • Potential employees can see actual site, meet colleagues, etc. where they may work	• Offers of appointments usually have to be made quickly • If wrong appointment made, expensive and difficult to remove person • Selection process may differ from place to place • Applying for many different posts is laborious and time-consuming • Unsuccessful applicants 'start from scratch' each time with new application • Merely competent/mediocre staff more likely to become complacent

Figure 8.2   Possible advantages and disadvantages of autonomous/'free-market' systems

Within the different systems, actual methods of selection differ considerably according to either national regulations or national custom or culture, and sometimes to institutional variations. These can range from a battery of tests especially for posts involving any form of leadership, as often in the US and England, to interviews only as in Singapore. (Huber and Pashiardis, 2008)

For leaders in centralised systems, Bush (2008: 62) summarises the principle applied in many countries as being 'an essentially bureaucratic process'. This carries with it several of the problems suggested in Figure 8.1. For example, where many candidates have similar qualifications and years of experience, existing inequities in the system will often be confirmed, such as in age (more years in experience equals better), gender, and lack of representation of an ethnic minority (Bush and Moloi, 2007 (South Africa); Bush et al., 2007 (England); Manuel and Slate, 2003 (USA)).

Given all these issues, there remains for leaders the essential fact that, in recruiting and selecting high-quality staff, they are faced with the situation of one person (or persons) making an assessment of another as to their suitability for the specific role. If this seems a truism, it does remind us that:

- Education is a 'people business' and the constant appraisal of other people, whether colleagues, students, parents or others, is a regular part of that business.
- That a mistake in making a bad appointment is 'extremely costly, both in financial and human terms' (Middlewood, 1997b: 140).
- That the removal of all traces of subjectivity in what is meant to be an objective process is impossible (Bush and Middlewood, 2005).

Although some major research studies (Huber and Hiltmann, 2009; Huber and Pashiardis, 2008) address methods of selecting school leaders in a number of countries, less systematic attention is paid to how school leaders themselves select staff. However, given the recognition that removing all subjectivity is impossible, as above, there is evidence that at organisational level there are principles and strategies that can be applied for effective selection.

Recognition of the prejudices of self and other selectors

Lumby with Coleman (2007: 111) powerfully make the point that humans much more easily see the need for change in others than in themselves, 'that it is other people's attitudes … which require adjustment … Leaders assume that because they believe they do not intend discrimination, others do not experience it'.

It follows that leaders who can recognise the prejudices they themselves hold and who have a willingness to face them will have a better chance of minimising their impact on decisions based on impressions made on them. Some of these impressions and related prejudices are well researched, both in educational and also occupational psychology fields, and the selection interview, the most human interactive part of the selection process, is most prone to them. Examples include:

- Selectors often make up their minds about a candidate in the first few minutes of an interview.
- Selectors' judgements can be affected by speech, gender, appearance, race of candidates, either positively or negatively.
- Physically attractive candidates are more likely to be appointed.
- An average candidate who follows several poor ones is seen as good.
- Selectors cannot maintain focus and concentration at the same level over a prolonged period; thus several candidates interviewed one after another may not all receive the same attention.
- Selectors are likely to remember information at the beginning and closing of an interview and more likely to forget what was said between (summarised by Thomson, 1993, and Middlewood, 1997b).

Other impressions with a scope for fallibility include the 'halo effect', whereby when a selector is impressed by one characteristic of a person, he/she will tend to be positive about other characteristics and the 'logical error', whereby the selector assumes that because a person has one feature, (s)he must automatically have another, thus, a 'clever' person must be 'creative'!

Possibly the most important factor of all for school leaders is the 'similarity factor' (Byrne, 1971), where the leader tends to be attracted in selecting to someone who has similar characteristics to his/her own or similar to the person vacating the post. Research by Blackmore et al. (2006) and Grummell et al. (2009) has also stressed this 'homosociability' aspect of selection decisions, so that 'particular qualities of leadership are normalised'. (Grummel et al., 2009: 345). Hinton (1993) points out that at least the chances of appointing someone in 'one's own image' can be reduced to some extent by using a panel of selectors, rather than simply relying on the leader's own assessment. Even at a bureaucratic level, the National College of School Leadership (NCSL) in England found that governors most often sought 'for an individual as similar as possible to the previous school leader in post instead of focusing on the future needs of the school' (NCSL, 2006: 7).

This reference to the future needs of the organisation is crucial for educational leaders in a period of constantly changing circumstances. The 'contextual fit', urged by Huber and Pashiardis (2008: 156), is crucial if the right staff are to be in place for twenty-first century educational organisations. In England, the growth and development of a particular kind of community education in the form of Extended Schools led Middlewood and Parker (2009) to reflect upon approaches to recruitment and selection which had to be radically different from conventional ones. In institutions, where teachers, support staff, community workers, youth workers and professionals from other agencies all work with an impact on student learning, they conclude that leaders should never 'be assuming that like for like replacements are the best solutions to sudden or anticipated needs' (Middlewood and Parker, 2009: 64).

While research continues to explore the effectiveness of selection methods (Lumby et al., 2008), organisational leaders can increase the chances of successful staff appointments by regular evaluation of their own methods. Huber and Pashiardis (2008: 183–95) report that, as far as selection of principals was concerned, places such as Singapore and Germany appeared to carry out no evaluations of the selection process, there were no research findings from evaluations in Australia and the USA, while in England fewer than half of school governing bodies evaluated their methods. Funder (1987) drew attention to the fact that when a panel of selectors agreed on a person, the pleasure in finding agreement could blind them to the fact that the appointment might eventually be unsatisfactory and therefore to the success or otherwise of the actual selection process. Both Middlewood (1997b: 152) and Bush and Middlewood (2005: 137) noted that the success or otherwise of an appointment can only eventually be known through the appointee's subsequent performance.

Supporting, guiding and developing staff

For high performance to be achieved, it seems clear that people need to have job satisfaction to enable them to focus on that job without distraction and then, going beyond this, to be motivated to strive for better. While motivation and job satisfaction are understandably often linked together, they are quite different concepts. Herzberg's (1966) 'two factor theory' demonstrated that the removal of employees' 'dissatisfaction' did not lead to satisfaction or development. Thus, the meeting of at least the minimum in 'hygiene' factors (basic working conditions) would seem to be a prerequisite for leaders achieving staff satisfaction. Two points may however be proposed against this apparently simple assumption.

- The provision of even the basic of necessities can be beyond the power of the school leaders in some countries where the lack of such amenities is widespread. Parts of South Africa in the late 1990s are but one illustration, 'no water within walking distance at a quarter of all schools, power supplies in less than half … and toilets absent in many schools' (Department of Education, 1997).

- People can be highly motivated even when working in conditions of great adversity. Thus, for example, Mwamwenda (1995) found in a survey of Transkei schools that only 10–20 per cent of teachers were dissatisfied. As Lumby (2003: 155) notes: 'Any simple equation which assumes that motivation decreases in the face of poor conditions or increased adversity does not take account of human spirit'.

Bush and Middlewood (2005: 78) define the difference between job satisfaction and motivation as the former being the state affecting the work someone *currently* does, while the latter relates to the notion of *anticipation*, that is, looking forward to what will be achieved. For leaders, Blauner's (1964) four elements of job dissatisfaction remain a useful guide for elements to identify (and avoid) in work structuring:

- powerlessness (no influence in the job being done)
- meaninglessness (no point in the job being done)
- isolation (not fitting in with others)
- self-estrangement (not seeing the job as important).

There are several limitations that educational leaders need to be aware of in developing staff to feel motivated. These include:

- Centralist control, often including a prescribed curriculum. As discussed earlier concerning recruitment and selection, leaders' scope is similarly limited where the rewards and career progression are controlled by national bodies.
- The status conferred upon education and its workers by the society within which the institutions operate. For example, in the 1990s, one of the key factors identified in research by Lewis (1995) and Reynolds and Farrell (1996) into the educational success of Pacific-Rim societies was the high status and prestige of teachers and teaching.
- Cultural influences by which traditionally some factors have come to be seen as more important than others; as Fisher and Yuan's (1998) study found, the differences between China and Russia were significant in terms of what satisfied employees. Employees in both countries stated that being informed and

involved with decisions was important, but those in Russia valued recognition of achievement highly whereas Chinese employees rated financial reward and promotion as more significant.

However, research in the late twentieth and early twenty-first centuries has thrown more light on the complexities of human motivation and human learning and development, suggesting that there are specific things that educational leaders are able to do for effective leadership and management of staff motivation for performance.

- Recognising that motivation is a highly complex concept, leaders need to attempt to identify the factor in each individual's motivation, leading to what Middlewood and Lumby (1998) stated as two assumptions never to be made by leaders, that is, not to assume that what motivates one person will necessarily motivate another and, consequently, not to assume that what motivates the leader will necessarily motivate the led! Saiti's (2007) research among Greek primary teachers, for example, indicated typically that job satisfaction and motivation did not relate to financial factors, and Lam et al. (1997) found in Singapore that altruistic motives persisted despite concerns over financial rewards.
- Take account of individual variables such as stage of career and indeed of life.
- Take account of gender.
- Take account of cultural mix and ethnicity.
- Ensure that the focus remains on the key value that is shared by everyone involved in the educational institution – the quality of learning and teaching. Studies in post-statutory institutions in England and New Zealand (Briggs, 2002; Howse and MacPherson, 2001) in the 1990s revealed a lack of motivation in lecturers as a gap emerged between senior leaders and middle managers over what was important in those places. Following moves to autonomy of polytechnics and further education colleges, leaders had placed great emphasis on training everyone in managerialism and financial competence, leaving staff to complain that the values which were meant to be important and central to their roles, that is, related to student learning, were being neglected.

Having taken account of the variables and noted the individuality of human motivation, educational leaders would seem to need to develop a common sense of direction if the institution is to achieve high performance. It seems clear that the responsibility should lie with sufficient people to enable them to relate to a small enough group of people to allow a personal strategy to motivate the individual to be involved. This has implications for any line management structure and can be complicated by rigidity in leadership and management structures. A recent extensive global examination of leadership development led the editors to conclude that, despite many interesting and different approaches, 'hierarchy matters considerably in many cultures' (Lumby et al., 2008: 446)

The reference above to small groups or teams carries with it implications of shared and distributed leadership, a topic dealt with in Chapter 4. Here, its significance lies in the ownership that individuals are able to be given through working in small teams where scope for developing individual support and motivation can be greater.

Perhaps it is in supporting the learning and development of individuals that leaders can best enable them to be self-motivated for performance and thereby contribute to institutional achievement. The phrase 'learning and development' is used here because it implies concern for staff as people in their personal and/or professional learning, and thereby a degree of ownership of the learning by the individual. However, in centralist controlled education systems, 'training' is actually a more accurate word to describe a process which can be 'highly specific, content driven and targeted programmes geared to knowledge acquisition and information giving' (Law and Glover, 2000: 247). It would be foolish to deny that, in cases where there is a focus on educational outcomes, usually owing to pressures from state and parents (for example, Moloi et al., 2005 on South Africa), teachers and lecturers are seen more as functionaries, and the scope for personal development can be much more limited.

There is growing interest in the understanding of the way in which an individual's life history is significant in the development of their work as professionals. Day (1999: 124) suggests that this work 'is bound up with their lives, their histories, the kind of person they have been and have become'.

Merriam's (2001) work on the understanding of adult learning, which she describes as an 'ever-changing mosaic', stresses this importance of adult learner's inner selves through which they seek self-direction and fulfilment. The implications for leaders, as Beatty (2006) explains, lie in the process for them of learning *with* others. Through this process, they recognise and empathise with the needs of the individuals whom they lead and thereby help to develop learning communities. As Beatty (2008: 154) proposes: 'Leaders who are assisted in becoming emotionally prepared for developing dynamic learning communities that embrace diversity and the diffusion of leadership throughout them, are better able to respond to the needs of *all* learners, including themselves'.

Writers such as Ribbins (2008) and Parker (2002) argue that this study of life histories can equally enable 'understanding of the lives and careers of school leaders' (Ribbins, 2008: 75), so that there is much to be gained by leaders themselves through an understanding of their staff as individuals and through addressing their needs and support to be given accordingly. Of course, for institutions with large numbers of staff, only by diffusion of leadership and the creation of small and probably regularly changing teams can this be at all possible.

Evaluating and giving feedback

Reflecting on the sections above, the leadership and management of people in an educational institution might be described as the task of motivating and supporting a body of people, recognising each of them as an individual with their own personal needs, characteristics and abilities, and yet uniting them with a common sense of direction and purpose through shared values to achieve high performance. A forbidding and formidable task indeed! However, in considering the area of evaluating and giving feedback about performance to staff, there is an overriding need to display a more uniform and consistent approach across the institution, while of course continuing to take account of individuality. This is because giving feedback inevitably involves a form of evaluation of performance at some points, and this evaluation (variously called appraisal, assessment, performance review, and so on) needs to be overtly practised for various reasons.

- The accountability which necessarily underpins evaluation of performance.
- The rewards which can be related to such evaluations.
- The need for a transparent sense of fairness in the operation.

Each of these needs to be considered briefly.

Accountability

The collective performance of schools and colleges is subject to intense external examination and comparison, often both at national level and at local levels by governors, parents and other community stakeholders. The chief accountability for this lies with the principal so that his/her accountability and the linked evaluation is primarily external. School and college leaders need to be conscious of this external examination as they develop effective means of staff evaluation with a focus on internal accountability. Even those proposing models of staff assessment which encourage team and organisational learning through feedback recognise the need for the institution to be demonstrating to those outside the school that such procedures are 'robust as well as reflective and can submit readily to scrutiny from external frameworks' (Middlewood et al., 2005: 13).

Rewards

In many countries, career progression in education is linked to staff having a regular appraisal or performance review before passing to the next stage with increased pay. Where national schemes apply, they run the risk of the assessment gaining 'no respect, there is no recognition and the salary progression quickly becomes automatic' (Ingvarson, 2001). The experience of this in Australia, England, New Zealand, Israel, South Africa and many other countries suggests that these 'rewards' offer leaders little opportunity for developing incentives for individual staff. The issue of rewards for performance in education remains contentious, especially when related to performance-related pay (PRP). The main argument against PRP is its scope for divisiveness in a profession where collegiality may be seen as the norm. Baxter's (2003) study of the allocation of financial rewards in schools in England suggested that anything other than an equal sharing of rewards resulted in resentment, while Wragg et al.'s (2004) research in England and Wales also found resentment of unfairness and bureaucracy. Parry's (1995) suggestion that the growth of legal challenges in the USA to performance review rewards was becoming a deterrent to employers' willingness to experiment may well have been accurate, since there is little evidence of PRP schemes for individuals being implemented in education in the twenty-first century's first decade.

The notion that assessment of performance can only be effectively carried out in an ethos of trust is widely accepted in the literature (Bush and Middlewood, 2005; Cardno and Piggot-Irvine, 1997; Middlewood, 2002; Thurlow, 2001; West-Burnham, 2001). This does not relate to the precision of the rules for assessment, because having a 'procedurally sound system alone will not necessarily produce effective, accurate, ethical performance ratings (Longnecker and Ludwig, 1990: 68). Rather it depends on a network of relationships 'fostered in a climate of tolerance, love of the heterodox, and relations of mutual care' (Strain, 2009: 81).

National schemes of assessment, especially in centralised educational systems, run significant risks in terms of being able to be effective, such as excessive bureaucracy in South Africa (Thurlow, 2001), neglect in the regions, in Greece (Middlewood, 2001) or of perceptions of irrelevance, in the Seychelles (Nancy, 2007). Furthermore they tend to focus on summative performance and use of quantitative data, and may offer leaders little scope for feedback which will stimulate staff and motivate better performance. Davis and Garner (2003) make it clear that formative evaluation serves as a tool for future development while summative evaluation is mainly a tool for accountability. Pashiardis and Brauckmann (2006: 265) neatly summarise this as, 'In short, formative evaluation has the person as the main focus whereas summative evaluation has the system as the main focus'.

In addition, national schemes which set criteria for so called standards-based evaluation tend to ignore two other critical factors. The first is what MacBeath and Myers (1999: 2) describe as the 'X factor – the surprise, the chemistry, the shift in perspective that may be brought (by the person) who does not fit the arithmetic but may, nonetheless, bring a magical quality to the task'.

The second is the importance of contextualisation in assessing performance. Thrupp's (1999) research into teacher effectiveness in schools in contrasting contexts with very different socio-economic conditions and widely differing pupil intake found that effective teaching in one context contrasted quite sharply with that in the other. However, each was an effective practice for pupil learning in its own specific context. It is the leader's task to assess staff in his/her own school or college according to their effectiveness there, and not according to how they might perform if they were in, for example, an 'easier' or 'more difficult' context. The leader's aim in evaluating and giving feedback is to achieve improvement by that individual in that particular institution. Of course, it is likely that excellent teachers would perform well in all types of schools and, equally, that weakest teachers would do poorly in most places. However, except in systems such as in Tokyo, where early career teachers are placed in different contexts for certain periods of time, leaders will focus exclusively on the individual person in the specific context. Two interviews carried out for this chapter were with principals of large secondary schools in reasonably affluent areas in England, each in their second principalship. Each had previously been head of a school in a much more challenging environment and both were adamant that they could not apply the same criteria on assessing performance.

I can think of twenty teachers here who would not have lasted very long at all where I was previously. But they are doing a first class job here and all any of us can do is the best for the students you have in front of you. That's what I have to do and it's what I ask of them. (Principal A)

There were staff in my previous school, who had developed all the 'tricks of the trade' in getting students motivated, despite the environment. Some of them would not know how to do that here. We need people keen to work in both kinds of environment and be effective, don't we? (Principal B)

In the twenty-first century, with moves towards personalised learning in some countries, greater understanding of the roles of others than teachers (for example, para-professionals, parents) in effective learning, increased use of technology bringing other learning sources to bear, the role of the teacher is undergoing major change. The leader's role is to develop forms of performance for feedback which recognise this, if such evaluation is not to be seen as irrelevant or merely a system requirement. Early career teachers interviewed by Middlewood (2002) favoured forms which would:

- take account of feedback from students, parents and colleagues
- emphasise team assessment rather than individual assessment
- use qualitative data as much as quantitative.

Despite much debate on and research into various forms of distributed or shared leadership (see Chapter 4), it is inescapable that the focus of research into evaluation of leaders is almost wholly focused on *individual* leaders (see Pashiardis and Brauckmann, 2008). This is probably because of the external scrutiny, previously mentioned. However, there is no reason why such procedures as 'team appraisal' should not be developed *within* schools or colleges. Middlewood and Parker (2009), researching into the features of extended schools in England, found examples of such practice, particularly in those schools where roles were blurred; teams comprised teachers, support staff, agency workers and so on, and any notion of applying different criteria to different roles within the team was inappropriate. They describe one learning team (2009: 80–1) where all team members received feedback from all the others, following both self-assessment and quantitative data analysis; both team and individual targets were set and opportunity still existed for confidential consultation if needed. Such team processes have been seen as appropriate for a collegial context such as an educational institution and argued for by O'Neill (1997), Draper (2000), Dimmock (2001) and Middlewood (2002). They appear to remain, however, a minority practice.

Conclusion

The task of leading and managing people to achieve high performance remains both the most exciting and the most challenging parts of the leadership role, and possibly the most crucial of all. 'I find working with people difficult. Working with people is also the most rewarding part of this job' (quoted in Fitzgerald, 2009: 63). It is exciting because relationships between people, at all levels and in all roles, remain at the centre of institutional effectiveness and the best resource for educational improvement. It is challenging because of the awareness that an effective school or college is more than a collection of individual performers, however talented they may be as individuals, and the leader will continue to be held accountable for the overall institutional performance, certainly for the foreseeable future.

There has not been space in this chapter to deal with the least rewarding and sometimes disagreeable aspects of people and performance management, that is, individuals' underperformance, disciplinary procedures and dismissal of staff. Furthermore, the context of responsibility for performance imposed upon institutions is often set out by external authorities, including national governments, in terms of control of others. Strain (2009: 71) sees, for example, that the UK government's demands on headteachers mean that 'Leadership is conceived by government as a device to change and mobilize teachers' behaviour in their professional relations and pursuits of purposes *chosen by others*'. This means that 'unequal social relations' (Strain, 2009: 71) are inevitable, with the perceptions of 'winners and losers' and more or less powerful people. Similarly, Ball (2003: 216) described what teachers saw as the 'terrors of performativity', influencing teachers' whole ethical and moral judgements concerning their professional work. In this context, the onus on leaders and managers is increasingly to develop a community based upon a culture of mutual trust, with respect for individuals regardless of their institutional status. In the UK there is increasing interest in 'executive heads', and even non-educationalists leading schools, all implying a distance between leaders and staff at operational level so that an overall, more detached strategic view can be taken. However, if we are to see educational institutions in the twenty-first century as learning communities with all those involved committed to their own and others' development, the case for the leaders being highly visible within the institutions is strong. Enabling staff to know the leaders personally, and vice versa, can often be a powerful supportive and motivational approach.

Even for what might be seen as 'selfish' reasons, leaders know that, in the context of being personally accountable for overall performance, they need most of all the help, support and respect of the people who are in the front line in the daily work of the school or college. Recognising, as quoted earlier, that too often leaders see the need for change in others rather than change in themselves, some may reflect on the adage, 'If you have a problem, look first at yourself!' The pressures on leaders do not encourage this kind of thinking and it is extremely challenging. Business management practice found that, especially in difficult times, 'the tendency of top management to isolate itself from the front line troops is fatal!' (Goldstein, 1998: 116). The principal's office is a safe haven and at least paperwork does not argue with you!

Educational leaders therefore need to 'capture the energy of people' (Slater, 2008: 67) and it is by drawing on these resources that change occurs. As much current thinking on leadership suggests, this requires emotionally intelligent leaders who are self-motivating and empathetic (Lambert, 2003), and with skills including listening, problem-solving, negotiating and conflict resolution (Hudson and Glomb, 1997). None of these detract from the importance of the leader's role where the need to direct at times and prompt people to move out of personal comfort zones remains crucial. As Slater (2008: 67) proposes, 'this may ultimately lead to the numbers of those inspired to become leaders themselves being a measure of leadership success'.

If research continues to emphasise the crucial importance of individual teachers' and leaders' life histories as being the key to their effective leadership and management, the courageous and effective leaders of the future may well be those who are able to form effective relationships with a significant number of staff, enabling them to develop their own capabilities in leading and managing others.

References

Ball, S. (2003) 'Performance and fabrication in the educational economy: towards the performative society', in D. Gleeson and G. Husbands (eds), *The Performing School*. London: Routledge.

Baxter, G. (2003) 'A fair distribution of rewards?', *Headship Matters*, 25: 5–6.

Beatty, B. (2006) 'Becoming emotionally prepared for leadership', *International Journal of Knowledge, Culture and Change*, 6(5): 1–19.

Beatty, B. (2008) 'Theories of learning', in J. Lumby, G. Crow and P. Pashiardis (eds), *International Handbook on the Preparation and Development of School Leaders*. London: Routledge. pp. 136–59.

Blackmore, J., Thomson, P. and Barty, K. (2006) 'Principal selection: homosociability, the search for security and the production of normalized principal identities', *Educational Management Administration and Leadership*, 34(3): 297–317.

Blauner, S. (1964) *Alienation and Freedom*. Chicago, IL: Chicago University Press.

Briggs, A. (2002) 'Facilitating the role of middle managers in further education', *Research in Post-Compulsory Education*, 7(1): 63–78.

Bush, T. (2008) *Leadership and Management Development in Education*. London: Sage.

Bush, T. and Middlewood, D. (2005) *Leading and Managing People in Education*. London: Sage.

Bush, T. and Moloi, K. (2007) 'Race, racism and discrimination in school leadership: evidence from England and South Africa', *International Studies in Educational Administration*, 35(1): 41–59.

Bush, T., Allen, T., Glover, D. and Sood, K. (2007) *Diversity and the National Professional Qualification for Headship*. Nottingham: National College for School Leadership.

Bush, T., Coleman, M. and Si, Z. (1998) 'Managing secondary schools in China', *Compare*, 28(2): 83–195.

Byrne, D. (1971) *The Attraction Paradigm*. New York: Academic Press.

Cardno, C. and Piggot-Irvine, E. (1993) 'Effective performance appraisal', *Integrating Accountability and Development in Staff Appraisal*. Auckland: Longman.

Davis, E. and Garner, E. (2003) *Current Practices of Evaluating Superintendents and Principals in a Standards Based Environment*. Technical Report 2002–2005. Pocatello, ID: ICEE.

Day, C. (1999) *Developing Teachers: The Challenges of Lifelong Learning*. London: Falmer Press.

Department of Education (1997) *The School Register of Needs Survey*. Pretoria: Department of Education.

Dimmock, C. (2001) *Managing the Learning Centred School*. London: Paul Chapman Publishing.

Draper, I. (2000) 'From appraisal to performance management', *Professional Development Today*, 3(2): 11–21.

Fisher, C. and Yuan, A. (1998) 'What motivates employees? A comparison of US and China', *International Journal of Human Resource Management*, 9(3): 516–28.

Fitzgerald, T. (2009) 'The tyranny of bureaucracy', *Educational Management Leadership and Administration*, 37(1): 51–65.

Funder, D. (1987) 'Errors and mistakes: evaluating the accuracy of social judgements', *Psychological Review*, 101: 75–90.

Goldstein, A. (1998) *Corporate Comeback*. New York: John Wiley and Sons.

Grummell, B., Devine, D. and Lynch, K. (2009) 'Appointing senior managers in education: homosociability, local logics and authenticity in the selection process', *Educational Management Administration and Leadership*, 37(3): 329–49.

Gurr, D., Drysdale, G. and Mulford, B. (2005) 'Successful principal leadership: Australian case studies', *Journal of Administration*, 43(6): 539–51.

Hallinger, P. and Heck, R. (1996) 'Re-assessing the principal's role in school effectiveness: a review of empirical research, 1980–1995', *Educational Administration Quarterly*, 32(1): 5–44.

Herzberg, F. (1966) *Work and the Nature of Man*. Cleveland, OH: World Publishing.

Hinton, P. (1993) *The Psychology of Inter-Personal Perception*. London: Routledge.

Howse, J. and MacPherson, R. (2001) 'New Zealand's educational administration and the strategic management of its polytechnics', in P. Pashiardis (ed.), *International Perspectives in Educational Leadership*. Hong Kong: CCEAM.

Huber, S. and Hiltmann, M. (2009) 'The recruitment and selection of school leaders – first findings of an international comparison', in S. Huber (ed.), *School Leadership – International Perspectives*. New York: Peter Lang.

Huber, S. and Pashiardis, P. (2008) 'The recruitment and selection of school leaders', in J. Lumby, G. Crow and P. Pashiardis (eds), *International Handbook on the Preparation of School Leaders and Development*. London: Routledge.

Hudson, P. and Glomb, N. (1997) 'If it takes two to tango, then why not teach both partners to dance?', *Journal of Learning Disabilities*, 30(4): 442–8.

Ifanti, A. (1995) 'Policy making, politics and administration in Greece', *Educational Management and Administration*, 23(4): 217–78.

Ingvarson, L. (2001) 'Developing standards and assessments for accomplished teaching', in D. Middlewood and C. Cardno (eds), *Managing Teacher Appraisal and Performance: A Comparative Approach*. London: RoutledgeFalmer.

Lam, P., Yeen, F. and Ngoh, M. (1997) 'Job satisfaction and withdrawal cognition among preservice teachers', in J. Tan, S. Copiathan and H. Kan (eds), *Education in Singapore*. Singapore: Prentice-Hall.

Lambert, L. (2003) *Leadership Capacity for Lasting School Improvement*. Alexandria, VA: Association for Supervision and Curriculum Development.

Law, S. and Glover, D. (2000) *Educational Leadership and Learning*. Buckingham: Open University Press.

Leithwood, K. and Levin, B. (2004) *Assessing School Leaders and Leadership Programme Effects on Pupil Learning: Conceptual and Methodological Challenges*. London: DfES.

Leithwood, K. and Riehl, C. (2005) 'What do we already know about educational leadership?', in W. Firestone and C. Riehl (eds), *A New Agenda for Research in Educational Leadership*. New York: Teachers College Press. pp. 2–27.

Leithwood, K., Day, C., Sammons, P., Harris, A. and Hopkins, D. (2006) *Seven Strong Claims About Successful School Leadership*. London: DfES.

Lewis, C. (1995) *Educating Hearts and Minds: Reflections on Japanese Pre-School and Elementary Education*. Cambridge: Cambridge University Press.

Longnecker, G. and Ludwig, D. (1990) 'Ethical dilemmas in performance appraisal revisited', in J. Holloway, J. Lewis and G. Mallory (eds), *Performance Measurement and Education*. London: Sage.

Lumby, J. (2003) 'Managing motivation', in J. Lumby, D. Middlewood and E. Kaabwe (eds), *Managing Human Resources in South African Schools*. London: Commonwealth Secretariat.

Lumby, J. with Coleman, M. (2007) *Leadership and Diversity: Challenging Theory and Practice in Education*. London: Sage.

Lumby, J., Crow, G. and Pashiardis, P. (2008) 'Epilogue', in J. Lumby, G. Crow and P. Pashiardis (eds), *International Handbook on the Preparation and Development of School Leaders*. London: Routledge.

MacBeath, J. and Myers, K. (1999) *Effective School Leaders*. London: FT/Prentice-Hall.

Manuel, M. and Slate, J. (2003) 'Hispanic female superintendents in America', doctoral dissertation, University of Texas at El Paso.

Merriam, S. (2001) *The New Update on Adult Learning Theory*. San Fransisco, CA: Jossey-Bass.

Middlewood, D. (1997a) 'Managing appraisal', in T. Bush and D. Middlewood (eds), *Managing People in Education*. London: Paul Chapman Publishing. pp. 169–87.

Middlewood, D. (1997b) 'Managing recruitment and selection', in T. Bush and D. Middlewood (eds), *Managing People in Education*. London: Paul Chapman Publishing. pp. 139–54.

Middlewood, D. (2001) 'The future of managing teacher performance and appraisal', in D. Middlewood and C. Cardno (eds), *Managing Teacher Appraisal and Performance: A Comparative Approach*. London: RoutledgeFalmer.

Middlewood, D. (2002) 'Appraisal and performance management', in T. Bush and L. Bell (eds), *The Principles and Practice of Educational Management*. London: Sage.

Middlewood, D. and Lumby, J. (1998) *Human Resource Management in Schools and Colleges*. London: Paul Chapman Publishing.

Middlewood, D. and Parker, R. (2009) *Leading and Managing Extended Schools: Ensuring Every Child Matters*. London: Sage.

Middlewood, D., Parker, R. and Beere, J. (2005) *Creating a Learning School*. London: Sage.

Moller, J., Eggen, A. and Fuglestad, O. (2005) 'Successful school leadership: the Norwegian case', *Journal of Educational Management*, 43(6): 584–94.

Moloi, C., Gravett, S. and Nduna, B (2005) 'Using resources for school improvement', in L. Anderson and J. Lumby (eds), *Managing Finance and External Relations in South African Schools*. London: Commonwealth Secretariat.

Mwamwenda, T. (1995) 'Job satisfaction among secondary school teachers in Transkei', *South African Journal of Education*, 19(2): 84–7.

Nancy, M. (2007) 'Leadership and teacher appraisal: challenges for school leaders in improving appraising practice in the Seychelles secondary schools', unpublished MA dissertation, University of Warwick.

National College of School Leadership (NCSL) (2006) *Recruiting Head Teachers and Senior Leaders: Overview of Research Findings*. Nottingham: NCSL.

O'Neill, J. (1997) 'Teach, learn, appraise: the impossible triangle', in J. O'Neill (ed.), *Teacher Appraisal in New Zealand*. Palmerston North: ERDC.

Parker, R. (2002) *Passion and Intuition: The Impact of Life History on Leadership*. Nottingham: National College for School Leadership.

Parry, G. (1995) 'Concerns and issues related to teacher appraisal in the USA', *Education and the Law*, 7(1): 17–29.

Pashiardis, P. (2001) 'Secondary principals in Cyprus: views of the principals versus the views of the teachers: a case study', *International Studies in Educational Administration*, 29(3): 11–23.

Pashiardis, P. and Brauckmann, M. (2008) 'The evaluation of school principals', in J. Lumby, G. Crow and P. Pashiardis (eds), *International Handbook on the Preparation and Development of School Leaders*. London: Routledge.

Reynolds, D. and Farrell, S. (1996) *Worlds Apart*. London: HMSO.

Ribbins, P. (2008) 'A life and career based framework for the study of leaders in education', in J. Lumby, G. Crow and P. Pashiardis (eds), *International Handbook on the Preparation and Development of School Leaders*. London: Routledge.

Saiti, A. (2007) 'Main factors of job satisfaction among primary school educators: factor analysis of the Greek reality', *Management in Education*, 21(2): 23–7.

Slater, L. (2008) 'Pathways to building leadership capacity', *Educational Management, Administration and Leadership*, 36(1): 55–69.

Strain, M. (2009) 'Some ethical and cultural implications of leadership turn in education: on the distinction between performance and performativity', *Educational Management Leadership and Administration*, 37(1): 67–84.

Thomson, R. (1993) *Managing People*. Oxford: Butterworth-Heinemann.

Thrupp, M. (1999) *Schools Making a Difference. Let's Be Realistic!* Buckingham: Open University Press.

Thurlow, M. (2001) 'Educator appraisal in South Africa', in D. Middlewood and C. Cardno (eds), *Managing Teacher Appraisal and Performance: A Comparative Approach*. London: RoutledgeFalmer.

West-Burnham, J. (2001) 'Appraising Headteachers or Developing Leaders?', in D. Middlewood and C. Cardno (eds), *Managing Teacher Appraisal and Performance: A Comparative Approach*. London: RoutledgeFalmer. pp. 19–28.

Wong, P. (2004) 'The professional development of school principals: insights from evaluating a programme in Hong Kong', *School Leadership and Management*, 24(2): 139–62.

Wragg, E., Haynes, G., Wragg, C. and Chamberlain, R. (2004) *Performance Pay for Teachers*. London: Routledge.

Section III

Leadership and Learning

CHAPTER 9

Leadership for Learning

Christopher Rhodes and Mark Brundrett

Introduction

Learning is central to the mission of educational institutions, indeed it is the reason for their existence and leaders in education have no more important role than that of enhancing the learning outcomes of the students in their care. The relationship between leadership and learning is increasingly accepted as being one of the most important issues in enhancing the effectiveness of educational organisations. For this reason theoretical and practical interest in examining processes that relate what leaders do and the ways in which they can make educational institutions more successful remains high both cross-sector and in international contexts. This is not surprising since leadership that has the potential to raise student outcomes in academic, personal and social development is the arcana that has been sought since the inception of academic interest in educational administration, and we consider this topic to be of key interest to practitioners, policy-makers and researchers.

In this chapter we commence by examining the problematic nature of the term 'leadership for learning', we then go on to explore the link between leadership and learning and set out key notions such as instructional leadership and learning-centred leadership. We subsequently progress to explore conceptions associated with the influence and impact of learning-centred leadership, learning communities and the importance of student voice. Finally, the chapter concludes with an examination of the leadership implications, challenges, opportunities and new and emerging agendas in leadership for learning.

The problematic nature of the term 'leadership for learning'

It is important to note that the term 'leadership for learning' is highly problematic despite the increasing ubiquity of its employment both in the literature and more colloquially. We may note, for instance, that MacBeath and Dempster (2009) point out that there is no firm definition of the term 'leadership for learning' either nationally or internationally, and usage is likely to be influenced by the immediate context of the educational organisation within which the discourse is located and the prevailing policy and cultural conditions of the country involved. For instance, in the tertiary sector in the UK great emphasis has been placed on the introduction of policies that take account of student voice in leadership and management processes have been recognised as important in encouraging greater engagement and proactivity on the part of learners (Collinson, 2007). Equally, in the higher education sector, enhanced learning outcomes facilitated by increased consultation with students continues to attract much international interest (Campbell and Li, 2008; Gaspar et al., 2008; Ozolins et al., 2008). Whereas in the schools sector, research into the linkages between management processes and learning outcomes has led to a recognition that leadership for learning can occur at all levels in the school and is fostered by opportunities to build professional learning communities (Fitzgerald and Gunter, 2006). In addition, there are others who argue that more distributed forms of leadership, in which teachers are encouraged to take a greater role in the leadership of change and innovation, are the key to better outcomes (Frost, 2008a).

It is the very complexity of the relationship between these variables that leads Knapp et al. (2003) to suggest that there is strong evidence for the interrelatedness of student learning and teacher learning in the US context. Equally, MacBeath and Dempster (2009) argue that there are five major principles that underpin leadership for learning, including: shared or distributed leadership; a focus on learning; creation of the conditions favourable for learning; creation of a dialogue about leadership and learning; and, the establishment of a shared sense of accountability. It is this complex nexus of leadership functions that constitute the key to the relationship between what leaders do and the achievement of educational organisations.

The link between leadership and learning

The impulse to improve the effectiveness of educational organisations in order to secure improved learner outcomes has been a key driver of change in many countries over several decades. Central government directives and local initiatives in schools and colleges and other educational organisations have sought to offer the necessary pressure and support to enable desired improvements to be realised. In many cases, the improvement focus has rightly encompassed the quality of teaching and learning as a major element in raising learner attainment. A firm focus on teacher and student learning in classrooms has emerged (see Harris and Hopkins, 1999). As part of this focus, inclusion has also emerged as an important element of school improvement as organisations seek to reduce the gap between the highest and lowest achievers (Cruddas, 2005) and learner engagement has come to the forefront in thinking about improvements in teaching and learning.

Despite the increasing emphasis on leadership and learning, both at the macro level of national policy and the micro level of individual schools, unpacking the ways in which leaders can impact on learning have been problematic. At least in part this is due to the fact that theories of learning have tended traditionally to offer two opposing views which emphasise either teacher-centred or pupil-centred approaches which can be characterised as 'top-down' or 'bottom-up' attitudes (Brundrett and Silcock, 2002). However, more recent work draws on developments in cognitive theory (see, for instance, the influential work of Shayer and Adey, 2002) in order to offer an alternative notion that attempts to resolve this dichotomy by supporting *co-constructivist* techniques (Broadfoot, 2000) whereby twin perspectives that are both 'top down' *and* 'bottom up' are encouraged (Biggs 1992). Such co-constructed forms of learning integrate teacher- or subject-centred systems with pupil-centred approaches into a third partnership approach (Silcock and Brundrett, 2006). These methods spring both from pupils' experientially based attitudes and capabilities and the special features of subjects being taught. Within this co-constructivist approach, all members of staff cooperate, negotiate, resolve differences, mediate between options, and generally act in a socially skilled manner to reach decisions that will enhance student learning. It follows that educators will also work in partnership with students in order to enable them to appreciate alternatives, experiment with radical positions, and show a tolerance usually untested within monocultural settings (Brundrett and Silcock, 2002: 91). This new architecture of learning theory has thus caused a revolution in the perceived role of school leaders at all levels in the system since it has become clear that new forms of leadership that accentuate collaboration and distribution of power and authority are themselves central to learning (Burton and Brundrett, 2005).

This better understanding of the ways in which students learn has enabled the relationship between high quality leadership and successful schools to become increasingly well established (see, for instance, the work of Bush, 2008a; Hargreaves and Fink, 2006; Southworth, 2004) and has led to an acceptance that leadership development is a key component of school improvement (Bush, 2008b). For this reason headteachers in schools and principals in colleges are encouraged increasingly to understand the importance of their role in enhancing the learning experience of students and to seek to ensure that the structures and systems to support teaching and learning are created as part of their leadership responsibility and accountability.

The link between leadership and learning is emphasised by Leithwood et al. (2006) who claim that school leadership is second only to classroom teaching as an influence on pupil learning. They conclude: 'As far as we are aware, there is not a single documented case of a school successfully turning around its pupil achievement trajectory in the absence of talented leadership' (2006: 5).

Similarly, PricewaterhouseCoopers (2007) suggest that the behaviours of school leaders have great impact on pupil performance and affirm that there is widespread recognition that school leaders have a vital role in raising the quality of teaching and learning within their schools. The adoption of a learner-centred approach to teaching and learning has been seen as having the potential to effect learner inclusion, engagement and improved achievement. Each learner will have, for example, a different life agenda, strengths, learning needs, learning styles and intelligences. Depending on the individual school or college, they will have some or maybe little voice with respect to their own learning and be disempowered by organisational structures and culture. It is teachers who are the leaders of teaching and learning in classrooms. Teachers need to know how to lead lessons, inspire learners, have high expectations, enable good learning experiences through planning and pursue inclusion and differentiation appropriately. They need to probe knowledge and understanding, monitor performance and give feedback. They need to maintain good relationships with learners and between learners so as to sustain learning. Because teachers are leaders of teaching and learning in classrooms, senior leaders need to help teachers to improve their own practice by enabling teachers to continue to learn themselves. A developing consensus suggests that school heads improve teaching and learning indirectly through their influence on staff motivation, development, well-being and working conditions.

The notion of becoming a 'learning-centred' institution has emerged as a term that denotes that schools or colleges place both student and staff learning at the core of their work. Staff learning may be collaborative and shared in the sense of a learning community to serve the organisation in its endeavours to change, improve and further support student learning outcomes. The leadership of such a venture may be termed *leadership for learning*. Offering a helpful overview, Swaffield and MacBeath (2009) suggest that linkages between leadership and learning may be seen in the learning of leaders as they engage in leadership over time and in their leadership actions to enable the learning of others. In some organisations, leadership for learning may be about empowering middle leaders and teachers to take a direct lead in teaching and learning within a trusting and collaborative culture (for example, Fitzgerald and Gunter, 2006; Frost, 2008a). Alternatively, understandings of leadership for learning may be characterised by senior leadership reliance upon assessment and outcome data to reward perceived good teacher performance as expressed in a desire for improved outcomes in the US conception of 'instructional leadership'.

Instructional leadership

The quality of teaching in schools and colleges has long been associated with the likelihood of successful student outcomes in many nations. Barber (1997: 79) comments: 'Research shows the quality of teaching to be the single most important factor in successful education'. For instance, in the USA, Elmore (2000) has used the term 'instructional leadership' to describe a focus on instructional (teaching) improvement with a view to improving learner outcomes. It is a term that has come to prominence both in practice and research terms over the past three decades (Sheppard, 1996; Spillane, 2004). Also in the USA, Blase and Blase (2004) report that school principals have tended to see instructional leadership as consisting of supervision, staff development and curriculum development. However, these authors do develop an understanding of instructional leadership that can and should embrace leadership actions that seek to enhance both instruction and also teacher learning and, in turn, student learning. They advocate that successful instructional leaders talk to teachers about their instruction, encourage collaboration between teachers and empower teachers to foster decision-making, professional growth, teacher leadership, status, autonomy, impact and self-efficacy. They see that successful instructional leaders are able to encourage those conditions that can constitute a professional learning community of students and teachers. The term 'instructional leadership' is now slowly being replaced by the term 'learning-focused leadership' (Knapp et al., 2006). Another example of this shift in thinking can be found in South Africa where the management of teaching and learning is seen as a key role of school principals (Bush and Glover, 2009). However, some principals, deputies and heads of department hold only a limited conceptualisation of their roles as instructional leaders (Bush and Heysteck, 2006). In some schools, teacher leadership and empowerment are underdeveloped and hence have only limited impact in securing improvements in teaching and learning (Grant, 2006). In particular, it has been identified that many heads of department need to be much more proactive in promoting and monitoring teaching and learning if gains in outcomes for all learners are to be realised against a backdrop of deep poverty which frequently dominates the lives of learners (Ali and Botha, 2006; Bush et al., 2008).

In the UK, Southworth (2002) has examined the notion of instructional leadership and offers a review showing that it is strongly connected with teaching and learning, including both student learning and the professional learning of teachers. The inclusion of teacher learning signifies pedagogic development and the development of an environment where teachers are confident to become learners (Southworth, 2000). The inclusion of student learning signifies achievement but also refers to the potential efficacy of enquiry into pupils' perspectives on their learning and uses this information to inform developments in pedagogy and learning (Fielding et al., 1999). The difference between a curriculum-centred view and associated transmission of content and a learning-centred view is explored by MacBeath et al. (2007). These authors contend that teaching to stimulate learning requires teachers to create environments supportive of learning mediated through their good working relationships with learners in the community and their ability to engage students though stimulating and well communicated interaction. The message here for heads and other leaders is their need for good and current understanding of both pedagogy and androgogy if both students and staff are to be enabled to learn well. They are charged with creating a culture that fosters learning though excellent teaching. Leadership which is alert to the wide variety of learning needs of students, teachers, support staff and the needs of the whole learning community can place teaching and learning at the centre of the organisation. There may well be implications for leaders' own professional learning and development.

With a firm focus on improving student outcomes through teaching and learning, instructional leadership requires teachers to adopt a focus on teaching and learning and to engage with their own pedagogic growth (Bush and Glover, 2002, 2009; Southworth, 2002). In these terms, instructional leadership represents an important advance towards the establishment of inclusive learning-centred leadership. When coupled with the leadership support necessary to empower teachers to become truly engaged with building fertile and sustainable organisational and inter-organisational learning environments for both staff and students, then the term leadership for learning becomes more appropriate. Leadership for learning may therefore be seen as subsuming and advancing the goals of instructional leadership by adopting learning-centred leadership approaches capable of finding positive and potent expression within the experience of all learners. Such leadership requires the establishment of both structural and cultural support to enable the necessary capacity to address the changes needed within the contexts, communities and intended futures within which these improvements are pursued.

Learning-centred leadership

Emphasising the importance of learning-centred leadership, Southworth (2004) examines how school leaders influence teaching and learning in classrooms and across the school. He states:

> For me it is the single most important task for school leaders. Indeed, it is a responsibility which marks them out as school leaders. A great deal of what heads, deputies, assistant heads and subject leaders do is similar to what is done by leaders in other organisations and employment sectors. However, what is distinctive about school leadership is the way leaders influence the quality of teaching and learning in classrooms. Unless leaders know how to do this and practise it they may not be making a strong contribution to the success of the school as a learning centre. (Southworth, 2004: 4)

Southworth (2004) goes on to explore six levels of learning across the school enabling the potential engagement and impact of leadership to be made more explicit. For example, at the *pupil level of learning*, leaders may use outcome data to make appropriate interventions and at the *teacher level of learning*, leaders may enable opportunities for teachers to learn from one another as a means to embed new and improved practices. This may extend to a *collaborative staff learning level* perhaps facilitated by the establishment of structural and cultural changes within the school. At an *organisational learning level*, professional growth may enable the characteristics of a learning community characterised by trust and openness to be established. Given the complexity of many of these tasks, leaders may actively distribute leadership responsibilities to enable a *leadership learning level* charged with the wider promotion of learning-centred leadership within the organisation. Finally, leaders may actively seek external input to further effect improvements in teaching and learning through reference to other schools and agencies, at this *learning networks level* the engagement of a variety of empowered staff is most likely to lead to the adoption of enhanced classroom learning opportunities.

In an impressive and important analysis Hallinger and Heck (1999) have suggested that learning-centred leaders influence learning and teaching in three ways. They may influence outcomes *directly* by personal intervention or *reciprocally* by their personal work along with teachers or, most likely; *indirectly* via the agency of other staff. Indirect working is most likely to emerge in larger schools linked to the inevitable issues of capacity and complexity. Mediation through others dictates that it is incumbent upon leaders to model the importance of a focus on improving teaching and learning, monitor teachers' work to ensure engagement and progress, and to talk to teachers so as to bring forward and share good ideas and good practices so that conventional thinking may be challenged. This may involve a coaching or mentoring role. It is clear from this analysis that learning-centred leadership truly does involve the learning of students and staff and also the learning of leaders themselves. The question emerges as to what practical steps can leaders take in order to make a difference to learning within their schools and colleges and what are the implications for the learning of leaders themselves?

A recent study in New Zealand (Timperley, 2006) points to three learning the challenges for leaders in developing leadership for learning within their schools. First, leaders need to learn what becoming a learning-centred leader means; secondly, they need to understand that establishing collaboration between teachers is insufficient if it does not lead to improved student outcomes and, thirdly, they need to assimilate that student outcome data has much potential in informing improvement in the quality of teaching and learning activities.

The influence and impact of learning-centred leaders

How, and the extent to which, the influence of intending learning-centred leaders may be expressed at organisational and classroom level will be subject to the framework established by the prevailing national political administration as it pertains to different sectors of the education system. It will also be subject to differing national perceptions of leadership roles and responsibilities within educational organisations. For example, in the UK schools sector, the national standards for headteachers in schools (DfES, 2004) and the Office for Standards in Education (OFSTED, 2005) framework for the inspection of schools state clear expectations of leaders and how they broadly may be expected to act to improve teaching and learning within their school. Accountability mechanisms promote an expectation of adherence to central policy directives coupled with space for some creativity, for example, in empowering teacher leaders or alternatively limiting their classroom autonomy. National variations to such a climate exist, for example, there is an established tradition of teacher autonomy in Greek schools and political directives may not be well received in other nations where there is a strong democratic tradition and an intolerance of hierarchy such as obtains in Norway and Denmark (Waterhouse and Dempster, 2009).

Given sector and international differences, many school heads and other senior leaders in education are very much involved in ensuring succession management internally to ensure that the right teacher gets into the right job at the right time. They are also involved in attracting and recruiting staff from the pool of teaching talent available external to the school. In short, a key role of senior leadership is to get good teachers capable of performing well with learners within the immediate school or college context and who thus make a strong contribution to teaching and learning success. Senior leaders provide support, learning opportunities and build staff capacity. They are aware of inclusion issues and take measures to encourage the engagement of all learners as their outcomes can be strongly influenced by other factors such as family socio-economic level and home environment. Learning-centred leaders maintain a strong focus on teaching and learning and appreciate that what constitutes effective teaching and learning may vary from context to context. They adjust their style to accommodate necessary teacher direction and personal accountability for outcomes against teacher empowerment, encouragement and release of their control. Leaders are ascribed with the task of helping to create an organisational culture that will foster organisational learning (Schein, 1992). This is by no means a trivial matter and is recognised to be difficult in cases where mistrust, poor capacity and Balkanisation prevail. Indeed, Lakomski (2001) cautions that the leaders themselves are also part of the organisational culture and will therefore have the difficulty of stepping out of it when required by circumstance. In a study of Australian secondary schools,

Mulford and Silins (2003) conclude that leadership impact is predominantly indirectly related to student outcomes via the more direct influence exerted upon the way in which teachers organise and conduct their instruction, their educational interactions with students, and the challenges and expectations teachers place on their pupils. In turn, pupils' positive perceptions of teachers' work directly promotes participation in school, academic self-concept and engagement with school and the possibility of good academic achievement. The study highlights that school context, the nature of the community environment from which students are drawn and the nature of links the school has with that community can be highly influential in how well students are engaged in learning and hence the level of their subsequent outcomes. In a recent UK study, Waterhouse (2008) reports on a 'Learning Catalysts' project created to further understand how learning aspirations are shaped and expressed at the interface of the school and the community. This important project so far indicates that volunteers acting as leaders of learning within their communities can forge dialogue aimed at raising the expectations of pupils and parents but further work is needed to carry this forward to school settings.

Leithwood et al. (2006) claim that school leaders improve teaching and learning indirectly and most powerfully through their influence on staff motivation, commitment and supportive working conditions. There is evidence that achieving good learning outcomes for pupils and good behaviour serves to further motivate teachers (see Addison and Brundrett, 2008). Leadership distribution can impact on teachers' decision-making capacity and motivation, and can act positively upon student learning and achievement. Southworth (2004) advocates the distribution of learning-centred leadership to increase the impact of the focus on teaching and learning throughout the organisation. He sees a learning-centred focus rolling out to engage staff and transmit key ideas and practices. He suggests that an important task of learning-centred leaders is to enable other leaders and other staff to exercise it. Hence, middle leaders are important in any strategy to develop learning-centred leadership in schools and colleges. The balance of trust, autonomy, empowerment and personal accountability resides within individual teams, and middle leaders need to be able to implement effective teaching and learning strategies. In addition to senior leaders, middle leaders also need to model and pursue a focus on teaching and learning. They are closer to students and can transmit strategies for inclusion, student engagement and high expectations for student achievement via their working relationships with their teams. Busher (2006) considers the creation of departmental subcultures to develop teaching and learning in which, for example, middle leaders may act as role models for team members to show effective teaching and learning. They may also seek to further engage pupils in learning through working with their team on curriculum development, feedback and relationships. This assumes that middle leaders have excellent working relationships with their team members.

To understand how students can learn better implies an understanding of how learning takes place and how it can be fostered. It implies good teaching and establishing that achievement is supported by good planning, resources, written and verbal feedback and approaches to behaviour management that enable access to learning and support for learner confidence and self-esteem. Leaders in schools and colleges can promote structures and systems that help enable these requirements to be met. For example, policies concerned with appropriate target-setting, marking, assessment, quality of feedback and planning can help unify approaches to improved teaching and learning which relate to the particular circumstances of the individual organisation. As already indicated, leadership distribution can enable more staff to contribute to and sustain learning-centred leadership. Learning is an individual as well as a social process and leaders need to promote learners' learning skills, learning autonomy and understand more about learners' perceptions of their own learning experience. In the UK, the notion of personalised learning has entered contemporary thinking about improving learner outcomes. The deeper focus on individual learners implied is intended to support those who are gifted and talented as well as seeking to enrich the learning experience of disadvantaged learners. Indeed, this is embodied in the *Every Child Matters* agenda (DfES, 2003).

In a recent study in the UK, Day et al. (2007) examined the impact of school leadership on pupil outcomes. The interim report indicates that heads are still perceived as the main source of leadership by key school staff. Although some did not agree that heads are closely involved in the details of curriculum and the improvement of pedagogy, many thought that the head's leadership had a direct effect on how they thought about their teaching and learning practices, which then indirectly impacted upon student outcomes. The study showed that success in improving student outcomes was associated with the establishment of achievement-focused school cultures in which care and trust were strong features, and that the head's high expectation for staff and students was a strong driver in developing teaching and learning programmes. Many staff in the study related their school's success in improving student outcomes to the head's strategic vision enabling the school to respond positively to change. They also associated improved student outcomes with whole-school approaches to behaviour management. In some schools, the incorporation of student leadership was considered to be a means of enhancing pupil outcomes. The study firmly links quality of leadership with improvement and confirms many of the key tenets of leadership for learning. In summary, many of the features prevalent with learning communities appear to foster the improvement of student outcomes and learner voice appears to be an element of such a community that is now more strongly entering both national strategic thinking as well as local thinking about leadership for learning.

Learning communities

There has been much interest and debate concerning the benefits to schools and other educational organisations of developing the characteristics of a learning community. Major benefits are perceived to be associated with learning that would enable them to respond quickly to unpredictable and changing environments (Stoll and Louis, 2007; Stoll et al., 2003), that they would better develop their staff (Stoll et al., 2006) and that they would become more effective and produce better outcomes (Cochran-Smith and Lytle, 1999; Roberts and Pruitt, 2003). Research by DuFour, (2004) has suggested that professional learning communities in schools emphasise three key components:

- collaborative work among the school's professionals
- a strong and consistent focus on teaching and learning with that collaborative work
- the collection and use of assessment and other data for shared inquiry into performance over time.

Bezzina (2008) reports on the successful actions of a school in Malta to become a learning community. In order to build strong relationships and a student-centred approach, the head distributed leadership and encouraged teacher leadership and decision-making in order to transmit a shared and collaborative focus on team-working, classroom practice and pupils' learning. In short, effective professional learning communities take collective responsibility for staff and student learning and need leadership and management focused on the set-up and maintenance of a professional learning community necessitating the need for shared values and vision, openness, inclusion and mutual trust and support. In the USA, Keedy (1999) has cautioned that without the recruitment, selection and training of principals who value teacher leadership, there is less likelihood of teachers transforming schools into learning communities and the attendant benefit of revitalising schools for all learners. Busher (2006) suggests that the dynamics of a school learning community involves the voices of leaders, teachers, pupils, support staff and other adults with the intention of working to foster student learning. He suggests that the learning community may be as small as a department or as big as the whole school. To secure trusting collaborations, leaders need to be aware of the staff involved and be open to the dialogue and discussion that emerge. This has implications for the ways in which leaders distribute power within communities that emerge. This work also emphasises the importance of pupil voice and the transmission and incorporation of their own experience of teaching and learning into efforts to improve learning and student outcomes. This latter point is a key theme that has emerged in recent years in relation to building learning communities and it is to the topic of student voice that we turn next.

Student voice

As noted earlier in this chapter, in the higher education sector student voice has been used to inform academic integration and improved learning experiences (Campbell and Li, 2008; Rhodes and Nevill, 2004) for students so as to enhance possibilities for progression, retention and success. In the UK tertiary sector, inclusion of student representation and participation is well established as a contributor to quality improvement (LSC, 2006). While suggesting that student voice has an important role to play in fostering improved learner engagement and proactivity, Collinson (2007) rightly identifies that student empowerment can have implications for leadership in this sector. The transition from students as recipients of information about leadership decisions to fuller collaboration with staff and assumption of responsibility for management decisions implies the emergence of a much higher level of student leadership in these organisations. Collinson (2007) also points out that there is little research on student involvement in this sector, and the complex relationship between learning and leadership in such distributed and collaborative terms remains under-explored.

In the schools sector, Whitty and Wisby (2007) identify the four main drivers for pupil voice as children's rights, active citizenship, school improvement and the greater personalisation of learning. In a study based in the USA, Mitra (2005) reports that student-voice initiatives aimed at providing opportunities to students to share in school decision-making can range from simply allowing students to voice opinions through to full collaboration with adults and in some cases to actually taking a lead on seeking change. However, Frost and Holden (2008) establish that students' voices have not been as prominent as the voices of adults within schools and in an Australian study Lewis and Burman (2008) elaborate on areas of decision-making concerning classroom management that teachers would not feel comfortable in negotiating with students. The need for whole-hearted adult support and belief in the potential of student voice is advocated by Martin et al. (2005) who suggest that without such adult support the role and contribution of students to their learning communities will be diminished or unrealised. Adult inclusion of student voice may, in some circumstances, be hard to achieve. Rudduck and Flutter (2000: 53) suggest: 'it takes time and vary careful preparation to build a climate in which both teachers and pupils feel comfortable working together on a constructive view of aspects of teaching, learning and schooling' and Fielding (2001: 105) comments: 'For many teachers student voice is seen as either peripheral, irrelevant or corrosive of the already diminishing legitimacy of teacher professionalism'.

Despite this, the term 'pupil voice' has generally remained a limited conception of letting young people 'have a say' within the bounds of school constraints (MacBeath, 2006). Again in the UK, 'pupil voice' has been put forward as a common sense notion by Cruddas (2007), who suggests that if one wants to know what children want and if they are able to represent their own interests, then the simple way to access this 'voice' is to ask them. The research literature reveals examples of reported benefits of listening to 'pupil voice' in efforts to improve teaching and learning. For example, in a UK primary school, Papatheodorou (2002) established that pupils showed much awareness about the physical limitations of their learning environment and its importance to their learning experience. This contributed to discussion with teachers so that learning could be advanced. Also in the UK, student voice and the engagement of students in shaping their educational experience have been extended to include work-related learning (WRL) programmes in schools (Hopkins, 2008). It is suggested that accessing the voices of disaffected and marginalised students is useful in finding out what these students see as the benefits of WRL programmes and how they can be made more re-engaging for disaffected students. In a study about the engagement of Greek secondary school students in discussions about teaching and learning, Mitsoni (2006) further established the importance of content relevance and active learner participation as a means to foster greater involvement. Adult support for 'pupil voice' is important in ensuring its success; however, this requirement may place additional demands upon those teachers who are not part of already established learning communities. Bragg (2007) emphasises the importance of developing the voices of teachers and other adults alongside those of pupils so that teacher's voice does not become undermined and they lose confidence in their professional judgement. In the UK, the *Every Child Matters* (DfES, 2003) agenda and increasing interest in personalised learning encourages pupils to take increasing ownership of their learning experiences and dialogue with teachers. Despite power differences, Arnot and Reay (2007) contend that students' voices are no more or less true than any other group, including adults in the educational community. Careful leadership and management are likely to be required in order to successfully incorporate the voices of all community members and Frost and Holden (2008) advocate that we need to build such learning relationships for the future.

The engagement of pupil voice in improving teaching and learning may have positive influences on reported outcomes such as examination results. However, the incorporation of pupil voice may also hold other, less measurable, but nevertheless important outcomes for individuals. Including pupil voice in decision-making may assist those struggling to avoid disaffection and improve co-operation and mutual trust between themselves and other learners and teachers (Angus, 2006). The creation of such enabling relationships and inclusion could also support rises in self-esteem, self-discipline, self-expression and interpersonal skills (Fielding, 2006). These outcomes are of value to all learners and, as such, strongly point to a place for pupil voice in learning-centred leadership and in leadership for learning itself.

Flutter and Rudduck (2004), drawing on Hart (1997), point the way to how leaders can seek to ascend a 'ladder' of pupil participation from pupils not being involved in consultation, to being listened to, to being active participants or researchers and, finally, to taking their place as fully active participants and co-researchers along with adults. In a recent US study, Mitra (2008) also points out that power imbalance between adults and students that may well need to be overcome so that intended student voice initiatives can be strengthened. She suggests that power differences may serve to inhibit deep understanding of school problems in communities of practice involving both adults and students. Two fundamental questions for leaders in schools are how far can pupils seek to question adult decision-making? And if they are allowed to become full partners with adults, what difficulties could emerge if adult leadership cannot deliver? If pupils genuinely have their voice and feel sufficiently empowered so as not to simply reproduce the views of teachers, the nature of relationships between pupils and staff would need to alter accordingly. Frost et al. (2009) suggest that in some schools a shift in organisational vision would be necessary if the voice of pupils is to be taken seriously. It is clear that leadership in each school will need to think of how quickly and on what scale progress up the 'ladder' might be possible, if indeed, it is possible at all. Nevertheless, Frost (2008b) contends that developing the place of student leadership is essential if leadership is to be truly distributed in school communities. Full engagement of student leadership and student voice suggests that schools can see value in fostering such developments for the benefit of improving teaching and learning, and in helping to engage students as active participants in their education, and in helping to develop the whole child. As Frost (2008b) indicates, this also implies that such schools accept that developing student voice is an extension of leadership distribution and that both voice and distribution offer an important element in the development of leadership for learning.

Conclusion

In this chapter we have suggested that the extent of leadership influence in organisations seeking to develop a leadership for learning approach will be delimited by sector and by the prevailing national political and policy environment. Nonetheless, it is clear that such an approach can offer benefits to individuals, the organisation and the system as a whole, whatever the phase of education. In particular, this chapter has highlighted potential benefits connected with improved learner engagement, personal development and outcome success. It has also linked such an approach to possible learning benefits for leaders, teachers and overall organisational capacity given that the features associated with a professional learning community can emerge. We have argued that a focus on learning coupled with leadership distribution to middle leaders, teachers and learners through their own voice and involvement in leadership and decision-making suggests a collaborative approach within a supportive culture that can cross organisational boundaries and foster community engagement. In these terms, leadership for learning can encourage 'bottom-up' initiatives, foster innovation, enable joint responses to the needs of learners and help address the gap between high and low achievers though better learner integration.

However, despite the clear implication of the potential 'moral good' of such approaches, a leadership for learning approach will present significant challenges to leaders, staff and learners themselves. For instance, individual organisational readiness will be influenced by present notions of hierarchy and the prevailing pedagogic culture of an educational institution. Student empowerment through an engagement with student voice and student leadership, mediated by fuller collaboration with staff in decision-making, may be perceived as presenting either exciting opportunities or professional threats to incumbent leaders and teachers. While leader-, teacher- and learner-shared perspectives imply a greater collective knowledge and understanding as a basis for change, traditional power differences between teachers and learners, and between leaders and teachers in some organisations, may well militate against the linkage of leadership and learning and inhibit rather than foster new and trusting relationships between stakeholders. It is clear that leaders need to adapt their style appropriately to connect with new conversations about leadership for learning and use self-evaluation and other outcome data as a basis upon which to advance.

Two major associated research and practice issues are emerging in relation to this topic. First, until comparatively recently, there has been a dearth of evidence that leadership distribution can make an impact upon raising outcomes for learners in schools and colleges. However, there is emerging evidence that distributing a larger portion of leadership activity to teachers has a positive influence on teacher effectiveness and teacher engagement (Leithwood and Jantzi, 2000). These authors conclude that teacher leadership has a significant effect on student engagement that far outweighs principal leadership effects after taking into account students' family backgrounds. In Australia, Silins and Mulford (2002) studied the effects of leadership on student learning and found that student outcomes are more likely to improve when leadership sources are distributed throughout the school community and when teachers are empowered in areas of importance to them. However, some school leaders may be better at distribution than others. This is confirmed as an issue in the UK, where PricewaterhouseCoopers (2007) suggest that some school leaders, judging on feedback provided by teachers and support staff, are distributing leadership much better than others and Hargreaves and

Fink (2006) caution that teachers to whom leadership is distributed need to be up to the required task if progress in these terms is to be made. Nevertheless, despite the growing body of research there is still only limited empirical evidence to substantiate the impact of leadership distribution on raising learner outcomes.

Secondly, although the precise connections between leadership and learning have yet to be delineated, there is ample corroboration of the potential for improving schools and the achievement of pupils by working more closely with local communities. Studies in the USA have shown how greater stakeholder involvement can contribute to improving student behaviour and learning outcomes, retention, attendance and drop-out rates; they also report improved access to physical and social services and provide convincing evidence that raised stakeholder involvement can foster better youth and adult relationships (Sanders and Lewis, 2005; Van Voorhis and Sheldon, 2004). However, the same studies also report the considerable challenges in securing long-term rather than temporary success for these developments. It is these two interconnected issues of delineating the ways in which leaders can impact on learning and the strategies by which permanent and positive change occur through stakeholder involvement that define the research agenda for the coming decade.

As this chapter shows, the linkage of leadership and learning and its translation into practice within educational organisations is not without difficulty and will necessarily vary in detail internationally and between different phases of education. It is a leadership that seeks to enable the learning of others with the goal of improving outcomes for all learners. Maintaining a focus on teaching and learning within individual organisations suggests that leaders are aware of internal strengths and weaknesses impinging upon such a focus and the structural and cultural changes that could help promote it. It also suggests that leaders are aware of opportunities and threats to their leadership for learning emerging from an external policy environment that is subject to continuing change. For example, the *Every Child Matters* (DfES, 2003) agenda in the UK recognises that schools have a critical role in raising the educational achievement of children in care and other groups that have consistently underachieved. Arising from this is the implementation of Extended Schools, through which key services can be organised directly by a school or in partnership with private or voluntary sector providers. Providing for greater integration of schools with their communities, the policy potentially enables the more effective provision of services to meet the needs of children, families and the local community, improved access to school facilities, greater parent and community involvement and enhanced learning opportunities for adults. Coupled with this, the DfES (2005) *Extended Schools Prospectus* suggests that by 2010 all schools should be offering a core set of extended services including childcare, parenting support and other specialist services. This requires school leaders of learning to collaborate effectively with other agencies to secure the delivery of these services and implies that other agencies may be represented on school leadership teams. Multi-agency teams will need to find ways of working together and will perhaps share the same aspirations for a focus on teaching and learning as a means to secure improved learner outcomes. As new ways of working emerge, successful school leaders should not lose sight of the need to pay close attention to the quality of teaching and learning in their schools. The authors conclude that given the potential benefits of a leadership for learning approach, we now also need to conduct research on 'new' models of leadership to assess the impact, if any, on student cognitive and non-cognitive outcomes.

Further reading

Blase, J. and Blase, J. (2004) *Handbook of Instructional Leadership: How Successful Principals Promote Teaching and Learning*. Thousand Oaks, CA: Corwin Press.
Law, S. and Glover, D. (2000) *Educational Leadership and Learning: Practice, Policy and Research*. Maidenhead: Open University Press.
MacBeath, J. and Cheng, Y.C. (eds) (2008) *Leadership for Learning: International Perspectives*. Rotterdam: Sense.
MacBeath, J. and Dempster, N. (eds) (2009) *Connecting Leadership and Learning: Principles for Practice*. London: Routledge.
Southworth, G. (2004) *Primary School Leadership in Context: Leading Small, Medium and Large Sized Schools*. London: RoutledgeFalmer.

References

Addison, R. and Brundrett, M. (2008) 'Motivation and demotivation of teachers in primary schools: the challenge of change', *Education 3–13*, 36(1): 79–94.
Ali, F. and Botha, N. (2006) *Evaluating the Role, Importance and Effectiveness of Heads of Department in Contributing to School Improvement in Public Secondary Schools in Gauteng*. Johannesburg: Matthew Goniwe School of Leadership and Governance.
Angus, L. (2006) 'Educational leadership and the imperative of including student voices, student interests, and students' lives in the mainstream', *International Journal of Leadership in Education*, 9(4): 369–79.
Arnot, M. and Reay, D. (2007) 'A sociology of pedagogic voice: power inequality and pupil consultation', *Discourse: Studies in the Cultural Politics of Education*, 28(3): 311–25.

Barber, M. (1997) *The Learning Game: Arguments for an Education Revolution*. London: Indigo.

Bezzina, C. (2008) 'Towards a learning community: the journey of a Maltese Catholic Church School', *Management in Education*, 22(3): 22–7.

Biggs, J.B. (1992) 'Returning to school: review and discussion', in A. Dimetriou, M. Shayer and A. E. Efklides (eds), *Neo-Paigetian Theories of Cognitive Development: Implications and Applications for Education*. London: Routledge.

Blase, J. and Blase, J. (2004) *Handbook of Instructional Leadership: How Successful Principals Promote Teaching and Learning*. Thousand Oaks, CA: Corwin Press.

Bragg, S. (2007) '"But I listen to children anyway!" Teacher perspectives on pupil voice', *Educational Action Research*, 15(4): 505–18.

Broadfoot, P. (2000) 'Liberating the learner through assessment', in J. Collins and D. Cook (eds), *Understanding Learning: Influences and Outcomes*. London: Paul Chapman/Open University Press.

Brundrett, M. and Silcock, P. (2002) *Achieving Competence, Success and Excellence in Teaching*. London: Routledge.

Burton, N. and Brundrett, M. (2005) *Leading the Curriculum in the Primary School*. London: Paul Chapman Publishing.

Bush, T. (2008a) 'Developing educational leaders – don't leave it to chance', *Educational Management Administration and Leadership*, 36(3): 307–9.

Bush, T. (2008b) *Leadership and Management Development in Education*. London: Sage.

Bush, T. and Glover, D. (2002) *School Leadership: Concepts and Evidence*. Nottingham: National College for School Leadership.

Bush, T. and Glover, D. (2009) *Managing Teaching and Learning: A Concept Paper*. Johannesburg: Matthew Goniwe School of Leadership and Governance.

Bush, T. and Heystek, J. (2006) 'School leadership and management in South Africa: principals' perceptions', *International Studies in Educational Administration*, 34(3): 63–76.

Bush, T., Joubert, R., Kiggundu, E. and Van Rooyen, J. (2008) *Leading and Managing Literacy and Numeracy*. Johannesburg: Zenex Foundation.

Busher, H. (2006) *Understanding Educational Leadership: People, Power and Culture*. Maidenhead: Open University Press.

Campbell, J. and Li, M. (2008) 'Asian students' voices: an empirical study of Asian Students' learning experiences at a New Zealand university', *Journal of Studies in International Education*, 12(4): 375–96.

Cochran-Smith, M. and Lytle, S. (1999) 'Teacher learning communities', *Review of Research in Education*, 24: 24–32.

Collinson, D. (ed.) (2007) *Leadership and the Learner Voice*. Lancaster: Lancaster University Management School, Centre for Excellence in Leadership.

Cruddas, L. (2005) *Learning Mentors in Schools: Policy and Practice*. Stoke-on-Trent: Trentham Books.

Cruddas, L. (2007) 'Engaged voices – dialogic interaction and the construction of shared social meanings', *Educational Action Research*, 15(3): 479–88.

Day, C., Sammons, P., Hopkins, D., Harris, A., Leithwood, K., Qing, G., Penlington, C., Mehta, P. and Kington, A. (2007) *The Impact of School Leadership on Pupil Outcomes: Interim Report*. Research Report DCSF-RR018. Nottingham: University of Nottingham.

DfES (2003) *Every Child Matters* (CM5860). Norwich: HMSO.

DfES (2004) *National Standards for Head Teachers*. London: The Stationery Office.

DfES (2005) *Extended Schools: Access to Opportunities and Services for All*. Ref 1408–2005DOC-EN. Nottingham: DfES Publications.

DuFour, R. (2004) 'What is a Professional Learning Community?', *Educational Leadership*, 61(8): 6–11.

Elmore, R. (2000) *Building a New Structure for School Leadership*. Washington, DC: Albert Shanker Institute.

Fielding, M. (2001) 'Beyond the rhetoric of student voice: new departures or new constraints in the transformation of 21st century schooling', *Forum for Providing 13–19 Comprehensive Education*, 43(2): 100–10.

Fielding, M. (2006) 'Leadership, radical student engagement and the necessity of person-centred education', *International Journal of Leadership in Education*, 9(4): 299–313.

Fielding, M., Fuller, A. and Loose, T. (1999) 'Taking pupil perspectives seriously: the central place of pupil voice in primary school improvement', in G. Southworth and P. Lincoln (eds), *Supporting Improving Primary Schools: The Role of Heads and LEAs*. London: Falmer. pp. 107–21.

Fitzgerald, T. and Gunter, H. (2006) 'Leading learning: middle leadership in schools in England and New Zealand', *Management in Education*, 20: 6–8.

Flutter, J. and Rudduck, J. (2004) *Consulting Pupils: What's In It for Schools?* London: RoutledgeFalmer.

Frost, D. (2008a) 'Teacher Leadership: values and voice', *School Leadership and Management*, 28(4): 337–52.

Frost, R. (2008b) 'Developing student participation, research and leadership: the HCD Student Partnership', *School Leadership and Management*, 28(4): 353–68.

Frost, R. and Holden, G. (2008) 'Student voice and future schools: building partnerships for student participation', *Improving Schools*, 11(1): 83–95.

Frost, D., Frost, R., MacBeath, J. and Pedder, D. (2009) 'The influence and participation of children and young people in their learning (IPiL) project', International Congress for School Effectiveness and Improvement, Vancouver, BC Canada, 4–7 January, pp. 1–14.

Gaspar, M., Pinto, A., da Conceicao, H. and da Silva, J. (2008) 'A questionnaire for listening to students' voices in the assessment of teaching quality in a classical medical school', *Assessment and Evaluation in Higher Education*, 33(4): 445–53.

Grant, C. (2006) 'Teacher leadership emerging voices on teacher leadership: some South African views', *Educational Management Administration and Leadership*, 34(4): 511–32.

Hallinger, P. and Heck, R. (1999) 'Can leadership enhance school effectiveness', in T. Bush, L. Bell, R. Bolam, R. Glatter and P. Ribbins (eds), *Educational Management: Redefining Theory, Policy and Practice*. London: Paul Chapman Publishing.

Hargreaves, A. and Fink, D. (2006) *Sustainable Leadership*. San Francisco CA: Jossey-Bass.

Harris, A. and Hopkins, D. (1999) 'Teaching and learning and the challenge of educational reform', *School Effectiveness and School Improvement*, 10: 257–67.

Hart, R.A. (1997) *Children's Participation: The Theory and Practice of Involving Young Citizens in Community Development and Environmental Care*. London: Earthscan Publications.

Hopkins, E.A. (2008) 'Work-related learning: hearing students' voices', *Educational Action Research*, 16(2): 209–19.

Keedy, J.L. (1999) 'Examining teacher instructional leadership within the small-group dynamics of collegial groups', *Teaching and Teacher Education*, 15: 785–99.

Knapp, M., Copland, M. and Talbert, J. (2003) *Leading for Learning: Reflective Tools for School and District Leaders*. Washington, DC: Center for the Study of Teaching and Policy, University of Washington.

Knapp, M., Copeland, M., Portin, B. and Plecki, M. (2006) 'Building coherent leadership systems in education: roles, resources, information and authority to act', paper presented at the Annual Meeting of the American Educational Research Association, 7–11 April.

Lakomski, G. (2001) 'Organizational change, leadership and learning: culture as a cognitive process', *International Journal of Educational Management*, 15(2): 68–77.

Leithwood, K. and Jantzi, D. (2000) 'The effects of different sources of leadership on student engagement in school', in K. Riley and K.S. Louis (eds), *Leadership for Change and School Reform: International Perspectives*. New York: RoutledgeFalmer.

Leithwood, K., Day, C., Sammons, P., Harris, A. and Hopkins, D. (2006) *Seven Strong Claims about Successful School Leadership*. Nottingham: National College for School Leadership.

Lewis, R. and Burman, E. (2008) 'Providing for student voice in classroom management: teachers' views', *International Journal of Inclusive Education*, 12(2): 151–67.

LSC (2006) *Framework for Excellence*. http://www.ffe.gov.uk

MacBeath, J. (2006) 'Finding a voice, finding self', *Educational Review*, 58(2): 195–207.

MacBeath, J. and Dempster, N. (eds) (2009) *Connecting Leadership and Learning: Principles for Practice*. London: Routledge.

MacBeath, J., Gray, J., Cullen, J., Frost, D., Steward, S. and Swaffield, S. (2007) *Schools on the Edge: Responding to Challenging Circumstances*. London: Paul Chapman Publishing.

Martin, N., Worrall, N. and Dutson-Steinfeld, A. (2005) 'Student voice: Pandora's box or philosopher's stone?', paper presented at the International Congress for School Effectiveness and School Improvement, Barcelona, 2–5 January.

Mitra, D. (2005) 'Increasing student voice and moving towards youth leadership', *The Prevention Researcher*, 13(1): 7–10.

Mitra, D. (2008) 'Balancing power in communities of practice: an examination of increasing student voice through school-based youth–adult partnerships', *Journal of Educational Change*, 9: 221–42.

Mitsoni, F. (2006) '"I get bored when we don't have the opportunity to say our opinion": learning about teaching from students', *Educational Review*, 58(2): 159–70.

Mulford, B. and Silins, H. (2003) 'Leadership for organisational learning and improved student outcomes – what do we know?', *Cambridge Journal of Education*, 33(2): 175–195.

OFSTED (2005) *Framework for the Inspection of Schools in England from September 2005*. http://www.ofsted.gov.uk

Ozolins, L., Hall, H. and Peterson, R. (2008) 'The student voice: recognising the hidden and informal curriculum in medicine', *Medical Teacher*, 30(6): 606–11.

Papatheodorou, T. (2002) '"How we like our school to be" … pupils' voices', *European Educational Research Journal*, 1(3): 445–67.

PricewaterhouseCoopers (2007) *Independent Study into School Leadership RB818*. Nottingham: DfES Publications.

Rhodes, C. and Nevill, A. (2004) 'Academic and social integration in higher education: a survey of satisfaction and dissatisfaction within a first-year education studies cohort at a new university', *Journal of Further and Higher Education*, 28(2): 179–93.

Roberts, S. and Pruitt, E. (2003) *Schools as Professional Learning Communities*. London: Sage.

Rudduck, J. and Flutter, J. (2000) 'Pupil participation and perspective: "Carving a new order of experience"', *Cambridge Journal of Education*, 30(1): 75–89.

Sanders, M.G. and Lewis, K.C. (2005) 'Building bridges toward excellence: community involvement in high schools', *The High School Journal*, February/March: 1–9.

Schein, E. (1992) *Organizational Culture and Leadership*. San Francisco, CA: Jossey-Bass.

Shayer, M. and Adey, P. (eds) *Learning Intelligence*. Buckingham: Open University Press.

Sheppard, B. (1996) 'Exploring the transformational nature of instructional leadership', *Alberta Journal of Educational Research*, 42(4): 325–44.

Silcock, P. and Brundrett, M. (2006) 'Pedagogy at Key Stage 2: teaching through pupil–teacher partnership', in R. Webb (ed.), *Changing Teaching and Learning in the Primary School*. Maidenhead: Open University Press. pp. 92–102.

Silins, H. and Mulford, B. (2002) 'Leadership and school results', in K. Leithwood, P. Hallinger, K.S. Louis, P. Furman-Brown, P. Gronn, W. Mulford and K. Riley (eds), *Second International Handbook of Educational Leadership and Administration*. Dordrecht: Kluwer.

Southworth, G. (2000) 'How primary schools learn', *Research Papers in Education*, 15(3): 275–91.

Southworth, G. (2002) 'Instructional leadership in school: reflections and empirical evidence', *School Leadership and Management*, 22(1): 73–91.

Southworth, G. (2004) *Primary School Leadership in Context: Leading Small, Medium and Large Sized Schools*. London: RoutledgeFalmer.

Spillane, J. (2004) 'Educational leadership', *Educational Evaluation and Policy Analysis*, 26(2): 169–72.

Stoll, L. and Louis, K.S. (2007) *Professional Learning Communities: Divergence, Depths and Dilemmas*. Maidenhead: Open University Press.

Stoll, L., Bolam, R., McMahon, A., Thomas, S., Wallace, M., Greenwood, A. and Hawkey, K. (2006) *What is a Professional Learning Community? A Summary*. DfES-0187-2006. London: DfES.

Stoll, L., Fink, D. and Earl, L. (2003) *It's All about Learning and It's about Time*. Buckingham: Open University Press.

Swaffield, S. and MacBeath, J. (2009) 'Leadership for learning', in J. MacBeath and N. Dempster (eds), *Connecting Leadership and Learning: Principles for Practice*. London: Routledge.

Timperley, H. (2006) 'Learning challenges involved in developing leading for learning', *Educational Management Administration and Leadership*, 34(4): 546–63.

Van Voorhis, F. and Sheldon, S. (2004) 'Principals' roles in the development of US programs of school, family, and community partnerships', *International Journal of Educational Research*, 41: 55–70.

Waterhouse, J. (2008) 'Raising aspirations within school communities: the Learning Catalysts project', *School Leadership and Management*, 28(4): 369–84.

Waterhouse, J. and Dempster, N. (2009) 'Seven countries, eight sites, 24 schools', in J. MacBeath and N. Dempster (eds), *Connecting Leadership and Learning: Principles for Practice*. London: Routledge.

Whitty, G. and Wisby, E. (2007) 'Whose voice? An exploration of the current policy interest in school decision-making', *International Studies in Sociology of Education*, 17(3): 303–19.

CHAPTER 10

Building and Leading Learning Cultures[1]

Allan Walker

Successful leaders make a difference to school outcomes indirectly rather than directly (Day and Leithwood, 2007; Hallinger and Heck, 1999). In other words, successful leaders exert a positive influence on student learning and lives by working through and with others in the school (Southworth, 2004). They do this through shaping the form, meaning and substance of key school conditions that have a direct and verifiable influence on learning within a particular context. Leithwood (2007) calls these conditions mediating variables. He points out that 'while there is a considerable body of evidence about classroom and school conditions more or less directly influencing student learning, much less is known about how principals successfully influence these conditions' (2007: 8).

The message is that although we now have a reasonably solid grasp of ways to help students learn in the classroom, and of the organisational conditions that facilitate this, we know less about how school leaders can make these learning conditions happen across the school. This calls for increased understanding of how to connect coherently what we know about effective classroom learning with supportive organisational conditions, and with leadership practice.

The purpose of this chapter is to discuss what leaders can do to build and sustain learning cultures in schools. Interest in building such cultures has grown markedly over the last decade with the flood of research into professional learning cultures, communities of practice and learning communities.

This chapter has four main sections. The first section unveils the concept of culture, and the second, the notion of a learning culture. An understanding of these ideas is necessary to frame discussion of possible ways to build and nurture learning cultures. Both sections attempt no more than an introduction to these complex areas. Section three outlines a number of organisational 'learning conditions'. These conditions represent assumptions which, when shared, underpin school life and therefore hold the potential to positively influence practice. The fourth section focuses on leading learning cultures, or the actions school leaders might take to influence student and teacher learning.

Culture

The use of culture as an organisational identifier has been part of the literature at least since the classic work of Waller in the 1930s (Waller, 1932). Over the years it has become one of the most discussed concepts in the organisation literature, particularly in terms of how organisations really work and, consequently, how they can change. Hofstede (1991) describes culture as the 'software of the mind'.

Academic discussion aside, people living and working together have always been aware that their society, clan, group or settlement was different and somewhat unique – but could not always easily articulate how or why this was so. In schools, for example, teachers know that their work is much more than a detached collection of material things such as procedures, manuals and work schedules. They know that beneath their formal work resides an indefinable though commonly understood force that determines not just whether they do their work, but what they do, how well they do it, how much they like it and who they do it with. As Deal and Peterson (1999: 3) state: 'Beneath the conscious awareness of everyday life in schools, there is a stream of thought and activity. This underground flow of feelings and folkways wends its way within schools, dragging people, programs, and ideas toward often-unstated purposes'.

Given the attention culture has received, it is unsurprising that no single agreed-upon definition dominates. Although there is some general consensus that a culture is 'the way of life of a given collectivity (or organization) particularly as reflected in shared values, norms, symbols and traditions' (Mitchell and Willower, 1992: 6), there endures basic disagreement about whether a culture is something an organisation *is* or *has*. It is worth outlining this debate.

Seeing culture as something that a school *is* positions culture as a root metaphor (for example, a machine, an organism, a prison, a rap band). In organisational terms a metaphor serves to highlight characteristics ignored by observers, such as the underlying assumptions that drive behaviour and the shared interpretive schema of members.

This implies that culture cannot be observed directly but exists only in the minds of those associated with the organisation, or those immersed in it for a long time. Conversely, seeing culture as something that a school *has* takes a more instrumental premise and suggests that culture is an attribute associated with other organisational variables and can therefore be manipulated or shaped by leaders. It is important to note that cultures operate at different levels, and that multiple cultures are nested and layered. Culture can be applied in big picture terms to nations, societies, religious or ethnic groups. In schools, they flourish within different formal groups such as subject departments, as well as through various informal groupings. People belong to more than one culture and are influenced by these cultures to a greater or lesser degree.

Schein's (1985, 1993, 1996) definition of culture is among the most widely accepted. It attempts to integrate both the *is* and *has* positions. In Schein's own words:

> (Culture) is a pattern of basic assumptions – invented, discovered, or developed by a given group as it learns to cope with problems … that has worked well enough to be considered valid and, therefore, to be taught to new members as the correct way to perceive, think, and feel in relation to those problems. (Schein, 1985: 9)

This model defines culture as something that an organisation *is*, in that it focuses primarily on the level of basic assumptions, but also as something an organisation *has*, through its focus on artefacts and values. As such, Schein's model comprises three distinct but closely related levels: artefacts, values and basic underlying assumptions.

Artefacts comprise the visible signatures of the culture – the physical environment, the photos, the displays of student work, trophies or dress codes. *Values* refer to the philosophies that form the 'articulated, publicly announced principles and values that the group claims it is trying to achieve' (Schein, 1995: 9). As such, they are the visible yet intangible manifestations of an organisation's driving beliefs and assumptions. These philosophies may include, for example, intangible policies, rituals, procedures and networks of relationships. Assemblies, celebrations, reward systems, how people support each other or whether people walk freely into others' classrooms are examples of this level of values in schools.

The *basic assumptions* that underpin organisational life and shape its norms reside at level three. These are the 'invisible' workings of schools, consisting of unconscious, taken for granted beliefs that help to solve problems encountered by organisational members. Such beliefs may focus, for example, on the centrality of equity and respect for all; or that people only deserve what they 'earn' in the world of the classroom.

A learning culture

The concept of culture and its influence on organisational life is clearly established. Some authors hold that a learning-orientated culture sets the context for everything an organisation does (Lopez, 2000). For example, while discussing the nexus between organisational culture and the creation of new knowledge (learning), De Long and Fahey (2000: 126) suggest that culture 'creates the context for social interaction that determines how knowledge is used in particular situations and shapes the processes by which new knowledge is created, legitimated and distributed'.

Much recent discussion of the potential of culture to effect school change comes wrapped in discussion of professional communities (Lieberman and Miller, 2008), communities of practice (Wenger, 1999), learning communities (Sullivan and Glanz, 2006) and professional learning communities (Dufour et al., 2006). This chapter draws on but does not review these constructions explicitly; the literature is far too large and diverse. It should be noted, however, that without exception all these discussions underscore the importance of culture to meaningful learning and change. They also stress that one of the main reasons why some schools have not been as successful as hoped is because cultural, contextual and pedagogical aspects are out of alignment. This criticism is explicated below.

A basic argument underpinning interest in learning cultures is the apparent inability of numerous well-intentioned and generously resourced reforms to make a significant and sustainable difference to student learning. Much of this failure is attributed to basic incompatibilities between ingrained teacher cultures and reform intentions, and how systems and leaders express and link the value of learning and increased capacity. Recent research in Australia, for example, suggests that cultures that drive school revitalisation carefully align values and practices around the vision and realities of teachers' work (Crowther et al., 2008).

In the USA, Elmore (2004, cited in Fullan, 2006) targeted the lack of coherence between what teachers know and how they work. He lamented that:

> there is almost no opportunity for teachers to engage in continuous improvement and sustained learning about their practice in the settings in which they actually work ... confronting similar

problems of practice. This disconnection between the requirements of learning to teach well and the structure of teachers' work
life is fatal to any sustained process of instructional improvement.
(Elmore, 2004, cited in Fullan, 2006: 4)

In a similar vein, after an extensive review of the comprehensive
school reform literature, Bain (2007) concluded that reforms had
largely been unsuccessful because their overall designs were incom-
plete. He suggested that too many reforms have targeted some areas
of organisational life only and have failed to connect to teachers'
lives. His claim is that change is too often viewed as a rational
process and that discussions in the area generally miss 'overwhelm-
ing evidence from the literature on school culture that shows the
instability in the values and beliefs of teachers about critical issues
that underpin decision making about change' (Bain, 2007: 30). Issues
include teacher beliefs about autonomy, change, the place of data in
informing practice and the meaning of collaboration.

The argument proposed so far is that even though culture is an
intangible and complex phenomenon, it not only 'exists' but influences human thought and behaviour at every turn. In organisational
terms, the cultures that are determined by and determine behaviour
have a powerful effect on school success. Leaders influence this success directly and indirectly through the conditions they nurture in
the school; the culture of the school is an overarching condition.
Many schools have not been as successful as hoped and one of the
main reasons for this is that the cultural conditions are missing, mis-
aligned or misunderstood. In other words, how formal organisation
works interactively with informal norms can play an important role
in changing culture (Elmore, 2008).

Learning conditions

A learning culture is in effect the synergistic effects generated through
the establishment and embedment of a set of interrelated conditions
that promote and encourage learning as a way of professional life.
Processes used to nurture learning conditions interact on existing
values and norms. Through harnessing these conditions, leaders
work to indirectly and directly influence learning across the school.
In effect, the conditions represent assumptions which, when shared,
underpin school life and operation, and therefore hold the potential
to positively influence practice. The work of leaders is to hold up,
debate and champion these learning processes in order to influence

action. In other words, they instantiate the assumptions held within and across the conditions as they emerge and take root.

As will become apparent, the conditions paint a contradictory and somewhat messy picture. This is understandable given that much of what we know about change remains tentative, and leadership actions are by necessity applied across very different contexts by very different people. As such, any discussion of culture is unavoidably muddled because of the complexity and unpredictability of human relationships and social groupings. The conditions outlined below are by no means finite, but appear important for framing learning cultures (Walker and Quong, 2008):

- witnessing learning
- staying fresh
- becoming resilient
- framing scaffolding
- catching learning
- finding voice
- trusting intuition
- remaining curious.

Witnessing learning

Learning is most effective when embedded within social interaction. People are more likely to engage in meaningful learning when they witness and have someone to witness their work. Witnessing underpins the process of continuously providing meaningful feedback. Supportively framed, honest feedback is fundamental to any learning culture in that it provides personal and collective avenues for critique, reflection, celebration and experimentation. A witness takes on the role of a formal and informal assessor who sees the ups and downs colleagues experience. Witnessing involves shared expertise, debriefing after stressful episodes, commiserating when things don't quite work out and helping celebrate successes. This can only be done when colleagues are in touch with what each other are doing and are willing to watch, listen and share.

Staying fresh

Learning grinds down when educators and communities lose the ability or desire to see their work in new and different ways – when they lose the 'freshness of a beginner's mind'. Forgetting what it is like to be a 'beginner' has at least two somewhat contradictory faces. The first is that learning-geared cultures do not blindly adopt packages of 'best practice' which constantly bombard schools. The second is that even though experienced-based knowledge is extremely valuable, it is unwise to engage in practices just because 'they have always worked before'.

First, Glatter and Kydd (2003: 236) hold that successful learning cultures are, 'logically incompatible with the notion of "best practice"'. Almost by definition, learning demands active experimentation, which implies that practice can never be 'best'. Relying on what others (or a collection of others) claim works 'best' denies the place of context and learning through experimentation, and the inevitable failures associated with trying something new (Walker and Quong, 2005). In fact, Chapman (2002: 59) claims, paradoxically, that if we don't learn from failures, then failures will continue. 'This suggests that the potential for learning from unsuccessful practice may be at least as great as that from practice which is perceived to have been successful' (Glatter and Kydd, 2003: 237).

Second, although there is no doubting the value of experience-based knowledge, a careless over-reliance on 'what worked for me/us before' hinders learning. Very basic questions can be asked about whether the best way forward is always to go back. Whereas personal and shared experience is important because it forms how we learn, it also has the potential to sustain resistance to new ideas. Such resistance is rarely openly articulated, or even intentional, but is evidenced by the obstruction of possibilities or automatic rejection of the new or different. Anyone working in a school knows that situations are *never exactly the same*; that the leader is not the same person who addressed a similar problem five years ago or even last week. In other words, although experience is invaluable to inform learning, in reality, we never enter the same stream twice.

A caveat is important here. Keeping the freshness of a beginner's mind does not mean that learning ignores what has worked elsewhere or before; this is a gross oversimplification. Knowing and sharing research-informed knowledge and respecting experience are irreplaceable qualities for learning cultures. But unless communities are open to new ideas, willing to try something different or critique their own and others' practice, learning will not flourish and conformity may rule.

Becoming resilient

Learning requires resilience – the ability to not only survive, but also continue learning through adversity, to persist in the face of challenge and tolerate the feeling of 'not knowing'. The importance of resilience is built on the notion that professional learning is unavoidably an emotional experience. Learning in schools is not a distant 'academic exercise', but a commitment to personally altering practice where it counts – in the school. If learners lack resilience, when times get tough, the tendency is to revert to standard, imported solutions and so lose the drive to learn.

Framing scaffolding

An essential learning condition is scaffolding. Scaffolding provides the keys that help teachers decide the knowledge and skills needed to enhance learning: their own, their colleagues and their students. This involves uncovering the codes that underpin learning by breaking down knowledge into forms that can be understood and practised in context. Dimmock's (2000) notion of backward mapping holds relevance here. Scaffolding is also provided, for example, by research into effective learning, cultural nuance and curriculum. The use of scaffolds however, as noted earlier, is not about adopting someone else's framework unthinkingly; rather, it's about using them to frame or inform learning and so improve practice.

Catching learning

Learning is not something that necessarily comes automatically. If mindsets are not tuned to look for and make sense of what is happening around them, people miss much of what experience and interaction offer. In other words, if people do not *catch* themselves learning, they forgo the frequent subtle messages that have the potential to inform their practice, and so drive improvement (Velsor et al., 2004). Catching learning is about moving beyond simple exposure to new skills and techniques (although these remain important) toward challenging 'why' people do things as they do. In this way, catching learning is about consciously acknowledging, affirming, and reflecting on practice in order to provide capacity-building feedback.

Whereas catching learning appears a simple process, it is far from it. Too often, people forfeit learning opportunities because they see the experience as only happening in certain situations. For example, some associate learning with involvement in 'formal' occasions only. These may include workshops, team meetings or even academic reading. Whereas these are obviously useful learning places (or at least, should be) many other opportunities remain untapped because we fail to stop and capture their potential.

It can be difficult to catch yourself learning for a number of pragmatic and personal reasons. These may include our long-ingrained habits, the fact that everything else seems more urgent, a natural tendency to avoid the anxiety accompanying the 'new', or a realisation that formal systems do not provide sufficient encouragement or reward for learning (Velsor et al., 2004). All too often these reasons form artificial divisions between work and learning.

Bredeson (2003) points out that learning opportunities abound, and that professionals attempt to capture these opportunities at every turn, and then apply their learning to improve schools. He claims that learning is first and foremost about seeing it as work, or challenging the convention that 'work' and 'learning' are separate entities. According to Bredeson, the learning net can be cast equally 'in', 'at', 'outside' and 'beyond' work.

Finding voice

To learn to improve practice, teachers and leaders maintain a healthy belief in their own abilities; what can be labelled 'voice'. Let us be clear up front: finding voice does not equate to blind arrogance. It is about a belief in ability, but carefully tempered with a healthy dose of humility. In essence, finding voice depends on clarification of an authentic core of beliefs, values and actions, which in turn demand active self-evaluation and ongoing learning. If they do not find voice, teachers risk blindly following someone else's path rather than discovering what is needed to help students in context. In other words, successful leaders believe in themselves, know what they believe, and importantly, articulate why they hold those beliefs. If leaders do not make their beliefs explicit, learning is unlikely to happen (Eraut, 1999; Walker, 2007).

Legitimate voice develops only when practice is aligned with reality, when the requisite knowledge is identified and reliable, and when learners are 'open to available facts, knowledge, information, data and feedback'. Then one can openly ask, 'What needs to be done?' Finding voice in cultural terms suggests that teachers decide together what is important for their students, an approach that can lead to greater consistency, predictability and coherence. These elements in turn encourage trust, a key component for finding voice.

The need for trust runs along and through all the learning conditions. For teachers to find their voices, they need to trust their abilities. To feel this trust, they need to know that the system they work for actually believes in them. If teachers are unsure how they are judged, or if they do not feel valued, suspicion rather than trust will reign. This suspicion can be accompanied by high levels of professional cynicism that distort the aims of professional practice and damage confidence.

Trusting intuition

Although learning cultures call for research-based knowledge, a case remains for the place of intuition. Intuition is how teachers translate their experience into action. In line with related conditions, intuition stems from learning through both success and failure over a period of time, as well as from the discoveries that partner these experiences. Intuition is neither magical nor mystical; it is learned, and over time produces a level of automaticity. Klein (2003) puts it nicely by explaining that intuition is, 'a muscular rather than a magical or mystical view' – and is therefore something that can be acquired. As he says: 'Intuitive decision making improves as we acquire more patterns, larger repertoires of action scripts, and richer mental models' (2003: 11).

Remaining curious

Learning resides in the extensive contradictory evidence confronting schools. Although this often produces stress, the strain created by being uncomfortable, or 'not knowing' can produce a creative conflict. Cognitive conflict is the tension that is created when what a person believes they know and value is challenged by what actually is, or by alternate positions. Engaging with tension produces a form of cognitive conflict that prompts active curiosity. Curiosity, in turn, leads to new learning and different ways to proceed in practice. Such tension often emerges when we critically reflect on new data. That is, when people are exposed to new data, they can realise that there is a difference between what they think they know and what is being revealed. As used here, curiosity has a number of characteristics. It requires learners to maintain an open mind, actively wonder about things, ask lots of questions, and be interested in the possibility that things are not always as they seem at first glance (Walker and Quong, 2008).

Leading learning cultures

In basic terms, school success depends on a number of interrelated factors. First, a successful school has a shared and articulated understanding of what it wants to achieve (purpose), why it wants to achieve it (reason), and how the school community goes about doing it (practice). Second, shared purpose, reason, and practice are values driven and coherently aligned (connection); they do not work against each other unnecessarily. Third, as well as being values-based, purpose, reason and practice are deliberately informed by research ('big-picture' and school-based inquiry) and accumulated tacit knowledge. Fourth, successful leaders have a clear focus on learning for continuous improvement, which feeds back into purpose, reason and practice through an intentional design.

The leader's job then is to actively connect and align purpose, reason and practice for the benefit of students. Southworth (2004: 78) explains that 'whatever (the) leaders wish to see happening is contingent on others actually putting it into practice … They (leaders) do this through a range of strategies and processes'. If this is true, a number of questions quickly form, such as, how can leaders build and embed a commonly agreed dedication to ongoing learning? How can they create the conditions that encourage their communities to want to learn? How do they learn and help others learn? What strategies do they use? The discussion now turns specifically to leaders as culture builders and nurturers.

Productive learning cultures exhibit two features. First, there is shared agreement on 'what's important to us as a school' [what Bain (2007) calls 'simple rules']. This shared agreement focuses on school-wide learning. Second is the level of congruence between beliefs and actions at all levels, and how passionately people pursue this. The bottom line is that success is dependent on what, why and how people do their jobs; how they lead, teach, interact, care, and so on. Leaders play a range of roles to make this happen, and these roles come together to influence practice directly and indirectly through creating conditions that foster meaning, commitment and learning.

Whereas our working definition of culture is the assumptions, values, beliefs and norms that underpin school life, the culture aspired to is one within which learning becomes a natural driver of professional life. In reality, a culture cannot be built just by leaders getting everyone to agree on a shared set of values; these must be used to drive action. To clarify, leaders influence what happens in schools using two broad groups of connective strategies. These strategies can be called *structural connectors* and *cultural connectors* (Table 10.1), and they combine to energise, shape and co-ordinate action.

Table 10.1 General connective strategies

Structural connectors	Cultural connectors
Written rules, students' handbooks, formal mission statements, teacher and student groupings, formal reporting and accountability lines, formal curriculum, performance management systems, timetables, disciplinary procedures, timetables, defined positions, formal power relationships	Values, beliefs, norms, expectations, informal sanctions, relationships

Structural connectors are the formal mechanisms leaders use to bind and influence. These include written rules, teacher and student groupings, formal reporting and accountability lines, performance management systems, timetables, disciplinary procedures, and so on. Cultural connectors are the values, beliefs, norms, expectations and informal sanctions that underpin and guide school life. These may, for example, take the form of shared understandings that 'we are *all* responsible for *all* students', 'we don't ever humiliate kids at this school', 'we trust what our colleagues do in the classroom' or 'you can come and watch anytime you like'.

Although connectors can be separated into formal and informal lines for the purposes of discussion and understanding, in the actuality of schools they are intractably twinned; both depend on the relationships leaders develop with, within and even beyond their units or schools (Elmore, 2008). If leaders do not connect values and structures coherently, it is highly unlikely that schools will be successful. The message here is that building learning cultures is really about successful relationships that are values-based, learning-focused, human-centred and action-oriented.

I turn now to some of the ways leaders might work to build and sustain learning cultures. The strategies introduced are not intended to be comprehensive. There may be many other approaches, and as such, they cut across the learning conditions interactively, often in very uneven ways. The strategies include:

- modelling, monitoring and dialogue
- intentional design
- a common schema
- simple rules
- similarity at scale
- emergent feedback
- dispersed control.

Modelling, monitoring and dialogue

In a careful review of relevant literature, Southworth (2005: 78) found that 'ultimately, school leaders influence through three interrelated strategies: modelling, monitoring and dialogue'. Modelling, or the *power of example*, means that if leaders want the rest of the school community to value learning, they must not just claim the value, but show this clearly to others. An important consideration here for leaders is that they reflect carefully on their own beliefs and actions and can plainly articulate 'what they stand for'.

Monitoring, or the *power of watching and feeding-back* means that leaders keep careful track of hard data (for example, test scores), as well as the softer more veiled aspects of school life, such as the stories teachers tell about their work, and the stories students tell about their learning and feelings. Careful monitoring informs decision-making at all levels of operation, provides a form of ongoing needs analysis, and builds trust and understanding. Part of building a learning culture is about ensuring that all students receive the education they deserve. This cannot happen in leaders unaware of what is happening in the school. Data gleaning through monitoring forms the substance upon which the all-important feedback is based.

In simple terms: 'Dialogue is about creating opportunities for teachers to talk with their colleagues about learning and teaching' (Southworth, 2005: 80). It is the *power of talk*. Cultures that value dialogue favour focused discussion, knowledge sharing, exchange and debate (Davenport and Prusak, 1997). Dialogue in practice can entail gathering data from diverse sources, exercising shared judgement built around this data and using accumulated knowledge to inform practice. Again, successful dialogue implies tight, embedded feedback mechanisms.

Southworth (2005: 82) states that: 'The three strategies of modelling, monitoring and dialogue interrelate and overlap. Each makes a difference, but it is their combined effect which really matters'. As such, the strategies are iterative and reciprocal. They work tenaciously together to develop the trust that learning cultures need to take root. While extolling their power, however, Southworth points out that he is not promoting the vision of a heroic, charismatic leader moulding a culture based on personal charisma and personality. The essence of his argument is that leaders work at the nexus of the formal and informal, and as such, building a learning culture is as much about structures and systems as it is purely about values and beliefs. Culture without structure and system, no matter how sweet, may have little influence on learning.

The remaining group of strategies draws on Bain's (2007) research into self-organising schools. As with Southworth's ideas, the strategies only work interactively, and so challenge leaders to connect values, structures and actions in a coherent fashion, always targeted squarely at learning.

Intentional design

The construction and ongoing influence of a learning culture is dependent on an intentional and coherent design; learning cultures do not just happen. Intention is linked to strategy and requires formal infrastructure (Elmore, 2008). Culture cannot be crafted unless the school and leaders have debated, decided and articulated a strategy (Chatman and Cha, 2003). In our terms, to be relevant this strategy aims at making learning a way of organisational life in order to improve student lives and outcomes.

Using self-organising theory (built around complex adaptive systems theory) as a basis for successful change, Bain (2007) argues for a coherent design that promotes constant adaptation, or ongoing learning. His six design principals are discussed later in this section. He explains: 'Self-organisation or any organisation does not occur naturally in schools ... The cornerstone of the theory of self-organising schools rests on the view that the principles of self-organisation can be applied intentionally to all human systems' (2007: 43). Bain justifies how schools can implement designs for the successful adoption of research-based practice at scale.

> Individuals in self-organising systems generate collaborative bottom up solutions by pooling their collective intelligence, and in doing so, they transcend their individual capacities. Further, they adapt to the demands of their environment and increase the likelihood of thriving ... These theories of self-organisation have generated great interest in organisations because they explain how systems can come up with new learning, innovations, solutions to problems, and better ways to address their needs without constant top-down intervention. (Bain, 2007: 43)

Using an architectural metaphor, Bredeson (2003: xv) argues for the 'compelling need for professional learning, both individual and collective, to be legitimised as professional work and embedded in the daily work of teachers and administrators'. He suggests a series of design principles to help this happen. In essence, these principles comprise a set of beliefs which Bredeson recommends leaders draw on to build a learning culture and community. The design principles are:

- professional development is about learning
- professional development is work
- professional expertise is a journey, not a credential
- opportunities for professional learning and improved practice are unbounded
- student learning, professional development, and organisational mission are intimately related
- professional development is about people, not programmes (Bredeson, 2003: 8–12).

There is a wide range of useful approaches for designing learning cultures not discussed here. The central message cutting across these approaches is the desirability of an intentional, coherent approach to crafting culture if the key ideas, processes and practices are to be reinforced and reproduced irrespective of which part of the design is engaged, or who engages it.

A common schema

A schema is an abstract framework that defines how people interact with the world (Bain, 2007). A *common schema* is a framework shared by a group, in this case a school, which helps them to work out what's important. In cultural terms it is assumptions that guide school learning and life, and therefore channel actions, interactions, relationships and roles in the school.

A schema can take the form(s) of a common language, shared jargon, consistent discipline and counselling approaches or shared beliefs about teaching. In very simple terms, a schema allows everyone involved with a school to 'speak the same language' or to work 'on the same page' so that they can effect change focused on improving learning. Although this sounds straightforward enough, it is unwise for leaders to assume that a common schema exists in the school.

The leader's job is not to simply impose a schema: that will not work. Rather, it is to use his or her influence and relationship skills to help colleagues form common understandings of where to focus, what success means, the shape of professional development and where research-based knowledge, curriculum, pedagogy and technology fit in in the school. The leader works to help others apply the schema at various levels of practice and explicitness. After the schema has been negotiated and has started to bind action towards improved learning, leaders work to embed the shared beliefs through a common language, identifiable symbols and modelling.

The leader knows that learning a schema is a dynamic process; it needs to be simultaneously elastic and resilient. Schemas adjust and shift in reaction to discussion, feedback and experimentation. Bain (2007) explains that any schema is in constant receipt of information about itself that determines not only its success, but also whether it endures, is modified or ultimately discarded. In learning cultures, this means establishing a shared basis and context for learning rather than just aimless talk.

Simple rules

As noted, learning cultures are incredibly complex. They have to be, since they involve collections of individuals and various sized groups working in uncertain environments and different contexts. This does not mean, however, that the beliefs guiding life and learning need to be complex. In fact, the opposite is true. Bain (2007) labels the beliefs driving learning and action in schools as 'simple rules'. Drawing again on complex adaptive systems theory, the notion is that simple but explicit rules produce complex behaviour, and that overloading a system with formal rules reduces its adaptability and relevance.

Simple rules are about doing less, well, to accomplish or to learn more (Bain, 2007). As such, simple rules oblige leaders to guide their communities to assign a value to what they believe about learning and success, and in doing so, prioritise the limited energy needed for achievement. Effort focused through a manageable set of beliefs and actions energises the schema needed to drive learning, build capacity and meet students' needs. Examples of simple rules developed collaboratively in schools might be 'learning is co-operative', 'research is important' or 'learning is an individual and group responsibility'.

Similarity at scale

'Similarity at scale' is when the schema is embedded at all levels of the organisation, thereby reproducing a system similar to itself (Bain, 2007). This is particularly important as leaders work to sustain the necessary level of learning and related action across the different subcultures within the school. To ensure cultural coherence they connect the different groups (such as subject departments or level constellations) through embedding self-repeating patterns at different levels, or scales. This cultural coherence depends on how successful leaders are at nurturing a 'common language', and how far understandings are similarly exhibited even within the roles of different agents and groups.

'Scaling up' good practice is a key task for leaders in learning cultures. This task is about spreading and sustaining successful practice throughout the school, not just in isolated pockets. Leaders know that too many good practices remain useful only in secluded corners of the building because they are neither critiqued nor shared.

It should be noted that similarity of scale is not about everything being the same. Far from any notions of conformity, similarity of scale values context as vital. Similarity of scale spreads a common basis for learning and improvement (a common schema) across levels and networks within and beyond the school. In short, the similarity of scale principle offers a way for leaders to 'scale up' and extend their scope of influence to the broader level.

Emergent feedback

The importance of feedback in effective learning cultures is widely acknowledged. Feedback is how complex systems talk to themselves. Bain (2007: 29) describes it 'as a network of constant exchange among individuals and groups'. This can take innumerable forms in schools, from team teaching and peer review to 'learning-focused' staff meetings, to student 'comment forums' and examination analysis debates.

Common schema is revised continually as a function of feedback and exchange. The feedback referred to here is not the procedural time-dependent form often required as part of performance management systems. Rather, it is a form of constant dialogue embedded in all parts of the school and focused purposefully on learning and improved practice.

The leader's job is to fashion and nurture structures; for example, time allocation or team teaching, through which feedback about improvement becomes part of 'how things are done here', that is, its common schema. As feedback becomes a key component of school life, individuals and groups are encouraged to constantly exchange information about student learning and other issues, thereby making learning an integral part of how the community works.

Dispersed control

An effective learning culture is dependent on co-operation, trust, dialogue and collaboration, without which learning does not happen. The ultimate aim of leaders building learning cultures is to create self-organising systems. Collaborative learning is more sustainable through dispersed control in smaller but connected groups working at different levels. These groups permit a ready flow of feedback. Bain explains that the rationale here for leaders is that relationships in smaller 'levelled' (normally hierarchical) systems such as teams are stronger because of the shorter distance between members; learning travels better over shorter distances.

Levels are more learning-effective both within and between subgroups when leaders create common edges or interfaces with other individuals or groups. In effect, this means that good practice developed by one team can be more readily shared with others. The dispersed structure shortens the professional and communicative distance between learners.

Examples of different approaches to dispersed control may be drawn from the recent 'distributed leadership' literature (Southworth, 2004). In simple terms, it is about helping colleagues work together in small teams, thereby allowing closer communication on learning-related issues. These teams can then be 'hooked' together by different members depending on their common purpose, thereby maintaining the shortened levels in larger learning networks.

Conclusion

A number of interrelated messages flow from the discussion of leading learning cultures:

- Culture comprises the values, beliefs and expectations shared by the school community. Shared values and beliefs are reflected in the patterns of norms, relationships, actions and behaviours visible in the school. In strong cultures, values, formal structures and actions are aligned; they work in concert.
- Culture influences (and is influenced by) what happens in schools, including, for example, how the community, staff and students view learning, how they treat each other and the chances they take in classrooms.
- Leaders play a key role in shaping a learning culture. The values they project, model and nurture can determine the place and importance of ongoing, personal and collective learning.
- Leaders work to establish and embed an interactive set of conditions that support learning in all corners of the school. These include witnessing learning, staying fresh, becoming resilient, framing scaffolding, catching learning, finding voice, trusting intuition and remaining curious.
- Leaders simultaneously align cultural and structural connectors to make learning happen.
- Leaders work deliberately and explicitly to build and sustain learning cultures. Useful interactive strategies for this work include modelling, monitoring and dialogue; having an intentional design; embedding a common schema built around simple rules; dispersing control; emergent feedback and similarity at scale.

This chapter has aimed to introduce the concept of culture specifically as it relates to leaders infusing a dedication to learning across a school. Many important issues have remained untouched; for example, how the type of leadership shifts as learning cultures take hold (Elmore, 2008), the different but complementary roles of middle and teacher leaders and the importance of system leadership (Hopkins, 2007), and the secrets of relationship building and trust (Duignan, 2006). What has been discussed, however, holds considerable importance for all school leaders.

There is no recipe or guidebook for building learning cultures; it is not that simple. Rather, leaders find their own ways, their own values, vocabulary and strategies for building the relationships and conditions that promote learning across all levels of the school. Existing theories can both inform and draw wisdom from this process.

Further reading

Bain, A. (2007) *The Self-organizing School: Next Generation Comprehensive School Reforms*. Lanham, MD: Rowman and Littlefield Education.
Crowther, F., Ferguson, M. and Hann, L. (2008) *Developing Teacher Leaders: How Teacher Leadership Enhances School Success*. Thousand Oaks, CA : Corwin Press.
Lieberman, A. and Miller, L. (eds) (2008) *Teachers in Professional Communities: Improving Teaching and Learning*. New York: Teachers College Press, Teachers College, Columbia University.

Note

1. I wish to acknowledge the support of the Research Grants Council of Hong Kong for its support through an Earmarked Grant (CUHK 4514/07).

References

Bain, A. (2007) *The Self-organizing School: Next Generation Comprehensive School Reforms*. Lanham, MD: Rowman and Littlefield Education.
Bredeson, P.V. (2003) *Designs for Learning: A New Architecture for Professional Development in Schools*. Thousand Oaks, CA: Corwin Press.
Chapman, J. (2002) *System Failure: Why Governments Must Learn to Think Differently*. London: Demos.
Chatman, J.A. and Cha, S.E. (2003) 'Leading by leveraging culture', *California Management Review,* 45(4): 20–33.
Crowther, F., Ferguson, M. and Hann, L. (2008) *Developing Teacher Leaders: How Teacher Leadership Enhances School Success*. Thousand Oaks, CA: Corwin Press.
Davenport, T.H. and Prusak, L. (1997) *Information Ecology: Mastering the Information Knowledge Environment*. New York: Open University Press.
Day, C. and Leithwood, K. (eds) (2007) *Successful Principal Leadership in Times of Change: An International Perspective*. Dordrecht: Springer.
De Long, D.W. and Fahey, L. (2000) 'Diagnosing cultural barriers to knowledge management', *Academy of Management Executive,* 14(4): 113–27.
Deal, T.E. and Peterson, K.D. (1999) *Shaping School Culture: The Heart of Leadership*. San Francisco, CA: Jossey-Bass.
Dimmock, C. (2000) *Designing the Learning-centred School: A Cross-cultural Perspective*. London: Falmer Press.

Dufour, R., DuFour, R., Eaker, R. and Many, T. (2006) *Learning by Doing: A Handbook for Professional Learning Communities at Work*. Bloomington, IN: Solution Tree.

Duignan, P. (2006) *Educational Leadership: Key Challenges and Educational Issues*. Melbourne: Cambridge University Press.

Elmore, R. (2004) *School Reform from the Inside Out: Policy, Practice and Performance*. Cambridge, MA: Harvard University Press.

Elmore, R.F. (2008) 'Leadership as the practice of improvement', in B. Pont, D. Nusche and D. Hopkins (eds), *Improving School Leadership – Volume 2: Case Studies on System Leadership*. Paris: OECD.

Eraut, M. (1999) 'Non-formal learning in the workplace – the hidden dimension of lifelong learning: a framework for analysis and the problems it poses for the researcher', paper presented to the First International Conference on Researching Work and Learning, Leeds.

Fullan, M. (2006) 'Leading professional learning', *The School Administrator*, 63(10): www.aasa.org/publications/saarticledetail.cfm? Item Number=7565&snItem Number =950&tnItemNumber=on (retrieved 9 February 2009)

Glatter, R. and Kydd, L. (2003) 'Best practice in educational leadership and management: can we identify it and learn from it?' *Educational Management & Administration*, 31(3): 231–43.

Hallinger, P. and Heck, P. (1999) 'Can leadership enhance school effectiveness?', in T. Bush, R. Glatter, R. Bolam, P. Ribbins and L. Bell (eds), *Educational Management: Redefining Theory, Policy and Practice*. London: Paul Chapman Publishing. pp. 178–90.

Hofstede, G. (1991) *Culture and Organizations: Software of the Mind*. London: Profile Books.

Hopkins, D. (2007) *Every School a Great School: Realizing the Potential of System Leadership*. Maidenhead: Open University Press.

Klein, G. (2003) *Intuition at Work*. New York: Currency Doubleday.

Lieberman, A. and Miller, L. (eds) (2008) *Teachers in Professional Communities: Improving Teaching and Learning*. New York: Teachers College Press, Teachers College, Columbia University.

Leithwood, K. (2007) 'Organizational conditions to support teaching and learning', in W. Hawley (ed.), *The Keys to Effective Schools: Education Reform as Continuous Improvement*. Thousand Oaks, CA: Corwin.

Lopez, D.F. (2000). 'Social cognitive influences on self-regulated learning: the impact of action-control beliefs and academic goals on achievement-related outcomes', *Learning and Individual Differences*, 11: 301–19.

Mitchell, J.T. and Willower, D.J. (1992) 'Organizational culture in a good high school', *Journal of Educational Administration*, 30 (6): 6–16.

Schein, E.H. (1985) *Organizational Culture and Leadership: A Dynamic View*. San Francisco, CA: Jossey-Bass.

Schein, E.H. (1993) 'SMR forum: how can organizations learn faster? How can organizations learn faster? The problem of entering the green room', *Sloan Management Review*, 34(2): 85–92.

Schein, E.H. (1995) 'The role of the founder in creating organizational cultures', *Family Business Review*, 8(3): 221–38.

Schein, E.H. (1996) 'Culture: the missing concept in organization studies', *Administrative Science Quarterly*, 41(2): 229–40.

Southworth, G. (2004) *Primary School Leadership in Context: Leading Small, Medium and Large Sized Schools*. London: RoutledgeFalmer.

Southworth, G. (2005) 'Learning-centred leadership', in B. Davies (ed.), *The Essentials of School Leadership*. London: Paul Chapman Publishing and Corwin Press. pp. 75–92.

Sullivan, S. and Glanz, J. (2006) *Building Effective Learning Communities: Strategies for Leadership, Learning and Collaboration*. Thousand Oaks, CA: Corwin Press.

Velsor, E.V., Moxley, R.S. and Bunker, K.A. (2004) 'The centre for creative leadership development process', in C.D. McCauley and E.V. Velsor (eds), *Handbook of Leadership Development*. San Francisco, CA: Jossey-Bass.

Walker, A. (2007) 'Leading authentically at the cross-roads of culture and context', *Journal of Educational Change*, 8(3): 257–73.

Walker, A. and Quong, T. (2005) 'Gateways to international leadership learning: beyond best practice', *Educational Research and Perspectives*, 32(2): 97–121.

Walker, A. and Quong, T. (2008) *Leading Upstream: A Professional Learning Programme for Front Line Leaders in International Schools – An Overview*. Hong Kong: Hong Kong Centre for the Development of Educational Leadership.

Walker, A. and Quong, T. (2008) *Leading Upstream: A Learning Programme for Front-line Leaders in International Schools – Phase 1 Booklet*. Hong Kong: Hong Kong Centre for the Development of Educational Leadership.

Waller, W. (1932) *The Sociology of Teaching*. New York: John Wiley & Sons.

Wenger, E. (1999) 'Communities of practice: the key to a knowledge strategy', *Knowledge Directions*, 1(2): 48–63. Reprinted in Lesser, E., Fontaine, M. and Slusher, J. (2000) *Knowledge and Communities*. Boston, MA: Butterworth-Heinemann.

CHAPTER 11

Managing Resources to Support Learning

Rosalind Levačić

This chapter concerns the management of resources within educational institutions in order to obtain the best feasible student learning outcomes. Given this stance, the chapter adopts the rational perspective that the purpose of educational resource management is to maximise student learning within given resource constraints. It is, of course, acknowledged that other management and organisational models, such as natural systems, collegial, political and ambiguity (see Bush, 2000) often explain actual management practice better than the rational model. However, as the purpose of this chapter is to inform educational leaders who wish to act rationally in using resources efficiently and equitably, this normative perspective is adopted. The chapter aims to introduce educational leaders/managers to what is known from research evidence about the relationship between resources and student learning. The evidence of only a weak relationship between resources and learning in practice and of variability in the efficiency of educational institutions, points to the importance of many other factors than the quantity or mix of resources in determining student attainment.

The chapter starts by defining key terms. In section 2 the context–input–process–output model of how resources are linked to student learning is outlined. Many factors mediate the relationship between resources and student learning. One is the degree of decentralisation of educational decision-making which, having started in developed countries (Caldwell, 2005), has continued to spread globally since the late 1990s, being advocated by the World Bank for transition and developing countries (World Bank, 2003). Decentralisation is a pre-requisite for educational leaders at institutional level being empowered to manage resources. The third section sets out the main criteria for judging the allocation of resources for public services – efficiency, equity and adequacy. Evidence on the relationship between the amount and mix of resources and student learning is summarised in section 4. Finally, given what we know about the resource-learning relationship, section 5 examines how resource allocation decisions can be made in order best to support learning.

1   Resources in education: defining terms

Resources are both 'real' and 'monetary'. Real resources are the actual inputs into the education process and are subdivided into human resources and material resources. The main categories of human resources are teachers, and non-teaching staff, subdivided into management and administration, student support staff and technical staff (such as those maintaining building services). Other personnel-related resources are expenditures on services, such as payroll and recruitment, and professional development of staff. Material resources are subdivided into those used directly in learning – materials, stationery, books, equipment, software, communication charges and extension activities such as school trips and those used indirectly to support of learning. This second group of material resources is required to sustain the physical environment in which teaching and learning occurs, mainly the cost of buildings and servicing them. A further distinction is between recurrent resources and capital. In principle, recurrent resources are those which need replacing at least annually, such as the services of staff, cleaning, stationery and capital resources are those that last longer than a year. In practice such a clear distinction is not drawn, as expenditures on books and equipment, which last longer than a year, are usually classified as recurrent. So is expenditure on professional development, even though it is really an investment in the stock of knowledge and skills possessed by staff.

Monetary resources (in the form of claims to units of account in the government treasury, bank deposits, or cash) are the means by which purchasing power is transferred from those who ultimately fund the education system (taxpayers, lenders, donors and fee-paying customers) to educational managers who, through budget allocation decisions, transfer monetary resources into real resources by employing staff and purchasing goods and other services needed to provide teaching and learning. Only a very small proportion of real resources is directly transferred to schools, such as gifts of computers, building materials or volunteers' time. Budgeting is the process of determining what real resources are acquired with the available monetary resources.

School-based management (SBM) of resources is a feature of decentralised education systems. The degree of decentralisation of resource management is directly reflected in the proportion of real resources that is initially received at the school/college level in the form of monetary resources, the spending of which is determined at this local level. In highly decentralised systems such as England and Victoria, Australia, schools receive virtually all their resources via delegated budgets, which include an allocation for capital expenditure. Many countries practise varying degrees of budget decentralisation for schools and colleges: in some, local governments can decide whether or not to introduce SBM of resources. This tends to appeal to the larger urban authorities (municipalities) in order to secure greater efficiency by giving the responsibility for managing resources to school leaders. Examples are Helsinki (Finland), Poznan and Kwydzin (Poland) and Tallinn (Estonia). In contrast, in a highly centralised system, as in Azerbaijan, schools receive all their resources in real terms: teachers are allocated by the local administrative unit (rayon), utilities are paid for directly by the rayon and other material resources are allocated by the rayon, if it has sufficient funds, using its own criteria. Schools in very centralised systems that cannot mobilise adequate resources for education are usually much more deprived of material than of human resources. In the developed economies, expenditure on non-human resources in pre-university education is on average 19 per cent of current expenditure (OECD, 2008a) whereas in middle- and low-income countries it makes up a considerably lower percentage – from 10 to even as low as 2 per cent (UNESCO, 2005).

It is not easy to obtain rigorous research evidence on whether school-based management results in better educational outcomes for students than centralised school systems. Such evidence as there is from a limited number of studies suggests a favourable impact on student learning, in particular if self-managing schools experience external evaluation of school performance. For example, a study (OECD, 2007) using data from the Programme for International Student Assessment (PISA) to control for student, school and system level factors found that education systems where schools have a higher degree of autonomy in budgeting students scored more highly in science.[1] Wößmann (2003b) using data from the Trends in

International Mathematics and Science Study (TIMSS) for 17 West European countries reported that school autonomy in personnel, budgetary and process decisions had positive impacts on student attainment provided that there was a centralised examination system. This result was replicated in a further study Wößmann (2003a) using TIMSS repeat data and by Fuchs and Wößmann (2004) using reading scores of primary children in 35 countries from the Progress in International Reading Literacy Study (PIRLS).

Thus decentralisation is a key contextual factor that influences the relationship between resources and student learning.

2   The context–input–process–outcome model

The relationship between resources and learning is complex because resources are only one of many factors that determine student learning. The complexity of the factors influencing student learning, including resources, is represented in the context–input–process–outcome (CIPO) model developed by school effectiveness researchers (for example Reynolds and Teddlie, 1999; Scheerens, 1997, 1999).

Defining learning outcomes

From a rational perspective the purpose of formal educational settings is to produce learning outcomes for students. Several kinds of learning outcomes are distinguished – cognitive and affective outcomes attained while students are at school and post-school outcomes. The latter are categorised into private benefits accruing to individuals and external benefits for society as a whole. Private monetary benefits are higher lifetime income, while non-monetary benefits include better physical and mental health and greater cultural enjoyment. For society the external benefits of better educated adults include higher general standards of living, improved public health, reduced crime, better parenting and greater participation in civil society.[2] A major complexity for educational leaders in utilising resources to support student learning is the many-faceted nature of learning outcomes. Some, in particular cognitive attainment, are relatively easy to measure and therefore more tangible. Affective outcomes – that is attitudes, behaviours and so-called 'soft-skills' – are more difficult, if not impossible, to measure. Accountability systems usually focus on cognitive attainment or indirect measures of school success, such as student completions and destinations as they are not only important but also easy to measure. Consequently, affective outcomes may get squeezed out unless valued by educational leaders. A further difficulty is that different stakeholders are likely to have different preferences over the range of potential student outcomes. If outcomes are complements then achieving one will also lead to the achievement of the others. But when outcomes are substitutes then choices must be made between which outcomes to promote and which to neglect. Choices between outcomes are made much less at school/college level when the curriculum is centrally set. Decisions about any locally determined parts of the curriculum, including the emphasis on affective outcomes and how to balance the learning needs of students who differ by age, abilities and interests, are made at local level. Articulating clearly the institutional level choice of intended learning outcomes and securing substantial support within the school/college community are prerequisites for using resources to their best effect.

The three other classifications of factors – context, inputs and processes – interact and determine student outcomes. The main elements within each of the factors and their interrelationship in the CIPO model are depicted in Figure 11.1. Only some of these are under the direct control of schools, of which resources are only one element. Contextual variables (see Teddlie and Reynolds, 1999) relate to the socio-economic characteristics of the community from which the school draws its students, the composition of the student body (age range, gender balance, ethnicity, extent of special educational needs, proportion of students from deprived backgrounds), the governance structures of the school, including its local authority, and the education policies and legislation with which it must comply.

Inputs into learning are divided into two categories – student inputs and resource inputs. The former consist of the personal characteristics of individual students, such as abilities and dispositions towards learning, both of which are highly influenced by family background, in particular parents' level of education, income and socio-economic group. Student and family background factors are by far the most important determinants of pupils' cognitive attainment, compared to which the school attended has on average a small or modest impact, a finding first publicised in the Coleman Report on Inequality (Coleman et al., 1966) and subsequently corroborated in many later studies (for example Blanden and Gregg, 2004; DfES, 2006; Haveman and Wolfe, 1995; OECD, 2005). Differences in the effectiveness of schools contribute at a maximum to 20 per cent of the variance in students' attainment, when

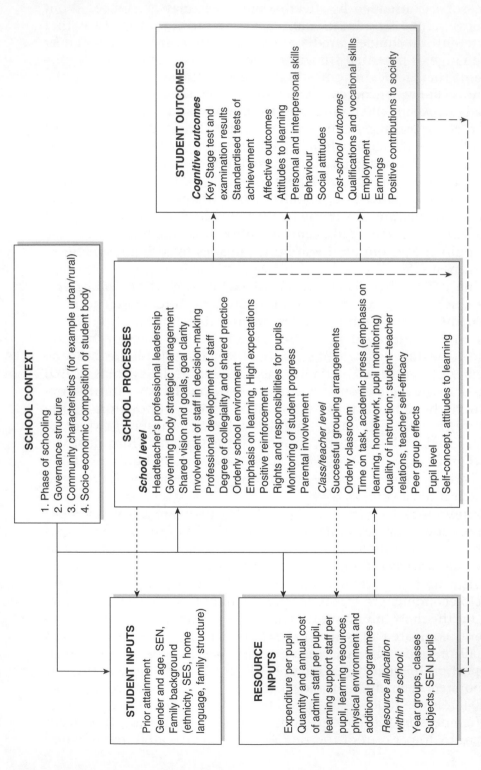

SCHOOL CONTEXT

1. Phase of schooling
2. Governance structure
3. Community characteristics (for example urban/rural)
4. Socio-economic composition of student body

SCHOOL PROCESSES

School level

Headteacher's professional leadership
Governing Body strategic management
Shared vision and goals, goal clarity
Involvement of staff in decision-making
Professional development of staff
Degree of collegiality and shared practice
Orderly school environment
Emphasis on learning, High expectations
Positive reinforcement
Rights and responsibilities for pupils
Monitoring of student progress
Parental involvement

Class/teacher level

Successful grouping arrangements
Orderly classroom
Time on task, academic press (emphasis on learning, homework, pupil monitoring)
Quality of instruction; student–teacher relations, teacher self-efficacy
Peer group effects

Pupil level

Self-concept, attitudes to learning

STUDENT OUTCOMES

Cognitive outcomes

Key Stage test and examination results
Standardised tests of achievement

Affective outcomes
Attitudes to learning
Personal and interpersonal skills
Behaviour
Social attitudes

Post-school outcomes

Qualifications and vocational skills
Employment
Earnings
Positive contributions to society

STUDENT INPUTS

Prior attainment
Gender and age, SEN,
Family background (ethnicity, SES, home language, family structure)

RESOURCE INPUTS

Expenditure per pupil
Quantity and annual cost of admin staff per pupil, learning support staff per pupil, learning resources, physical environment and additional programmes

Resource allocation within the school:

Year groups, classes
Subjects, SEN pupils

Figure 11.1   Context – input – process – outcome model of school effectiveness

social background factors and/or prior attainment are controlled for. The more usual amount of variance in student attainment contributed by school factors is 8–16 per cent (Levačić and Jenkins, 2006 (GCSE: 8 per cent); OECD, 2004 (Table 4.1b: maths 5 per cent); Sammons et al., 2008 (Table A7.1a KS2: maths 17 per cent, English 16 per cent)).

Resource inputs are listed again in Figure 11.1. This also includes how the different types of resources are allocated within schools between year groups, classes, subjects, and students with special needs. The key role for educational leaders is deciding how the resource inputs are utilised in creating the various processes of teaching and learning, some of which occur at school level and others at classroom and pupil level. Figure 11.1 lists under processes those that have emerged from school effectiveness research as the features of effective schools[3] (see Reynolds and Teddlie, 1999). Resource utilisation does not appear explicitly in any of the processes. Those that most obviously link to resources are professional development and quality of instruction, the latter dependent on the teacher quality and adequate learning resources.

Figure 11.1 shows how the main components of the CIPO model are linked. The unbroken double-line arrows pointing from left to right represent causal effects flowing from student and resource inputs to the processes of teaching and learning at all three levels of school, class/teacher and student: these processes determine student outcomes. There are also reverse lines of causality from student outcomes to inputs. One represents the effect of the school's reputation for student achievement on the decisions of parents to select the school for their child. Better educated, higher income and more socially skilled parents are likely to select schools with better student 'raw' outcomes. This affects not only the characteristics of the individual students but also the school context – shown in Figure 11.1 as affecting both student and resource inputs. In this way schools can, over time, influence their contexts. An alternative scenario – much more frequently practised in developed countries than others – is for state schools with lower student outcomes – due to the intake characteristics of their students – to receive additional state funding to supply additional resources to compensate for the additional costs of raising the attainment of students from disadvantaged backgrounds. The two-way nature of the causal links between resources and learning outcomes is fundamental to the problems faced by researchers in identifying and measuring the impact of resources on student learning – which I will return to.

3   Criteria for judging resource allocation decisions

At every level of decision-making about resources three main criteria apply. Are the resources:

- utilised efficiently
- distributed equitably
- adequate?

Efficiency

By efficiency is meant that a given expenditure – or cost – achieves the maximum feasible amount of output. Applying this definition to education is problematic for a number of reasons. First, education produces a variety of outcomes, which are not easy to measure and for which people's preferences differ. Even in the case of cognitive attainment, the output of a school must be measured in terms of the value added by the school to the student inputs it started with. Statistically, this means that in order to measure the amount of student learning attributable to the school, all the factors that are not directly under the influence of the school (student inputs and school context) must be controlled for. Explanations of techniques for arriving at value added measures of schools' student attainment can be found in OECD (2008b) and Ray (2006).

A much used approach to the problem of valuing outputs in education is to define a more limited version of efficiency – internal efficiency – which applies to the efficiency of a specific set of educational institutions producing a limited range of outputs, which are assumed to be socially valued (given the impossibility of arriving at a social consensus on the values on different learning outcomes). Internal efficiency occurs when the institution produces the highest feasible student attainment for a given cost of resources. (An equivalent definition is producing a given output at least cost.) The most used technique for assessing the efficiency of educational institutions (and other non-profit organisations) is data envelopment analysis (DEA). This compares a set of schools, say, which employ different combinations of staff and non-staff resources using different student inputs and produce several types of learning outcome. A recent study in England by Smith and Street (2006) used this technique to identify efficient secondary schools. As in all DEA studies, the efficiency of each school (firm) is measured relative to the most efficient schools that use the same combination of inputs. The inputs included were teachers, support staff and administrative and clerical staff – all per 1000 pupils – and expenditure on learning resources and on information and communication technology (ICT) per 1000 pupils. School context variables were percentages of pupils with special educational needs (SEN), English as an additional language and eligibility for free school meals and presence or not of a sixth form. One outcome measure was included – capped General Certificate of Secondary Education (GCSE) results. English secondary schools were found to be pretty efficient: average efficiency was 94 per cent, the lowest being 75 per cent (relative to the most efficient).

Equity

Equity refers to the fairness of resource allocation and applies both to the rules of distribution (procedural equity) and to the actual distribution of resources among groups and individuals – distributive equity. Two kinds of distributive equity are distinguished (Monk, 1990). Horizontal equity refers to treating equals equally. This implies that pupils with equal learning entitlements, such as students within a particular phase of education or studying similar courses, should be funded at the same level regardless of which school they attend or part of the country they live in. Vertical equity, on the other hand, refers to treating unequals unequally, in particular allocating additional resources to students who have greater learning needs. With the recent emphasis on personalised learning, educational leaders need to pay increasing attention to determining an equitable allocation of resources between different groups of students and different individuals.

Adequacy

The adequacy of resources for education is a difficult and, in the USA, a much-debated concept. Roughly, adequacy means that there are just sufficient resources for schools to achieve the standards of education expected of them by legislators. The problem is to define and measure what are 'sufficient resources' for specified educational outcomes. In the USA, where education policy is made through litigation, the courts have defined adequacy in terms of the minimum funding needed to sustain educational programmes that provide a specified standard of education. The problem is to make this definition operational. Four approaches have been used: professional judgement, best practice, cost functions and evidence-based (Picus and Blair, 2004).

Professional judgement involves a group of educational experts, perhaps also working with finance specialists, deciding what resources are needed by schools to ensure that the majority of children attain defined educational standards and then costing the resources. The professional judgement approach is also known as activity-led funding (Abu-Duhou, 1999). It is being used by an increasing number of English local authorities to determine per student allocations in their school funding formulae, for example Cambridge (Cambridgeshire Council, 2007).

The *best practice* method defines adequacy as the cost of the resources used by those schools or school districts with the best educational outcomes for students. To be valid the family background characteristics that determine children's academic attainment must be controlled for when selecting best practice settings and common measures of student outcomes used.

The *cost function approach* estimates the cost of achieving specified educational standards from data collected from schools on per student costs and other variables that determine student outcomes (Duncombe and Yinger, 1999; Ruggiero, 2007).

The *evidence-based* approach uses research evidence to identify and cost best practice in organising and resourcing student learning. Professional judgement is then applied to create a school design that reflects these best practices, for example 'Success for All' (Slavin et al., 1996).

Educational leaders should only expend effort on campaigning for additional resources for their own institutions if they are convinced that the latter are inadequate, otherwise it is more efficient to devote their time to ensuring resources are allocated and used efficiently and equitably.

4   Evidence on the relationship between resources and student learning

In high income countries resource levels are usually adequate: the main problems are to ensure efficiency and equity. For example, when developed OECD countries with similar average student scores in the PISA tests are compared, there is considerable variation in expenditure per student as a percentage of per capita national income. The correlation between higher spending per student and higher PISA scores is quite weak (OECD, 2008a: 306–7). Mingat (2007) reports similar variations in efficiency for sub-Saharan African countries, using expected years of completed schooling as the outcome measure.

Research seeking evidence on causal relationships between resources, such as expenditure per student or pupil–teacher ratios, and student attainment, faces a major methodological difficulty that the causal relationship runs both ways – as explained above in relation to the CIPO model (Levačić and Vignoles, 2002). The most common method of statistically estimating multivariate relationships between variables, Ordinary Least Squares, is liable to be biased when applied to estimating the relationship between student outcomes and resources using data from natural settings, which is the most frequently available type of data. For example, if parents with higher attaining children select better resourced schools then part of the observed positive correlation between attainment and resources per student is in fact due to student characteristics. Alternatively, if lower-attaining students have more spent on them or they are placed in smaller classes, then a negative correlation is observed between resourcing per student and attainment.[4] Researchers have a number of statistical techniques for attempting to produce unbiased estimates, though these are not fully reliable. The alternative approach is to generate data by conducting experiments in which students are randomly assigned to more or less resources. Because of the practical problems of conducting rigorous experiments in educational settings, few have been undertaken[5] nor is there a consensus that experimental evidence is better than that from natural settings.

Since the mid-1980s there has been considerable disagreement on whether evidence from studies on the resourcing-attainment relationship[6] – the majority from the USA – points to a systematic positive relationship. Hanushek (1986, 1997) has maintained that there is no such systematic relationship, a conclusion challenged by others (Hedges et al., 1994; Krueger, 2003). Those who argue for the absence of a systematic positive resource-learning relationship do not consider that resources do not matter for learning, but that a general increase in expenditure on education will have no effect on attainment unless educational institutions have incentives to be efficient, such as performance-related pay, accountability frameworks and school based management.

Reviews of more recent UK and European studies (Levačić, 2007; Levačić and Vignoles, 2002) concluded that these generally find some small to modest positive effects of resources on student attainment. Three studies of the relationship between expenditure per student commissioned by the Department for Children, Schools and Families (DCSF) (and its predecessor) found positive but modest resource effects for KS2, KS3 and GCSE results (Holmlund et al., 2008; Jenkins et al., 2005; Levačić et al., 2004).[7] From 1998 till the time of writing English schools experienced a doubling of expenditure per student (DCSF, 2008). Although test and examination results also improved over this period, given that other policy changes took place, one cannot attribute these improvements necessarily to increased expenditure. Descriptively, it has been shown that output per unit of resource has fallen since 1999 as inputs rose more rapidly than quality-adjusted output (UK Centre for the Measurement of Government Activity, 2006: 31).

Resource mix

For educational leaders at institutional level the most important issue in resource management is which mix of resources makes for the most efficient deployment of the school budget. Resource mix refers to the proportions of expenditure devoted to the different kinds of inputs that support learning- teachers, support staff, books, equipment, ICT and school buildings being the main types. Within any one category, such as teachers, questions arise such as whether it more efficient to have small classes, with teachers having less non-class contact or students less instruction time and teachers being paid less or to have larger classes but better paid teachers? Resource mixes are quite varied both internationally and within a single system. For example Korea and Luxembourg both spend a higher proportion of per student costs on teacher salaries than the OECD average, but Korea (which scores highly in PISA) has large classes and higher than average teacher salaries and Luxembourg the reverse (OECD, 2008a). Finland, one of the highest PISA performers, has just above average teacher salaries and above average class sizes. School benchmarking data for England (DCSF, 2009) shows quite wide variation in costs per student for different types of resource for schools of similar phase, size and student community.

Given the above variability in practice according to national and institutional context, it is not surprising that the research evidence on the relationship between quantities of specific resource types and attainment has produced few reliable generalisations. A thorough survey of the evidence on class size and attainment (Averett and McLennan, 2004: 363) concludes 'the weight of evidence indicates to us that smaller classes do result in higher achievement for some students and some classes'. They observe, as have many others, that the cost of reducing class size is high and is often not cost-effective on a large scale, as in California, where the resulting increased recruitment of teachers lowered teacher quality. For developing countries the evidence that more of any specific real input increases student attainment is mixed: it does in some cases but not others. 'The evidence suggests that the most effective forms of spending are likely to be those that respond to the inefficiencies of the school system' (Glewwe and Kremer, 2006: 1007). A programme providing extra textbooks in Kenya was only effective for the more able students since the rest could not understand them, whereas radio mathematics lessons in Nicaragua were effective because they compensated for teachers' lack of maths knowledge.

Practitioners are unlikely to be surprised that research confirms teacher quality is the school resource input with the most impact on attainment (Hanushek, 2005: 5). However, it has not proved possible to identify easily measurable characteristics of effective teachers, such as experience or paper qualifications, or to devise payment schemes which specifically reward effective teachers. (For a review see Levačić, 2009.)

Given the absence of a clear recipe for an efficient resource mix, utilising available resources to maximise their impact on learning in specific contexts relies on the quality of professional judgement exercised by educational leaders. Efficient resource management depends on making the right decisions about staff selection and the processes of teaching and learning and is inextricably interwoven with high-quality leadership and management of other functions.

5   Deciding how to allocate resources to support learning

School development planning (SDP) is advocated as the main way in which schools can link their financial planning and budget management to their educational objectives and hence student attainment (Audit Commission and OFSTED, 2000). Its purpose is 'to improve the quality of teaching and learning in a school through successful management of innovation and change' (Hargreaves and Hopkins, 1991: 91). It is not a comprehensive plan for the entire management of the school, but an orchestrated approach to identifying and implementing change, an important aspect of which is mobilising resources to support development. While there is no single view on the time scale a SDP should cover or on how comprehensive or detailed it should be, it is usual to consider the SDP as a medium-term plan (that is, for two to four years) that links the strategic direction of the school to the annual activities which take the school in the desired direction. It is reviewed and updated annually but only undergoes renewal every three years or so. The process of generating the SDP is important. It needs the active involvement of the school community – in particular teachers and governors. A plan that is only a paper document produced by the school principal or by the senior management team will not create a shared direction or sense of purpose for the school community.

The main elements of a SDP are:

- a statement of the aims of the school
- a review of the previous year's achievements of the plan's objectives
- proposed priorities for teaching and learning with a justification for their selection
- action plans for implementing the priorities, with timescale, named persons responsible and, most importantly, the costs of the actions and how they will be financed
- a set of measurable targets that will be used to evaluate achievements in next year's review.

The SDP is then implemented through a series of annual action plans, which are linked to the school budget.

Effective school development planning is one of the main features of efficient schools identified in the study by Dadd (2006). This is a valuable study of the features of efficient schools as the 30 English secondary schools studied were identified as efficient using DEA by Smith and Street (2006). Each of the 30 schools identified was the most efficient of at least 100 schools with similar inputs and student intakes. The study sought to find both the common characteristics of these efficient schools and aspects in which they differed. The common features included a dominant ethos focused on learning and strong leadership. The schools made extensive use of student performance data to set attainment targets and measure students' progress. Considerable emphasis was placed on recruiting high-quality staff, paying the salaries necessary to attract such staff. The schools were inclusive and spent additional funds on pastoral care and special units for 'at-risk' students. Teachers provided out-of-class teaching in the form of revision classes, small-group sessions and mentoring, usually without extra pay. Attention was paid to developing curricula to suit particular groups of students and, if necessary, to pay outside providers for specific vocational courses. The schools had very comprehensive SDPs covering many aspects of provision. There was also considerable investment in ICT.

However, these schools were not necessarily outstanding at the technical aspects of financial management, though all were at least satisfactory. Hence, it is the allocation of resources for educational purposes that is crucial, not financial management per se. A school can manage a budget to high standards of accounting, even if the budget is not well focused on improving learning. Nor were the governing bodies of the efficient schools necessarily high performing – emphasising the importance of the quality of leadership within the school. Furthermore, the efficient schools did not usually have a particularly good building or masses of new equipment. The schools also demonstrated considerable variability with respect to class sizes and setting.

Conclusion

The features of efficient schools found in Dadd's study are fully consistent with the messages emerging from the research literature. Due to the complexity and range of factors that interact to determine student attainment, no simple and direct relationships between quantities or mixes of resources and learning have been found. There is a considerable variability in the efficiency with which resources are utilised within schools and colleges both between and within national education systems. This implies that there is scope for improvements in the efficiency with which schools use resources, which can be achieved by school leaders who are both aware in general terms of research evidence about the effectiveness and efficiency of different ways of using resources and can also adapt this knowledge to their own contexts. Broadly the evidence points to lowering class size not being cost-effective, except for younger and more socially disadvantaged students. It has not yet been shown that raising the ratio of non-teaching staff to students produces positive effects on attainment. Increasingly, evidence is mounting that the most important resource is high-quality teachers. While school leaders can attempt to recruit the best teachers for their school, this will not improve teacher quality for the education system as a whole. To achieve this requires government policies to attract and retain effective teachers. School leaders can improve teacher effectiveness through appropriate professional development and by fostering school cultures that enhance teacher motivation.

In deciding what mix of resources is likely to support the highest and most equitable learning outcomes in specific settings, educational leaders need to develop and rely upon their own and their staff's professional judgements, which should not be based on uninformed beliefs but upon evidence. Educational leaders should as far as possible evaluate the consequences for student learning of the particular decisions their schools take about resource mixes and in this way develop an evidence base for their own practice which is supplemented by external evidence on the outcomes of particular uses of resources. Another key message from research evidence is that efficient resource management in education is inextricably linked with the quality of leadership and management of all the other aspects of teaching and learning. Effective human resource management and instructional leadership are inseparable from efficient resource management. This means the school budgeting needs to be fully integrated with teaching and learning. Key ways in which schools achieve this is by ensuring that their business/finance managers are part of the senior management team and linking school development planning, both formal and informal, with budgeting.

Further reading

Audit Commission (2009) *Valuable Lessons: Improving Economy and Efficiency in Schools*. London: Audit Commission.

Dadd, A. (2006) *Investigating the Effective Use of Resources in Secondary Schools: Research Report RR799*. London: DfES.

Levačić, R. (2007) 'The relationship between student attainment and school resources', in T. Townsend (ed.), *International Handbook of School Effectiveness and School Improvement*. Dordrecht: Springer Press. pp. 425–50.

Notes

1. One standard deviation increase in the index of school budgeting autonomy is related to an increase in the science score of 25.7 points (OECD, 2007: 267).
2. More highly educated individuals are not always beneficial to society: some can use their skills to perpetrate fraud and other 'white-collar' crimes. Nor do more better educated individuals necessarily contribute to higher economic growth if political and economic institutions fail to provide the appropriate incentives. Too much education of the wrong sort produces individuals who are 'over educated' that is, those who cannot obtain jobs that they perceive match the skills associated with their level of education.
3. An effective school is defined as one whose pupils make greater progress than would be expected given their prior attainment and other characteristics. See Mortimore, P. (1991).
4. This selection bias arises because most studies have inadequate data on all the pupil, family and school factors that determine attainment and even the data rich studies cannot measure all these factors, which remain therefore 'unobserved'.
5. The best known educational experiment is STAR, in which class sizes for early years pupils were reduced in Tennessee for a random sample of classes. Studies indicate some positive effect of smaller class size that persisted for socially disadvantaged students Krueger and Whitmore (2001).

6. This relationship is known as the education production function.
7. An increase of £100 p.a. per student would raise GCSE capped scores by 0.3 points (Jenkins et al., 2005). An increase of £1,000 per pupil (that is, of one third) would increase the number attaining KS2 level 4 or above by 2.2, 2.0 and 0.7 percentage points in English, Mathematics and Science respectively (Holmlund et al., 2008, p.3).

References

Abu-Duhou, I. (1999) 'Issues in funding basic allocations per pupil by grade level: activity led funding', in K. Ross and R. Levačić (eds), *Needs Based Resource Allocation in Education via Formula Funding of Schools*. Paris: International Institute of Educational Planning.

Audit Commission and OFSTED (2000) *Getting the Best from Your Budget: A Guide to the Effective Management of School Resources*. London: Audit Commission.

Averett, S. and McLennan, M. (2004) *Exploring the Effects of Class Size on Student Achievement: What Have We Learned over the Past Two Decades?* pp: 329–67. Cheltenham: Edward Elgar.

Blanden, J. and Gregg, P. (2004) 'Family income and educational attainment: a review of approaches and evidence for Britain', *Oxford Review of Economic Policy*, 20(2): 245–63.

Bush, T. (2000) 'Management styles: impact on finance and resources', in M. Coleman and L. Anderson (eds), *Managing Finance and Resources in Education*. London: Paul Chapman Publishing.

Caldwell, B. (2005) *School Based Management*. Paris: International Institute of Educational Planning.

Cambridgeshire Council (2007) '2007/8 Funding Formula', Available at: http://www.cambridgeshire.gov.uk/NR/rdonlyres/0322FF37-3C12-4586-8EFD-A513627B4085/0/200708FormulaTraining.pdf (last accessed 9 January 2009).

Coleman, J.S., Campbell, E.Q., Hobson, C.J., McPartland, J., Mood, A.M., Weinfeld, F.D. and York, R.L. (1966) *Equality of Educational Opportunity*. Washington, DC: Government Printing Office.

Dadd, A. (2006) *Investigating the Effective Use of Resources in Secondary Schools: Research Report RR799*. London: DfES.

DCSF (2008) *Department for Children, Schools and Families Departmental Report 2008*. London: DCSF.

DCSF (2009) *Financial Management Standards in Schools*. Available at: http://www.fmsis.info/ (last accessed 14 January 2009).

DfES (2006) 'Trends in attainment gaps: 2005', *Statistics of Education Bulletin*. London: Department for Education and Skills.

Duncombe, W. and Yinger, J. (1999) 'Performance standards and educational cost indices', in H.E. Ladd (ed.), *Equity and Adequacy in School Finance: Issues and Perspectives*. Washington, DC: National Academy Press. pp. 260–97.

Fuchs, T. and Wößmann, L. (2004) 'What accounts for international differences in student performance? A re-examination using PISA data', *CESifo Working Paper 1235*.

Glewwe, P. and Kremer, M. (2006) 'Schools, teachers and educational outcomes in developing countries', in E. Hanushek and F. Welch (eds), *Handbook on the Economics of Education*. Amsterdam: Elsevier.

Hanushek, E.A. (1986) 'The economics of schooling: production and efficiency in public schools', *Journal of Economic Literature*, 24(3): 1141–77.

Hanushek, E.A. (1997) 'Assessing the effects of school resources on student performance: an update', *Education Evaluation and Policy Analysis,* 19(2): 141–64.

Hanushek, E. (2005) *Economic Outcomes and School Quality.* Paris: International Institute of Educational Planning. www.unesco.org/iiep.

Hargreaves, D. and Hopkins, D. (1991) *The Empowered School.* London: Cassell.

Haveman, R. and Wolfe, B. (1995) 'The determinants of children's attainments: a review of methods and findings', *Journal of Economic Literature, 33:* 1829–78.

Hedges, L.V., Laine, R.D. and Greenwald, R. (1994) 'Does money matter? A meta analysis of studies of the effects of differential school inputs on student outcomes', *Educational Researcher,* 23: 5–14.

Holmlund, H., McNally, S. and Viarengo, M. (2008) *Impact of School Resources on Attainment at Key Stage 2.* DCSF-RBO43. London: DCSF.

Jenkins, A., Levačić, R. and Vignoles, A. (2005) 'Estimating the relationships between school resources and pupil attainment at GCSE', *DfES Research Report* RR727. London: DfES.

Krueger, A. (2003) 'Economic considerations and class size', *Economic Journal,* 113 (485): F34–F63.

Krueger, A. and Whitmore, D.M. (2001) 'The effect of attending small classes in the early grades of college test-taking and middle school test results: evidence from Project STAR', *The Economic Journal,* 111 (January): 1–28.

Levačić, R. (2007) 'The relationship between student attainment and school resources', in T. Townsend (ed.), *International Handbook of School Effectiveness and School Improvement.* Dordrecht: Springer. pp. 425–50.

Levačić, R. (2009) 'Teacher incentives and performance: an application of principal–agent theory', *Oxford Development Studies,* 37(1): 33–46.

Levačić, R. and Jenkins, A. (2006) 'Evaluating the effectiveness of specialist schools in England', *School Effectiveness and School Improvement,* 17(3): 229–54.

Levačić, R. and Vignoles, A. (2002) 'Researching the links between school resources and student outcomes in the UK: a review of issues and evidence', *Education Economics,* 10(3): 312–31.

Levačić, R., Jenkins, A. and Vignoles, A. (2004) 'Estimating the relationships between school resources and pupil attainment at Key Stage 3', *DfES Research Report 679.*

Mingat, A. (2007) 'Cost and financing of education and its impact on coverage and quality of services and efficiency and equity in Sub-Saharan African countries', in T. Townsend (ed.), *International Handbook of School Effectiveness and School Improvement.* Dordrecht: Springer. pp. 425–50.

Monk, D. (1990) *Educational Finance: An Economic Approach.* New York: McGraw-Hill.

Mortimore, P. (1991) 'The nature and findings of school effectiveness research in the primary sector', in S. Riddell and S. Brown (eds), *School Effectiveness Research: Its Messages for School Improvement.* London: HMSO.

OECD (2004) *Learning for Tomorrow's World: First Results from PISA 2003.* Paris: OECD. www.pisa.oecd.org.

OECD (2005) *School Factors Related to Quality and Equity: Results from PISA 2000.* Paris: OECD.

OECD (2007) *PISA 2006: Science Competencies for Tomorrow's World Vol 1.* Paris: OECD.

OECD (2008a) *Education at a Glance.* Paris: OECD.

OECD (2008b) *Measuring Improvements in Learning Outcomes: Best Practices to Assess the Value Added of Schools.* Paris: OECD.

Picus, L.O. and Blair. (2004) 'School finance adequacy: the state role', *Insights on Education Policy, Practice and Research,* 16 (March): 1–12.

Ray, A. (2006) 'School value added measures in England', A paper for the OECD Project on the Development of Value-Added Models in Education Systems.

Reynolds, D. and Teddlie, C. (1999) 'The process of school effectiveness', in C. Teddlie and D. Reynolds (eds), *The International Handbook of School Effectiveness Research*. London: RoutledgeFalmer.

Ruggiero, J. (2007) 'Measuring the cost of minimum educational standards: an application of data envelopment analysis', *Education Economics*, 15(1): 1–13.

Sammons, P., Sylva, K., Melhuish, E., Siraj-Blatchford, I., Taggart, B. and Hunt, S. (2008) *Influences on Children's Attainment and Progress in Key Stage 2: Cognitive Outcomes in Year 6: Effective Pre-school and Primary Education 3–11 Project (EPPE 3–11) Research Report DCSF-RR048*. London: DCSF.

Scheerens, J. (1997) 'Conceptual models and theory-embedded principles on effective schooling', *School Effectiveness and School Improvement*, 8(3): 269–310.

Scheerens, J. (1999) 'Concepts and theories of school effectiveness', in A.J. Visscher (ed.), *Managing Schools Towards High Performance*. Lisse: Swets and Zeitlinger. pp. 37–70.

Slavin, R., Madden, N., Dolan, L.J. and Wasik, B.H. (1996) *Every Child, Every School: Success For All*. Thousand Oaks, CA: Corwin Press.

Smith, P.C. and Street, A. (2006) *Analysis of Secondary School Efficiency: Final Report: Research Report RR788*. London: DfES.

Teddlie, C. and Reynolds, D. (eds) (1999) *The International Handbook of School Effectiveness Research*. London: RoutledgeFalmer.

UK Centre for the Measurement of Government Activity (2006) 'Public sector productivity: examining changes in output and productivity of government expenditure on education', *Economic Trends, ONS*, 626 (January): 13–47.

UNESCO (2005) *Education Trends in Perspective: Analysis of the World Education Indicators*. Paris: UNESCO Institute of Statistics.

Wößmann, L. (2003a) 'Central exit exams and student achievement: international evidence', in P.E. Peterson and M.R. West (eds), *No Child Left Behind: The Policy and Practice of School Accountability*. Washington, DC: Brookings Institution Press.

Wößmann, L. (2003b) 'Schooling resources, educational institutions and student performance: the international evidence', *Oxford Bulletin of Economics and Statistics*.

World Bank (2003) *World Development Report (2004) Making Services Work for Poor People*. Washington, DC: World Bank. www.worldbank.org.

Section IV

Leadership for Inclusion

CHAPTER 12

Leadership for Diversity and Inclusion

Jacky Lumby

Introduction

Each of the words of the title of this chapter has multiple and contested meanings. How we understand leadership is, of course, one of the primary concerns of the volume. Conceptualisations are legion. The words 'diversity' and 'inclusion' are also commonly used in practitioner discourse and in policy documents at organisational, local and national levels. How the terms are understood is as contested and varied as is leadership. This chapter begins by considering the multiple ways in which these key elements are conceived. It explores how diversity has been researched and therefore how relevant knowledge has been generated. Finally, it considers how leaders can act to lead for and with diversity and to be inclusive, and what preparation or support might aid them.

There is a very large and wide range of literature focused on issues of diversity and inclusion related to both staff and learners. The chapter has not space to address in detail the specific issues that may arise in relation to individuals or groups of staff or learners with particular needs, such as a physical or learning impairment, or who encounter disadvantage in relation to a particular characteristic, such as their ethnic heritage. Rather it sets out the overarching ideas, relevant research and actions which leaders might consider to achieve a strategic orientation to leading for diversity and inclusion.

Definitions and understandings

How we understand who are leaders and what activity constitutes leadership is an important foundation for the chapter. Identifying leaders is contextually sensitive. While theories of distributed leadership have found a following in many anglophone areas of the world, in other countries a more hierarchical approach is the norm, with 'leader' understood as the person who formally has a role invested with authority. For the purposes of this chapter, an inclusive but also partial approach is taken. Leaders are assumed to be all those in schools and other educational organisations who deliberately create and transmit the organisation's values and use influence to ensure that values inform practice. Such action is arguably the most fundamental act of leadership (Begley, 2003). The latter may involve more than this, but the question of values is particularly pertinent to diversity issues, and so is selected here as the heart of leadership. Potentially, therefore, all staff and students may play a leadership role in this area, though some research has suggested that those in roles of authority may have more power and so be more influential (Ng, 2008).

Diversity is a term which is used ubiquitously and variously. It is sometimes used as synonymous with ethnicity or race. Sometimes it is used to indicate the presence of individuals with the range of characteristics embedded in equality legislation such as ethnicity, gender, disability and age; sometimes it is used to acknowledge the very wide range of characteristics which differentiate human beings, including both visible and non-visible attributes of the physical person and their background, preferences and beliefs (You-Ta et al., 2004). How diversity is conceived has an impact on how leaders construct action in response. Diversity is defined here as the range of human characteristics which result in socially-constructed advantage and disadvantage (DiTomaso and Hooijberg, 1996); that is, it is not, for example, being black or fe/male or having a disability which is critical. What matters is how others react to the characteristic and by their reaction create unjustified advantage or disadvantage. Reynolds and Trehan, (2003: 167) put it succinctly: 'differences that matter and those that do not, depending on whether they reinforce inequality'.

Inclusion is the final concept central to the chapter. It can be related to multiple strategies to achieve particular outcomes for staff and learners, including equal opportunities, affirmative action, multiculturalism, and capabilities approaches. The differing terminologies and desired outcomes relate to varied understandings of fairness and social inclusion. Rather than adopt a single definition, the chapter explores the different goals related to alternative understandings of what inclusion might mean.

Researching diversity

Addressing issues related to diversity can draw on many disciplines, including, for example, social psychology, cultural anthropology and socio-biology. It can also consider neuro-epistemological theories about the degree of agency leaders may have to adjust the fundamental thinking processes which underpin attitudes to diversity and inclusion. The relevant literature can focus on single characteristics, as does feminist literature and critical race theory or, increasingly, can adopt intersectionality approaches which insist on understanding the effect of each individual's multiple characteristics in synergy.

With every area of inquiry, there is a relationship between knowledge production, theory and practice. In relation to diversity, McCall (2005) suggests three different approaches. The first is anti-categorical complexity, that is, rejection of the notion that it is possible to meaningfully research human beings using categories. Litvin (1997) argues this strongly. She believes that categorising people, for example into ethnic groups, inappropriately adopts a biological taxonomy approach. 'The categories constructed through the discourse of workforce diversity as natural and obvious are hard pressed to accommodate the complexity of real people' (1997: 202). While it may be possible to order plant species, humans cannot be analysed in the same way. Even the most apparently incontrovertible category, that of gender, is challenged by queer theory which attacks essentialist notions of gender and insists gender is a variable and constructed performance that is related to other characteristics (Sloop, 2007). McCall's second approach is inter-categorical complexity, using historic categories of disadvantage as an organising framework. Many individuals and groups assert that it is extremely important to consider groups, such as black people or girls/women or those who have a particular disability, as groups, because that is how they are often seen by others and stereotyped as a result. Membership of the group is therefore one root of the disadvantage they experience. The final approach, intra-categorical complexity, explores the nature of the making of categories and boundaries and their effects on research, knowledge and practice. Why we create groups and the effect of the group on how we see people is therefore another area of knowledge production.

The links to policy and action are evident. If leaders resist categorising people into groups, then their response to diversity and inclusion is likely to stress the need to consider each individual as a unique being. Leaders of schools for learners with special learning needs might adopt this understanding of diversity. By contrast, leaders of schools in inner cities might believe it is crucial to focus on equality and inclusion for a particular ethnic group, for example, African Caribbean youths in England or Latinos/Latinas in the USA. In South Africa, school, college or university leaders might believe it necessary to focus on addressing the effect on students of intersections of characteristics, such as ethnicity, language, gender and religion (Lumby and Heystek, 2008). In each case different conceptions of diversity call on different kinds of research/ literature which in turn lead to different goals and orientations to practice.

Identifying goals

For diversity

Leading *for* diversity, that is, achieving a representative profile of staff or students, is still a widely adopted goal internationally (Bush et al., 2006; Hartle and Thomas, 2003). It is seen to offer measurable progress and by accepting people into areas from which they have previously been excluded, potentially to redress the prior imbalance of power. There are, however, issues with such a goal. First, while it is widely adopted in relation to staff, it is far from universal in relation to learners. Schools may engineer their intake in various ways, and having a profile of learners which reflects, for example, the ethnicity or socio-economic background or prior attainment of the local or national population is not always the intention. For many staff and parents a 'good' school is one which has an intake skewed towards learners with a more advantaged background and higher prior attainment. By contrast, throughout the world many schools take professional pride in meeting the needs of all the children who live locally, who may have no option but to attend their local school. There is no question of engineering intake. Diversity (defined as representation), or lack of it, is a property of the local population reflected in the school. For other schools, fee payment or selection processes may aim at an unrepresentative learner body. Elite universities in the UK experience pressure from central government to ensure a range of socio economic backgrounds in their intake. Such a goal is far from accepted by many (Spencer, 2008). Representation is therefore a goal which is much more widely adopted in relation to staff. The result is potentially a dissonance between a staff body which is currently, or in aspiration, representative of the local and/or national population and a learner body which is not, or vice versa. Such disparity may constitute a hidden message which undermines any intended communication of commitment to diversity and inclusion (Lumby and Heystek, 2008).

The second issue is deciding of what population staff or learners are to be representative and which characteristics are most pertinent. A gender balance often appears more likely to be seen as relevant and achievable than, for example, a staff profile which is representative of the number of people nationally who are minority ethnic or have a disability, particularly if the local population is perceived as 'not diverse' (Lumby et al., 2005). Whether representation is in relation to the local or the national population becomes a key choice.

A third issue is controversy about what representation in itself achieves. If staff or learners are recruited who are perceived as different to the majority or a usually unstated norm, but the culture and practice of leadership, or teaching and learning remain static, representation may be achieved at the cost of assimilation, where the dominant group of people may consciously or unconsciously impose on all their own parameters for values, thinking and practice (Lumby with Coleman, 2007). The progress indicated by increasing representation is seen therefore as apparent only; 'entryism' (Davies, 1990: 16), that is, merely injecting under-represented people without attention to an inclusive culture (Grogan, 1999). As a consequence, for example, women and men may feel obliged to lead in a masculine mode and to adopt a masculine lifestyle such as lengthy working hours, whatever the gender representation among leaders (Coleman, 2002; Stott and Lawson, 1997); those from a particular faith or culture may find their values overridden. An example is the tension between staff whose culture gives primacy to maintaining family ties above educational continuity and those who prioritise education attendance above family commitments (Lumby and Heystek, 2008). Others argue that representation is an important goal, despite the issues it raises, and that a first step to greater equality is for those previously excluded to at least have the chance to progress to formal leadership roles and to influence practice and outcomes.

How far the goal of representation is achieved is hard to assess. The data on the degree of representation amongst educational leaders is difficult to come by, even in Organisation for Economic

Co-operation and Development (OECD) countries such as Australia, Canada and the UK (Cruikshank, 2004; Sobehart, 2008). Increasingly the goal is seen as representation plus; that representation may both be preceded by and support further the consideration of how culture and practice can be inclusive of all those currently in the school, college or university community and of potential future members (Milliken and Martins, 1996).

Leading with diversity

The term 'inclusion' is used as ubiquitously as diversity and often with as undefined a meaning. In relation to learners, in the UK the Office for Standards in Education's definition describes inclusion as equal opportunities for all, and goes on to identify particular groups requiring attention to ensure they have equal chances, such as children in care, or those of a particular ethnic background. By contrast, another kind of definition focuses on how the individual experiences the organisation, rather than the supplier's intention to offer equality:

> When individual and group differences are regarded as valued resources, as in an inclusive environment, differences no longer need to be suppressed. Those who cannot fit into the old monocultural model no longer need waste their energy trying to be what they are not, and those who can successfully suppress or hide their differences no longer need waste their energy doing so. (Miller and Katz, 2002: 17)

It is essentially all experiencing a sense of belonging which characterises inclusion for Miller and Katz.

This approach echoes the capabilites approach to equality which has emerged from the work of writers such as Sen (1984) and Nussbaum (1999). The approach insists that there is an interaction and symbiosis between people's talents, their education and the environment in which they ultimately use their developed skills and attitudes in both employment and personal life. The external context must offer opportunities fairly and this is suggested to be as important as internal individual development and empowerment. The goal is seen not as representativeness, for example an equal number of girls and boys studying physics in higher education, but rather as each individual being enabled to live a life which they value. Such a goal is relevant to both learners and staff.

Those leading for diversity and inclusion therefore face an important initial task in agreeing with others how diversity is conceived and what the goal(s) might be. Is the target particularly 'differences that matter' (Reynolds and Trehan, 2003: 167)? Are the groups with characteristics enshrined in equality legislation to be the focus? Is progress to be assessed by increasing the representation of those employed at all levels or, for learners, a more representative profile of those studying particular subjects, achieving accredited outcomes and progressing to further education or training? In many parts of the world, white men disproportionately hold senior posts, therefore, in such a context representation may be a key goal. Similarly the gulf between the achievement of some learner groups and others might demand specific attention to redress imbalance in outcomes. For example, Shields (2008) reports the huge discrepancies of funding for white and black students in Chicago, USA and in South Africa:

> In the Chicago area, for example, the highest per pupil expenditure of $17,291 is to be found in Highland Park and Deerfield, districts with a 90% White population and only 8% low income students, while in Chicago itself, with 85% low income students and 87% Black and Hispanic, the per pupil expenditure is $8,482 … . Similarly, in South Africa, Dunn (1998) reported that 'for every dollar spent on a black student, seven were spent on each white' (p. 2). (Shields, 2008: 5)

Leaders of schools in such inequitable contexts will indeed feel the pressure to address particularly 'differences that matter' (Shields, 2008). By contrast, in schools or colleges where there are multiple sources of disadvantage which intersect to heighten or lessen disadvantage, leaders might feel that to support all individuals, staff and learners, to be enabled to live a life they value, both in the present and the future, is the appropriate goal. In such a case, progress is more likely to be assessed by the satisfaction people feel with their experience, and particularly with the quality of their relationships and the support to achieve what they may, as much as the accredited outcomes they achieve. This is not to condone complacency about attainment outcomes, but to emphasise that how learners experience the process of education and training may matter as much as the final outcome (Lumby and Morrison, 2009).

Development of leaders for future diverse and inclusive schools, colleges and universities

There are very many guidance documents emerging from public sector bodies, interest groups, national reviews and local working groups. These offer a range of possible actions to increase equality, representation, family-friendliness, physical access and other goals. They focus outwards on action. This chapter goes on to consider such outward-orientated action, but first looks inwards. There is much evidence that inequality is embedded not only in structures but most profoundly in the attitudes of individuals, including educational leaders (Bush et al., 2006; Cushman, 2005; Decuir and Dixson, 2004; Rusch, 2004).

The majority of leaders would assert a commitment to equality, however they understand the term, in relation to both learners and staff. Yet there is historical and universal evidence of sexism, racism and other forms of discrimination (Gillborn, 2005; Walker 2005). Such behaviour is often not a conscious choice, but an arguably instinctive (Sapolsky, 2002) or socially embedded reaction (Simons and Pelled, 1999). An encounter with another who is perceived as different to oneself evokes uncertainty, which in its turn leads to anxiety. Cognitive processes habitually deal with such anxiety by avoidance or by a quick fix adoption of stereotyping, which allows categorisation of an individual and shapes the response to take account of what is 'known' about the stereotyped group. Stone and Colella (1996: 358) define stereotypes as 'largely false "overgeneralized" beliefs about members of a category that are typically negative'. Once a stereotyping process has been initiated, the leader's capacity to react to the person as an individual becomes limited:

> Cognitively anxiety leads to biases in how we process information. The more anxious we are, the more likely we will focus on the behaviours we expect to see, such as those based on our stereotypes, and the more likely we are to confirm these expectations and not recognize behaviour which is inconsistent with our expectations. (Gudykunst, 1995: 14)

There is no panacea for replacing such responses amongst oneself, other staff and learners with a more accurate and mindful interaction with the individual as a unique person, rather than as a member of a group. Lakomski (2001) and Allix and Gronn (2005) both argue that what needs to change is neurological patterns which may have been established by repetition over a lifetime. As a consequence, learned responses are 'highly resistant to eradication, or forgetting ... implicit learning gives rise to a phenomenal sense of intuition in that subjects respond the way they do because it simply "feels right", or natural' (Allix and Gronn, 2005: 187). Token 'sheep dip' training days will do little to shift deeply embedded attitudes, which are often unconscious and in contradiction to consciously held beliefs. A much more persistent range of strategies is needed to embed ongoing pressure to shift thinking.

One might hope that the presence of those perceived as 'other' might offer help in challenging such thinking patterns, but there are obstacles. Those who are disadvantaged by a particular characteristic or characteristics may adopt strategies to disguise their 'otherness' rather than foreground their distinctive nature. Gurin and Nagda (2006), writing in a US context, identify ways students (and potentially staff) may deal with minority status. They may de-categorise, emphasising that they are not to be seen as a member of a disadvantaged group, such as black or a woman, but as an individual: distinctively Parvati or Youssef. Such de-categorisation aims to encourage the in-group to see the individual as such, and not as a member of an out-group. Re-categorisation draws the out-group into the in-group, in order to create one single group: not Parvati, but a member of the senior leadership team, or of a class or set of children. If those who are disadvantaged adopt such strategies in order to blend with the majority or those who are dominant, they are not likely to offer the kind of information and support which helps understand difference. Rather, the latter is minimised as far as possible. The stigmatised characteristic is subject to misdirection, as a magician will attempt to divert attention away from what he or she does not want the audience to see (Goffman, 1986). The result may be to encourage blindness to difference and its significance. Colour blindness is one result. White staff do not focus on their whiteness as a significant characteristic. They also may not see the ethnicity of others as relevant (Cochrane-Smith, 1995; Mabokela and Madsen, 2003). The assertion that an individual 'does not notice colour' in others is widespread (Walker, 2005). In this way those who view themselves as the norm collude with those who are perceived as different, to maintain that difference does not matter. Leaders may need consistently to insist that people are different, that difference matters in a range of ways, and that some differences matter more than others in the advantage or disadvantage they accrue.

Key actions to achieve a diverse leadership

In order to lead in a diverse society and to foreground differences among learners and staff in a way that is positive, leaders may need intercultural competence skills, and to reconsider the purpose of leadership if the transformation of society is a goal (Stier, 2006). The preparation of leaders in relation to diversity and inclusion is generally inadequate. Drawing on a study of 11 leadership centres in seven countries (Australia, Canada, Hong Kong, New Zealand, Singapore, Sweden and the USA), Bush and Jackson (2002) noted that the focus and content were very similar. The issues of diversity and inclusion usually do not appear. Where they do, they are often peripheral to the main business of the programme. There are of course exceptions where preparation programmes make diversity and inclusion central to leader preparation (McClellan and Dominguez, 2006), but this is far from the norm in many parts of the world. Leaders who are seriously committed to inclusion therefore have an obligation to educate themselves and to deliberately practice the skills of relating to 'other'. Iles and Kaur Hayers (1997: 105) describe cultural fluency involving three dimensions, 'cognitive complexity, emotional energy and psychological maturity'. Their work draws on research concerning transnational corporations, but increasingly the intercultural competence needed in such contexts is equally relevant to the diverse communities served by many schools, colleges and universities. The kind of inner strength and moral energy depicted as necessary is a long way from the leader development which hinges on short-term training or guidance documents. The latter have a place, but are only likely to be effective if they are founded on a bedrock of the kind of 'mindfulness' described by Gudykunst (1995: 16). Rather than actions which focus outward on other staff or learners, the leader's first task may be to look inward and over time to continue to challenge one's own stance.

The stance of other staff and the purpose and structures of the organisations may also require attention. As outlined earlier in the chapter there are, of course, very many possible goals and actions.

Key areas of action for leading for diversity and inclusion

There are many prescriptions of how to achieve 'equality', deriving from national governments, from advisory bodies, and from research. Synthesising the content, some key questions emerge. The first is the location of responsibility. In some cases, the principal/headteacher may take personal responsibility, believing the area is foundational, and therefore rightly a part of the principal's brief. More often, the organisation may embed a diversity role as part of a member of the senior leadership team's portfolio. In larger organisations, such as colleges or universities, there may be a diversity manager, often situated within a human resource department, or a diversity champion/multicultural co-ordinator within the teaching and learning staff structure. If the role is low status, that is, perceived by the majority as not central to the success of the organisation, then wherever responsibility is placed, diversity will remain a minor issue. In a study of colleges in the UK, a diversity manager placed high in the organisation hierarchy nevertheless felt, 'You're a lone voice in an ocean ... a bolt-on to the business of the college' (Lumby et al., 2007). The locus of responsibility alone will not achieve diversity issues being perceived as high priority, but it could contribute to achieving such an aim. Responsibility for diversity issues placed with a junior role with little time or resource will give a clear message about its unimportance. Placing it higher will not necessarily give the contrary message unless linked to a degree of resource indicative of its importance. It may be a matter of changing culture and Schein identifies what he terms 'primary embedding mechanisms'.

> People calculate what is important and therefore what they need to give energy to by observing, amongst other things:
>
> - What leaders pay attention to, measure, and control on a regular basis
> - Observed criteria by which leaders allocate scarce resources. (Schein, 1997: 231)

He suggests that, ultimately, people cannot be fooled by rhetoric into believing something is important for long, when senior leaders do not consider it so, and that this is discerned by where the most careful attention and substantial funds go. Appointing/allocating someone to address diversity issues is of itself unlikely to bring about much change. Other signals will be deciphered to interpret the meaning of such action. Similarly, many organisations collect diversity data of various kinds. Collection in itself may achieve little. The attention paid to the kind of data and the use made of it signals whether the activity is ritual compliance with legislative requirements, or a matter of genuine concern to those who hold status in the school or college. Data monitoring as a displacement activity for real change is a common strategy (Deem and Morley, 2006). The implications of Schein's analysis of culture change is that commitment to a direction for change cannot be faked, or at least not for long. Both staff and learners will read the runes to decipher attitudes to diversity and the necessity for change or otherwise.

Assuming that there is a real intention to move towards greater equality, and that how this is understood has been discussed and agreed by staff and learners, there are many sources of ideas for action. Norte (1999) suggests a five-point framework for developing school practice for inclusion; that policy and practice be considered in relation to:

1. Content: the subject matter of focus (including vision, curriculum and support/counselling services for learners).

2. Process: how people engage the subject matter (planning, use of data, consultation engagement with all staff, student and local communities).

3. Structure: how time, space and people are organised and con-figured (encouragement of interaction between individuals and between school or community groups).

4. Staffing: the roles to which personnel are assigned (recruitment and selection, promotion, development opportunities and support, employment conditions and personal security).

5. Infrastructure: the physical setting (safety, accessibility and a positive environment and facilities for all).

If leaders reviewed each of these aspects of the school, college or university to consider their support of diversity and inclusion, sub-stantial change is likely to be indicated. For example, if staff are unrepresentative of the local or school community, changing the situation may demand determination and creativity. Existing staff may be resistant, arguing against what they erroneously perceive as unfair positive discrimination (Lumby et al., 2005). The criteria of appointment may be unconsciously favourable to the current hege-monic group. The racism or sexism of those involved in appoint-ment may need to be supportively challenged. This is just one exemplar area of action. A long-term and detailed strategy might emerge to address attitudes and practice if each of the five points were considered in all aspects.

Aguirre and Martinez (2007) present two options for responding to diversity which they term co-option and transformational strate-gies. There is evidence that much leadership for and with diversity in many parts of the world is co-option; that is, it treats diversity as a relatively minor issue which can be tacked on to other more central policies and acted upon periodically (Dass and Parker, 1999). Transformation approaches which place diversity as central are less frequent.

The practice gulf

While many, perhaps most, educational leaders recognise that there may be issues of inequality in their organisation related to particular individuals or groups of learners or staff, progress in addressing them is inhibited by the gulf between intention, enactment and experience. Evans (2003: 419) distinguishes 'policy espoused', 'policy enacted' and the impact on individuals' and groups' lives as 'policy experienced'. Official policy documents, policy espoused, generally commit to increasing equality of opportunity or social justice. The enactment of such policy is weak in many schools, colleges and universities. There is lack of action, peripheral tokenistic action or action primarily driven by compliance with legislation, which results in systems that do not impact deeply on people's attitudes and daily practice. The locus of both the existence of significant inequality and the responsibility for addressing it is often placed elsewhere. A kind of double-think is in existence, where leaders acknowledge that, for example, racism exists everywhere, but also that it is not particularly pertinent among their own staff or in their own practice. Numerous studies in different parts of the world suggest otherwise; that inequality is deeply and universally embedded and persistent, and that many staff and leaders consider diversity issues either irrelevant or low priority, or are actively hostile to them (Phendla, 2008; Rusch, 2004; Sinclair, 2000; Walker and Walker, 1998). There is a widespread overestimation of the impact of action. Research in the UK (Bush et al., 2006; Fazil et al., 2002), in South Africa (Lumby and Heystek, 2008; Phendla, 2008), in the USA (Lugg, 2003), in Canada and Australia (Gaskell and Taylor, 2003) and in Korea (Brooker and Ha, 2005), among many other countries, reveals persisting unjustified disadvantage and consequent underperformance resulting from attitudes to ethnicity, gender, sexual orientation, disability and socio-economic class, among other characteristics. There are, of course, exceptions where individuals and organisations have fully embraced the necessity to engage with issues of diversity in a positive and determined fashion (Lumby et al., 2005). One case study college provides evidence of such leadership in action, where the principal focused on and, evidence suggests, achieved:

- a focus on diversity issues as fundamental to organisational development
- a senior management team representative of the local community gender and ethnic profile
- responsibility for diversity and inclusion both embedded in the whole senior team and in specific roles
- a detailed and well-resourced equality action plan
- frequent and rigorous scrutiny and response to diversity data analysis
- ongoing and frequent development activities for all staff both in relation to generic leadership (in which diversity is foundational) and particular diversity issues
- participation in organisational, local and national networks supporting individuals and groups working towards greater equality (Lumby, in press).

Staff of varied levels in the case study perceived diversity as integrated within every aspect of their own and organisational practice. There are also examples of leadership preparation and development programmes which are innovative and stress diversity as a central issue (McClellan and Dominguez, 2006). However, the research cited in this section suggests that the majority of those leading and those preparing leaders who might identify with such practice are likely to be over-optimistic. The main thrust of this chapter has been to outline not only what might be done to address issues related to diversity, but also to stress what a long way remains to go.

Further reading

Lumby, J. with Coleman, M. (2007) *Leadership and Diversity: Challenging Theory and Practice in Education*. London: Sage.

Orte, E. (1999) '"Structures beneath the skin": how school leaders use their power and authority to create institutional opportunities for developing positive interethnic communities', *Journal of Negro Education*, 68(4): 466–85.

References

Aguirre, A. Jr and Martinez, R.O. (2007) 'Diversity leadership in higher education', *ASHE Higher Education Report*, 32(3), San Francisco, CA: Jossey-Bass.

Allix, P. and Gronn, P. (2005) '"Leadership" as knowledge', *Educational Management, Leadership and Administration*, 33(2): 181–96.

Begley, P. (2003) 'In pursuit of authentic school leadership practices', in P. Begley and O. Johansson (eds), *The Ethical Dimensions of School Leadership*. London: Kluwer Academic.

Brooker, L. and Ha, S.J. (2005) 'The cooking teacher: investigating gender stereotypes in a Korean kindergarten', *Early Years*, 25(1): 17–30.

Bush, T. and Jackson, D. (2002) 'Preparation for school leadership: international perspectives', *Educational Management and Administration*, 30(4): 417–29.

Bush, T., Glover, D. and Sood, K. (2006) 'Black and minority ethnic leaders in England: a portrait', *School Leadership and Management*, 26(3): 289–305.

Cochrane-Smith, M. (1995) 'Color blindness and basket making are not the answers: confronting the dilemmas of race, culture, and language diversity in teacher education', *American Educational Research Journal*, 32(3): 493–522.

Coleman, M. (2002) *Women as Head Teachers: Striking the Balance*. Stoke-on-Trent: Trentham.

Cruikshank, K. (2004) 'Towards diversity in teacher education: teacher preparation of immigrant teachers', *International Journal of Teacher Education*, 27(2): 125–38.

Cushman, P. (2005) 'It's just not a real bloke's job: male teachers in the primary school', *Asia-Pacific Journal of Teacher Education*, 33(3): 321–38.

Dass, P. and Parker, B. (1999) 'Strategies for managing human resource diversity: from resistance to learning', *Academy of Management Executive*, 13(2): 68–80.

Davies, L. (1990) *Equity and Efficiency? School Management in an International Context*. London: Falmer Press.

Decuir, J. and Dixson, A. (2004) '"So when it comes out, they aren't that surprised that it is there": using critical race theory as a tool of analysis of race and racism in education', *Educational Researcher*, 33(5): 26–31.

Deem, R. and Morley, L. (2006) 'Diversity in the academy? Staff perceptions of equality policies in six contemporary higher education institutions', *Policy Futures in Education*, 4(2): 185–202.

DiTomaso, N. and Hooijberg, R. (1996) 'Diversity and the demands of leadership', *The Leadership Quarterly*, 7(2): 163–87.

Evans, K. (2003) 'Uncertain frontiers: taking forward Edmund King's world perspectives on post-compulsory education', *Comparative Education*, 39(4): 415–22.

Fazil, Q., Bywaters, P., Ali, Z., Wallace, L. and Singh, G. (2002) 'Disadvantage and discrimination compounded: the experience of Pakastani and Bangladeshi parents of disabled children in the UK', *Disability and Society*, 17(3): 237–54.

Gaskell, J. and Taylor, S. (2003) 'The women's movement in Canadian and Australian education: from liberation and sexism to boys and social justice', *Gender and Education*, 15(2): 151–68.

Gillborn, D. (2005) 'Education policy as an act of white supremacy: whiteness, critical race theory and education reform', *Journal of Education Policy*, 20(4): 485–505.

Goffman, E. (1986) *Stigma: Notes on the Management of Spoiled Identity*. New York: Simon & Schuster.

Grogan, M. (1999) 'Equity/equality issues of gender, race and class', *Educational Administration Quarterly*, 35(4): 518–36.

Gudykunst, W. (1995) 'Anxiety/uncertainty management (AUM) theory', in R. Wiseman (ed.), *International Communication Theory Vol. XIX*. London: Sage.

Gurin, P. and Nagda, B.R.A. (2006) 'Getting to the what, how and why of diversity on campus', *Educational Researcher*, 35(1): 20–4.

Hartle, F. and Thomas, K. (2003) *Growing Tomorrow's School Leaders – The Challenge*. Nottingham: NCSL.

Iles, P. and Kaur Hayers, P. (1997) 'Managing diversity in transnational project teams: a tentative model and case study', *Journal of Managerial Psychology*, 1(2): 95–117.

Lakomski, G. (2001) 'Organizational change, leadership and learning: culture as cognitive process', *The International Journal of Educational Management*, 15(2): 68–77.

Litvin, D.R. (1997) 'The discourse of diversity: from biology to management', *Discourse and Organization*, 4(2): 187–209.

Lugg, C.A. (2003) 'Sissies, faggots, lezzies, and dykes: gender, sexual orientation, and a new politics of education?', *Educational Administration Quarterly*, 39(1): 95–134.

Lumby, J. (in press) 'Leaders' orientations to diversity: two cases from education', *Leadership*.

Lumby, J. and Heystek, J. (2008) 'Race, identity and leadership in South African and English schools', paper presented to the Biennial Conference of Commonwealth Council for Educational Administration and Management, 'Think Globally, Act Locally: A Challenge to Education Leaders', 8–12 September, Durban, South Africa.

Lumby, J. and Morrison, M. (2009) 'Youth perspectives: schooling, capabilities frameworks and human rights', *International Journal of Inclusive Education*. First article: 1–15. http://dx.doi.org/10.1080/13603110801995920 (accessed 5 May 2009).

Lumby, J., Bhopal, K., Dyke, M., Maringe, F. and Morrison, M. (2007) *Integrating diversity in Leadership in Further Education*. London: Centre for Excellence in Leadership.

Lumby, J., Harris, A., Morrison, M., Muijs, D., Sood, K., Glover, D. and Wilson, M. with Briggs, A.R.J. and Middlewood, D. (2005) *Leadership, Development and Diversity in the Learning and Skills Sector*. London: LSDA.

Lumby, J. with Coleman, M. (2007) *Leadership and Diversity: Challenging Theory and Practice in Education*. London: Sage.

Mabokela, R.O. and Madsen, J. (2003) '"Color-blind" leadership and intergroup conflict', *Journal of School Leadership*, 13(2): 130–58.

McCall, M. (2005) 'The complexity of intersectionality', *Signs: Journal of Women in Culture and Society*, 33(3): 1771–96.

McClellan, R. and Dominguez, R. (2006) 'The uneven march toward social justice: diversity, conflict, and complexity in educational administration programs', *Journal of Educational Administration*, 44(3): 225–38.

Miller, F.A. and Katz, J.H. (2002) *The Inclusion Breakthrough: Unleashing the Real Power of Diversity*. San Francisco, CA: Berrett-Koehler.

Milliken, Frances J. and Martins, Luis L. (1996) 'Searching for common threads: understanding the multiple effects of diversity in organizational groups', *Academy of Management Review*, 21(2): 1–32. http://search.epnet.com/dierct.asp?an=9605060217 &db=buh (accessed 6 May 2004).

Ng, E.S.W. (2008) 'Why organizations choose to manage diversity. Toward a leadership-based theoretical framework', *Human Resource Development Review*, 7(1):58–78.

Norte, E. (1999) '"Structures beneath the skin": how school leaders use their power and authority to create institutional opportunities for developing positive interethnic communities', *Journal of Negro Education*, 68(4): 466–85.

Nussbaum, M. (1999) 'Women and equality: the capabilities approach', *International Labour Review*, 138(3): 227–45.

Phendla, T. (2008) 'The paradox of Luselo–Lufhanga metaphors: African women defining leadership for social justice', *International Studies in Educational Leadership*, 36(1): 22–40.

Reynolds, M. and Trehan, K. (2003) 'Learning from difference?', *Management Learning*, 34(2): 163–80.

Rusch, E. (2004) 'Gender and race in leadership preparation: a constrained discourse', *Educational Administration Quarterly*, 40(1): 16–48.

Sapolsky, R. (2002) 'Cheaters and chumps', *Natural History*, 111(5): 1–7. http://weblinks2.epnet.com/citation.asp? (accessed 23 May 2006).

Schein, E. (1997) *Organizational Culture and Leadership*. 2nd edn. San Francisco, CA: Jossey-Bass.

Sen, A. (1984) *Resources, Values and Development*. Cambridge, MA: Harvard University Press.

Shields, C. (2008) 'Levelling the playing field in racialized contexts: leaders speaking out about difficult issues', paper presented to the Biennial Conference of Commonwealth Council for Educational Administration and Management, 'Think Globally Act Locally: A Challenge to Education Leaders', 8–12 September, Durban, South Africa

Simons, T. and Pelled, L.H. (1999) 'Understanding executive diversity: more than meets the eye', *Human Resource Planning*, 22(2): 49–51.

Sinclair, A. (2000) 'Women within diversity: risks and possibilities', *Women In Management Review*, 15(5/6): 237–45.

Sloop, J. (2007) 'In queer time and place and race: intersectionality comes of age', *Quarterly Journal of Speech*, 91(3): 312–26.

Sobehart, H. (ed.) (2008) *Women Leading Education Across the Continents: Sharing the Spirit, Fanning the Flame*. Lantham, MD and Toronto: Rowman and Littlefield.

Spencer, D. (2008) 'UK: Widening participation debate heats up', *University World News*. http://www.universityworldnews.com/article.php?story=20081002151757844 (accessed 3 December 2008).

Stier, J. (2006) 'Internationalisation, intercultural communication and intercultural competence', *Journal of Intercultural Communication*, 11: 1–12. http://www.immi.se/intercultural/ (accessed 14 July 2006).

Stone, D. and Colella, A. (1996) 'A model of factors affecting the treatment of disabled individuals in organizations', *Academy of Management Review*, 12(2): 352–401.

Stott, C. and Lawson, L. (1997) *Women at the Top in Further Education*, London: Further Education Development Agency.

Walker, M. (2005) 'Race is nowhere and race is everywhere', *British Journal of the Sociology of Education*, 26(1): 41–55.

Walker, A. and Walker, J. (1998) 'Challenging the boundaries of sameness: leadership through valuing difference', *Journal of Educational Administration*, 36(1): 8–28.

You-Ta, C., Church, R. and Zikic, J. (2004) 'Organizational culture, group diversity and intra-group conflict', *Team Performance Management*, 10(1): 26–34.

CHAPTER 13

Leading Educational Partnerships: New Models for Leadership?

Ann R.J. Briggs

Introduction

Educational leadership is not only carried out within individual schools, colleges, universities and other settings; it is also carried out collaboratively, in partnership with other leaders, to give children, young people and adults access to a range of educational provision. Current models of educational leadership largely have a single organisation focus, where external collaboration may be conceptualised as a necessary extension of leading the single organisation, particularly at senior leadership level. However, where institutions are working in partnership under conditions of joint accountability, the enactment of leadership across the partner organisations is potentially more complex, involving collaborative leadership of the partnership in addition to single-organisation leadership.

Collaborative leadership is not simply a 'bigger model' of single-organisation leadership. Single-organisation leadership may be delegated or dispersed in complex ways, and may include elements of joint leadership and joint responsibility with partner organisations, but its primary focus is upon the accountability of the single organisation. Collaborative leadership has joint responsibility and joint accountability for a wide range of partnership outcomes. Even where organisations have agreed to work in partnership, there may be issues of competition, misunderstanding or mistrust between them, and there may be historic differences in purpose and culture. Leadership across a range of organisations is therefore difficult to enact, and the stability of individual institutions may seem to be threatened by partnership working. Leaders may consequently act to maintain internal coherence within their own institution, instead of striving for the more difficult external coherence of working with partners. Leaders who have developed their professional experience in single-institution models may find it hard to adapt to such strongly collaborative ways of working. If partnership provision of education is to become more widespread, the conceptualisation of leadership may have to change.

Research context

This chapter draws upon published research data and experience of current practice in England, in a range of settings including school federations, networked learning communities, school improvement partnerships and collaborative provision for 14–19-year-old learners. In particular, it draws upon data from three research-based projects which investigated provision of 14–19 education in England:

- The baseline study for 14–19 education in England, funded by the Qualifications and Curriculum Authority (QCA) in 2007–08 (Gorard et al., 2009).
- Leading partnerships for 14–19 education: research funded by the Centre for Excellence in Leadership (CEL) in 2006–07 (Briggs et al., 2007).
- Interim and final evaluations of the Flexible Curriculum Programme (FCP) in Tyne and Wear, funded through Gateshead Borough Council in 2007 and 2008 (Clark et al., 2008; Hall and Briggs, 2007).

Each project had a mixed methodology, and together they comprise research at national, regional and sub-regional levels in England. The QCA baseline study involved 45 case studies across the nine English government regions, collecting statistical data on curriculum provision and achievement, and survey, documentary and interview data from a range of stakeholders, including young people, on the range, effectiveness and perceived equity of current 14–19 educational provision. The CEL project examined the leadership of 14–19 educational partnerships through four regional case studies in the North-East of England, drawing on interview data from learning partnership members, school and college leaders and groups of learners, together with a national survey of learning partnership co-ordinators across England. The FCP project comprised two studies which evaluated the effectiveness of flexible curriculum programmes in Tyne and Wear, based upon case studies of provision at sub-regional level, including interviews with learners and providers, and an analysis of attendance and achievement data. All three projects collected data on educational partnerships.

From this knowledge base, this chapter discusses the relatively new phenomenon of leading across partnerships. It examines the benefits and tensions of partnership working, and proposes new models for considering the nature of collaborative leadership. While the examples cited in the chapter are drawn from the UK educational context, the conceptualisation of collaborative leadership, its benefits and difficulties, may be applied more broadly in a range of international contexts. The models presented in the chapter are offered as thinking tools in this respect, for readers to interrogate and adapt to their own circumstances.

What are educational partnerships?

There is no agreed definition of educational partnerships: Powell and Dowling (2006: 305) describe them as 'the indefinable in pursuit of the unachievable'. Dhillon (2005: 4) observes that 'the term is used to cover a range of working arrangements, which involve multiple organisations, agencies, groups and individuals working collaboratively or co-operatively to achieve common goals or purposes (Audit Commission, 1998; Stuart, 2002)'.

In the English context, partnerships may be perceived as having two main drivers, external–political and internal–social. The strong external driver is current government policy, which for more than 10 years has encouraged and imposed collaboration as a basis for key educational initiatives. To take a range of examples, the framework for post-16 learning set out in the White Paper *Learning to Succeed* is 'based on partnership and co-operation between individuals, businesses and communities, as well as institutions' (DfEE, 1999: 4); in the White Paper *Schools Achieving Success,* partnerships for school improvement are encouraged 'with other successful schools, the voluntary sector, faith groups and the private sector', in order to spread specialist knowledge (DfES, 2001: 44); in the *Five Year Strategy for Children and Learners,* partnership and collaboration are seen as the way forward for school improvement, with Foundation Partnerships of secondary schools having 'responsibility for school improvement across the partnership ... flexible sharing of resources across the partnership and freedom about where and what support services to access' (DfES, 2004: 42). Partnership is also at the heart of a further range of educational initiatives, including school federations, children's centres, extended schools, new school and college buildings and the new Diploma curriculum for 14–19-year-old learners.

The internal driver is the shared resolve between organisations to work together for the collective benefit of the learners within (usually) a cohesive geographical region. The rationale for partnership is based upon a commitment to working collaboratively in order to achieve shared goals for learners, and a belief in the benefit of the processes of social learning for staff. In this respect, Dhillon (2005: 215) envisages partnership as the 'social glue' for achieving shared goals, enabling organisations to achieve more collectively than could be achieved severally. As will be discussed later in this chapter, the 'glue' has to be strong if it is to withstand conflicting influences such as market forces and counter-strands of government policy which create a context of competition between educational providers.

Given the complexity of the contexts which both encourage and impede collaboration, there is a range of levels at which educational partners collaborate. Educational partners may seek and achieve varying degrees of collaboration, depending upon their contexts for partnership. A number of typologies for collaboration have been offered to enable further understanding and analysis of partnership activity (see Atkinson et al., 2007: 9–12 for examples). Woods et al. (2006: 59), based upon their evaluation of Diversity Pathfinder schools in England, suggest the following criteria for assessing the relative degrees of collaboration between partners:

- degree of strategic vision
- degree of group identity/area identity
- enduring organisational structure of collaboration
- significant professional collaborative activity

- penetration below senior management levels
- strategic innovation
- normalisation of collaboration as part of the culture.

As Woods et al. note, there is overlap between these criteria, but together they indicate collaborative leadership practice which potentially goes beyond single-organisation thinking. If the factors listed above were strongly present within an educational partnership, both the culture and the operation of the individual partner organisations would be strongly aligned to the strategic aims, identity and activity of the partnership as a whole. Staff at all levels of the constituent organisations would be involved in partnership activity, for their own development and that of the learners, and the organisational structures would be adapted to accommodate this. At its most extreme, there would be joint accountability for the outcomes for learners. Ainscow et al. (2006: 200), when investigating collaboration as a strategy for improving schools in challenging circumstances, note that the most effective management and leadership of partnerships 'involves forms of shared accountability, often orchestrated through written agreements and then strengthened through experiences of learning how to work together'.

These criteria are further explored within the context of 14–19 education in England in a typology which models partnership at the weak and strong ends of the collaborative spectrum, devised through the work of the Nuffield Review of 14–19 Education and Training (2007). A selection of the dimensions of activity presented in the Nuffield Review typology is set out in Figure 13.1.

Factors to note from this typology which characterise strong collaboration are:

- a unified and integrated approach to learning
- holistic programmes across all types of learning
- strong sense of local professionalism, leadership and shared knowledge of the area
- reflective, locally generated approach to capacity-building
- pooled local and national funding.

It can readily be seen that these factors align with those of Woods et al. (2006) in relation to partners having shared strategic vision and capacity for strategic innovation, together with a sense of group

Dimensions	Weakly collaborative	Strongly collaborative
Vision, purposes and underpinning principles	Vision statements and learner entitlements largely confined to the government agenda of providing 'alternative learning experiences'.	Vision statements and learner entitlements cover all aspects of 14–19 learning, including GCSEs and A levels, and attempt to make a more unified and integrated approach to learning.
Curriculum, qualifications and assessment	Development of vocational pathways and programmes from 14+ for some learners. A primary goal is motivating disaffected 14–16 year-olds, using college and work-based provision.	Developing holistic programmes across all types of learning with a focus on more flexible, applied and practical approaches for all learners from 14+.
Professionalism, pedagogy and leadership	Conformity to government agenda without a strong professionally informed sense of what is required at the local level. Limited leadership and CPD, with a dependence on nationally generated support and key local individuals.	Strong sense of local professionalism, leadership and a shared knowledge of the area: a more reflective, longer-term, planned and locally generated approach to capacity-building using pooled local and national funding and locally agreed tariffs for local programmes.

Figure 13.1   Characteristics of weakly and strongly collaborative 14–19 learning systems

Source: Selected and adapted from Nuffield Review of 14–19 Education and Training (2007) Issues Paper 2

identity which fosters professional collaborative activity at all levels of the organisation. Ainscow et al. (2006: 199) note that this level of professional activity may be based upon an in-school culture of learning among colleagues: 'where those within a school community have already experienced the benefits of inter-dependent learning, it is more likely that they will be motivated to learn from and with colleagues in other schools'.

Collaborative leadership, as discussed in this chapter, is enacted across organisations for a shared educational purpose. In its most strongly developed forms it involves collaboratively developed strategy and provision for learning and learners across the partnership, and collective accountability for learner outcomes.

What are the benefits of educational partnerships?

Wherever partnership is discussed, there is general agreement on its principal benefits, for the organisation, for staff and for learners. As Arnold (2006: i–ii) notes in a review of federations, collegiates and partnerships between schools:

- Partnership is a structured way for schools to learn from one another and to share best practice.
- It gives the opportunity for collective planning, with the strengths of each constituent school knowing no boundaries.
- It makes possible 'individual learning pathways', through which a student's needs and aspirations can be met by drawing upon a wide range of expertise and specialisms.
- It allows a cost-effective and coherent curriculum, increasing the opportunity to fulfil individual students' needs.
- It creates joint staffing opportunities and wider career structures across the federation.
- It leads to improved senior and middle management.
- It has the advantage of economies of scale.
- It forms a basis for further partnerships with other providers, for example, 14–19, community services.

The benefits to the educational organisation can be seen in the rationale for the establishment of school federations: groups of two or more schools which formally agree to work together to 'raise standards, promote inclusion, find new ways of approaching teaching and learning and build capacity between schools in a coherent manner' (Lindsay et al., 2007: 5). A 'hard' federation involves structural changes in leadership and management, including in many cases joint senior leadership and governance. Different types of federation – including 'soft' looser federations – enable schools to undertake a range of degrees of collaboration for a variety of purposes according to their needs and priorities. A study of federated schools undertaken by Lindsay et al. (2007) indicates a likely positive impact upon pupil achievement, through the sharing of good practice among staff, leading to a higher level of 'collective intelligence'. The benefit of working in collaboration rather than in competition is seen in terms of support, especially for weaker schools within a federation, and in economies of scale, for example in relation to staff development.

The benefits for staff are also reported by Ainscow et al. (2006) who investigated the benefits of collaboration among schools facing challenging circumstances. Ainscow and his colleagues consider that schools working together are able to solve problems together, through sharing resources, including staffing, and through mutual support which includes working together on responses to negative circumstances. Interaction between staff from different schools serves also to raise staff expectations of learners, and to develop strategies for addressing the needs of vulnerable young people. Through groups of schools working together to plan and provide curriculum, an arrangement which often includes local colleges, the curriculum offer to learners can be considerably increased.

Similar benefits to staff are apparent in engagement with professional learning communities, which may operate within individual organizations, but may also extend beyond them. The Networked Learning Communities programme, for example, set up by the National College for School Leadership in England, enables teachers to engage in 'joint work founded upon learning principles that enables effective practice to be developed and tested within context through collaboration between institutions' (Jackson and Temperley, 2007: 46). The programme works upon the principle that each organisation on its own cannot provide adequate professional learning opportunities for its staff in a knowledge-rich world, and that purposeful collaboration between adult learners is more beneficial than competition (Jackson and Temperley, 2007). Ainscow et al. (2006) note that where competition within a region is seen as a limiting factor, it appears that successful collaboratives can be established between schools from different regions.

The advantage of partnership for learners is explored in the three studies of provision for 14–19-year-old learners in England, referred to in the 'Research context' section above and reported collectively in Briggs (2008). Leaders interviewed across the three research projects espouse the value that partnership work is undertaken for the benefit of the learners, both collectively and individually. Collective benefit for learners is seen in terms of raising the levels of education, aspiration and ultimately employment across a geographical region. The benefit to learners – and the attendant benefit to the local region – is apparent as the 'social glue' which keeps the partnership on track despite the difficulties of partnership working. The synthesis of findings from these projects concerning benefits to learners is presented as Figure 13.2.

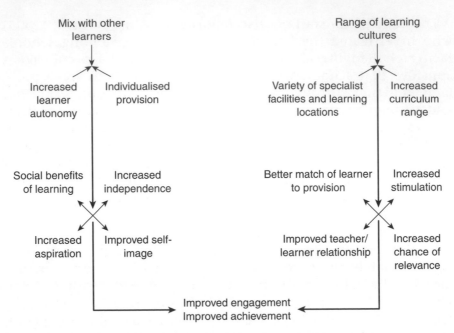

Figure 13.2   Potential benefits for learners of partnership provision

In the contexts investigated, learning opportunities are offered, or are planned to be offered, to 14–19 learners across a range of locations and facilities within a region. The potential advantages for learners of more specialised individual programmes, which give them access to new learning contexts and a different curriculum range, are seen in terms of increased relevance of learning to learners, improved relationship with teachers and higher levels of aspiration. These more favourable conditions for learning, accessible through partnership, can improve students' engagement with education and ultimately increase their levels of achievement. The three research studies are of partnerships largely at an early stage of development, available only to some learners in relation to specific subjects or levels of learning. These partnerships are at the stage of 'weak collaboration' described in Figure 13.1. Nevertheless, the actual and potential benefits experienced by learners and envisaged by leaders correlate with the findings of Arnold (2006) and Ainscow et al. (2006) above, as being the benefits of partnership collaboration. A further summary of the benefits of inter-school collaboration for schools, staff and pupils can be found in Atkinson et al. (2007: 72–3).

What are the tensions inherent in partnership working?

Partnership success comes at a cost. It involves resolving issues of resource and finance, handling logistics of staff development, staffing, timetabling and transport, and most significantly it involves partners in re-examining aspects of leadership, responsibility, ownership, equity and accountability. It involves taking risks which may affect the learning lives of significant numbers of people. Arnold (2006), reporting on the DfES conference 'School-to-School Collaboration for Transformation' in 2003, notes comments from the delegates which include:

Federations are about democracy but also delivery and sacrifice.

The key question is how you can have an equal partnership (rather than a dependency relationship) between schools which is fundamentally structured on inequality.

To take the notion of 'sacrifice' further, Lumby and Morrison (2006) propose that partnership is both an expression of, and an accommodation of, conflict. Leaders are involved in a choice process which involves players considering 'what their gain or advantage might be, if gaining it would rob other players of the reward, or whether a different co-operative strategy will offer the same or greater gain to all players' (Lumby and Morrison, 2006: 335). In England, government policy dictates that schools and colleges must achieve well in terms of inspection, examination results, league tables and effective use of funding: currently all these factors present constraints to many kinds of partnership working, impeding the goal of 'greater gain to all players'. Schools, colleges and universities exist in a competitive market environment where the strengths and achievements of individual organisations may be seen as assets for competition rather than as resource to be shared. Furthermore, as Styles et al. (2007) observe, there is currently no equitable, sustainable funding system to support partnership provision for young people. Government policy mechanisms serve to drive institutional self-interest (Nuffield Review of 14–19 Education and Training, 2007: 5).

Between partners, differing organisational cultures and conflicting agendas for partnership working can also act as stumbling blocks. As Connolly and James (2006: 80) note, 'expressions of professionalism vary across the educational sector', even within a single organisation teachers and leaders may espouse different values and interpretations of what makes 'good education,' and the context for collaboration may change during the life of the partnership, shifting the balance of activity. Studies of partnership working (for example, Ainscow et al., 2006; Atkinson et al., 2007) emphasise that since partnership working involves institutional and personal risk-taking, high levels of trust are needed for effective collaboration, especially where there are perceived to be weaker and stronger partners. A partnership which is newly convened in response to a recent government initiative may simply not have the time to reconcile issues and differences and establish trust within the lifetime of the initiative. The partnerships for 14–19 education in England, which bring together schools, colleges, training providers and a range of other agencies, have had to deal with a historical mismatch of mutual perceptions, understandings and values across the partners, as well as differential allocation of funding and public acknowledgement of their work. Partners interviewed in the three projects reported here, and in Briggs (2008), spoke of 'having to wash dirty linen' in the public arena of partnership meetings, in order to establish a better informed perception of each other's strengths, capabilities and value base. Figure 13.3 models the tensions, barriers and ambiguities which are evident in these 14–19 partnerships; these factors correlate well with those reported in other analyses of partnership working.

It is evident from a number of studies that two main causes of tensions, barriers and ambiguities are contradictory government policies (see, for example, Rodger et al., 2003) and single-institution models of strategy and operation (Hayward et al., 2006). These key factors are strongly evident in the three studies reported here, and are shown as inward-pointing arrows: contextual factors which can impede effective partnership working. Furthermore, schools, colleges, training providers and youth service providers have historically different cultures, arising out of their differing purposes and agendas. They may have misconceptions about the value base of each other's culture and purpose, which can impede partnership working; this is especially evident when difficulties of operation are encountered before mutual trust has been established. These further contextual factors – differing cultures and multiple agendas between partners – have to be reconciled before effective collaboration can take place.

The outward-pointing arrows in Figure 13.3 represent a range of issues which collaboration in partnerships may provoke or intensify. Each issue presents a significant challenge to partners, both

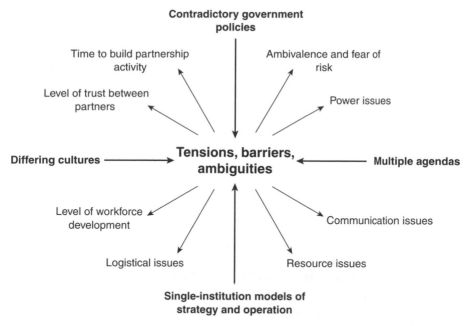

Figure 13.3 Tensions, barriers and ambiguities presented by collaborative leadership

individually and collectively. For example, the larger, more successful or more assertively led organisations within the partnership may be perceived as powerful: how is this to be reconciled with equitable partnership working? Where organisations are differentially resourced, and funding streams for partnership working are temporary or unclear, how is resource to be 'shared?' How can effective communication be established across a range of people at strategic and operational level across a number of separate types of institution? Is the collective workforce ready for collaborative working, involving different ways of learning? What logistical restructuring of curriculum, timetable, transport and student tracking systems is needed? Has enough time been spent establishing partnership understanding before partners have to act collectively, trusting each other's actions? It is little wonder that 'ambivalence and fear of risk' is reported by organisation leaders as an impediment to collaborative working. In partnerships, leadership tensions arise out of conflicting goals and unacceptable levels of risk for the individual organisations, and single-organisation lines of accountability and organisational structures impede the growth of joint-organisation ones.

These observations are similar to those noted by Rudd et al. (2004), where in partnership between education providers there was a fear of the unknown among staff required to work in new ways and open to perceived 'scrutiny' by others. The issues become intensified at operational level, where department leaders, teachers and trainers may not have time to establish mutual trust before they engage in collaborative work: indeed they may rarely meet. They may have little understanding of the partnership itself, the operational culture and goals of partners or the learning and teaching practices adopted by other partners. Communication may be difficult, and the logistical issues of placing, tracking and caring for students across multiple providers may be too difficult to manage. Multiple 'layers' of leadership across partnerships need to be understood, accommodated and nurtured. As Rodger et al. (2003: 61) comment: 'It has not always been recognised that partnership development, which involves cultural change and "changing hearts and minds", is a long term process. Everyone is at a different starting point and some are more able to deal with the practicalities and the politics than others'. The barriers to collaborative working are considerable, due to the competitive climate which exists between educational providers, fear of change and risk-taking, and the difficulty of establishing mutual understanding and trust within the necessary timeframe. Allegiance to a single organisation may of necessity be stronger than commitment to partnership. The model can be applied more broadly to collaborative leadership activity beyond the English 14–19 context: while the details of organisations and policies may differ, the fundamental issues of trust, power, communication and logistics remain.

New models of leadership?

Given the contexts discussed above, how can collaborative leadership succeed? There are clear messages from the research-based literature discussed in this chapter, which are applicable across a range of educational leadership contexts. Strong partnerships are not accidental and they do not arise out of goodwill or ad hoc projects (Watson and Fullan, 1992). Effective partnerships require new structures and activities, and involve each institution in re-thinking how it operates, as well as how it might work in partnership (Stoll et al., 2006). Successful leadership and management of partnerships involve shared accountability, strengthened through experiences of learning to work together. The leadership skills needed for collaborative leadership across schools are often apparent in senior leaders who have already established collaborative management arrangements within their own schools (Ainscow et al., 2006). In effective partnerships, stakeholders have a strong sense of ownership of the partnership. This involves an inclusive approach to decision-making, based upon trust, honesty and openness between the partners, together with a realistic acknowledgement of their individual strengths and weaknesses (Rudd et al., 2004). Partnerships exist which have gone beyond the notion of common curricula and shared resources, and have argued for common accountability in terms both of inspection and performance data (Arnold, 2006).

The findings outlined above suggest a potential for strongly collaborative, democratic leadership, dependent upon strength of partnership purpose, structures and systems, combined with an ethos of equity and inclusiveness among partner leaders which can accommodate both mutual and joint accountability. Figure 13.4 combines issues indicated above with the contextual factors discussed earlier in this chapter, to explore some of the aspects of collaborative leadership. Figure 13.4 proposes that a necessary starting-point for collaborative leadership is where government policy, and its associated resource, creates conditions for collective accountability and responsibility. Collaborative leadership could be of any kind of educational partnership: the English examples given in this chapter of federations, school improvement partnerships and 14–19 collaboration are simply a starting point. Organisational factors which are beneficial to collaboration are those which in a number of ways enable the partner institutions to 'mesh' together: a perception of mutual benefit to each organisation and its learners, a willingness to understand different cultures and purposes, and to accommodate difference; a preparedness to change and to learn together for mutual benefit.

Factors relating particularly to leaders and staff are also those of mutual accommodation: a focus on common purpose – in essence, successful, inclusive conditions for learning and teaching – which enables partners at all levels of the organisation to work in mutual trust. Trust extends to accepting the leadership of others who may be situated in partner organisations and to sharing expertise about learning and the contexts which support it. This implies that both leadership influence and 'ownership' of expertise are agreed to be distributed across the partners. These factors, and others which underpin them, create conditions for collective responsiveness and

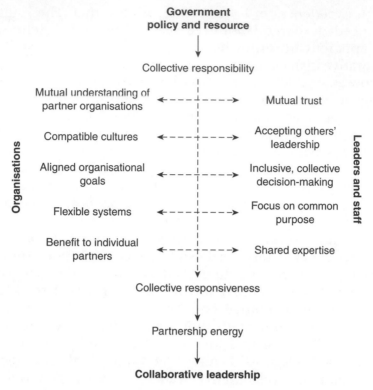

Figure 13.4   Beneficial conditions for collaborative leadership

inclusive, collective decision-making to achieve aligned organisational goals. The partnership energy, which is robustly evident in some of the partnerships investigated, can then more readily be translated into collective achievement for learners, brought about through collaborative leadership.

However, the issues identified at the beginning of this chapter still remain. Single institutional models of leadership are analysed, proposed and espoused because largely that is what exists. Current English government educational policy, however strongly it is based upon partnership, is largely enacted through funding to, and accountability of, single organisations. The benefits for learners of collaboration between providers are evident. At an individual local partnership level, where there is a clear focus on particular learner needs or a specific curriculum offer, collaboration can be strong, collective partnership energy and great and effective outcomes for learners can be achieved. But single-institution models of leadership and small-scale local partnerships do not fit the cultures and practices needed within large-scale systems of collaborative leadership, such as those envisaged in Figure 13.5.

Dimensions	Weakly collaborative	Strongly collaborative
Leadership and accountability	Focus is on the single organisation and its lines of accountability to central government, community and learners. Collaboration is undertaken 'outwards' from the organisation to improve response to these stakeholders.	Focus is on mutual accountability to partners and joint accountability to central government for learners across the locality and across a broad range of provision. Strong sense of joint leadership at all levels of the organisations, based on shared knowledge: a collective, reflective, locally generated approach to capacity-building.

Figure 13.5   Weakly and strongly collaborative leadership

Figure 13.5 takes the final row of the typology from Figure 13.1 and amplifies it for weakly and strongly collaborative leadership. Strong collaborative leadership is based upon both mutual accountability to partners and joint accountability to central government and to the learners. It involves leaders at different levels of the organisation, who work together to provide and support joint programmes of education and training. Leaders and staff draw on collective knowledge to seek mutual responses to a wide range of learner needs.

Collaborative leadership is therefore more multifaceted than single-organisation leadership. In operation, this web of leadership resembles a neural network, where leadership energy sparks and flows among participants in the partnership, where at any time one leader or cluster of leaders may move the partnership forward, while others are less active. The energy for the network is generated both externally, driven by appropriate policy frameworks, and internally, driven by the needs of the local economy and shared knowledge about local learners. Collaborative leaders learn to be dominant in the partnership where their energy and expertise is needed, but also co-operative and alert to the common purpose of the partnership and the leadership of others. Above all, mutual trust is needed, built over a length of time and upon mutually successful experience of working together.

Currently, we have few models of collaborative leadership in operation: the examples discussed in this chapter are drawn from local and regional responses to specific policy initiatives. However, particularly among senior leaders who are involved in substantial partnership working, there is a growing awareness of the distinctiveness of leadership in such contexts, and a consciousness that their previous understanding of the purposes and practice of leadership may not 'fit' the newly developing situation. There is the difficulty that collaborative leadership is not necessarily generic: leadership within a school federation may more closely resemble single-organisation leadership than leadership within a 14–19 partnership. Partnerships which focus upon the sharing and development of staff knowledge and expertise may need different types of collaborative leadership strategies from those which focus upon ways of meeting the multiple needs of very young children.

Exploring the democratic and facilitative styles of leadership which are needed within partnerships may enable us better to respond to the complexities of single-organisation leadership. The tensions and ambiguities discussed in this chapter, as well as the favourable conditions for collaborative leadership, may illuminate our understanding of leading partnership within, and outwards from, a single organisation. Leadership as a whole may be changing, in response to internal and external contexts of collaboration. In a report prepared for the Department for Education and Skills in 2003, success in collaborative educational practice was attributed to the partners' conscious efforts to achieve equity and commonality, which 'contrasts with the hierarchical and positional power-based roles and relationships so often in evidence' (DfES, 2003: 45). If single-organisation leadership is sometimes seen in terms of hierarchy, power and position, then collaborative leadership offers a fundamental conceptual shift to a focus upon equity, mutuality and shared educational purpose.

Acknowledgements

The work of the following research teams is gratefully acknowledged.

The baseline study for 14–19 education in England: Stephen Gorard, Jacky Lumby, Ann Briggs, Marlene Morrison, Ian Hall, Felix Maringe, Beng Huat See, Robina Shaheen and Susannah Wright. Universities of Birmingham, Southampton, Newcastle and Oxford Brookes.

Leading partnerships for 14–19 education: Ann Briggs, Chris Falzon, Ian Hall, David Mercer, Fay Smith, Trevor Swann: Newcastle University.

Interim and final evaluations of the Flexible Curriculum Programme (FCP) in Tyne and Wear: Ian Hall, Ann Briggs, Jill Clark, Colleen Cummings, Ulrike Thomas: Newcastle University.

References

Ainscow, M., Muijs, D. and West, M. (2006) 'Collaboration as a strategy for improving schools in challenging circumstances', *Improving Schools*, 9(3): 192–202.

Arnold, R. (2006) *Schools in Collaboration: Federations, Collegiates and Partnerships*. Coventry: EMIE.

Atkinson, M., Springate, I., Johnson, F. and Halsey, K. (2007) *Inter-school Collaboration: A Literature Review*. Slough: National Foundation for Educational Research.

Audit Commission (1998) *A Fruitful Partnership: Effective Partnership Working*. London: Audit Commission.

Briggs, A.R.J. (2008) 'Educational leaders as partners: new models of leadership?', presentation to the conference of the Commonwealth Council for Educational Administration and Management, Durban, September.

Briggs, A.R.J., Hall, I., Mercer, D., Smith, F., Swann, T. and Falzon, C. (2007) *Leading Partnerships for 14–19 Educational Provision*. Lancaster: Centre for Excellence in Leadership.

Clark, J., Thomas, U., Cummings, C., Briggs, A.R.J. and Hall, I. (2008) *Flexible Curriculum Programme for 14–19 Education*. Newcastle upon Tyne: Research Centre for Learning and Teaching, Newcastle University.

Connolly, M. and James, C. (2006) 'Collaboration for school improvement', *Educational Management and Administration*, 34(1): 69–87.

Department for Education and Employment (DfEE) (1999) *Learning to Succeed*. London: HMSO.

Department for Education and Skills (DfES) (2001) *Schools Achieving Success*. London: HMSO.

Department for Education and Skills (DfES) (2003) *Collaboration: Learning Partnerships and Stakeholders, a Guide*. London: HMSO.

Department for Education and Skills (DfES) (2004) *Five Year Strategy for Children and Learners*. London: HMSO.

Dhillon, J. (2005) 'The rhetoric and reality of partnership working', *Journal of Further and Higher Education*, 29(3): 211–19.

Hall, I. and Briggs, A.R.J. (2007) *14–19 FCP2 Interim Evaluation Report*. Gateshead: Gateshead Borough Council.

Hayward, G., Hodgson, A., Johnson, J., Oancea, A., Pring, R., Spours, K., Wilde, S. and Wright, S. (2006) *The Nuffield Review of 14–19 Education and Training: Annual Report 2005/06*. London: Nuffield Foundation.

Gorard, S., Lumby, J., Briggs, A.R.J., Morrison, M., Hall, I., Maringe, F., See, B.H., Shaheen, R. and Wright, S. (2009) *14–19 Reforms: QCA Centre Research Study, Commentary on the Baseline of Evidence 2007–2008*. London: Qualifications and Curriculum Authority.

Jackson, D. and Temperley, J. (2007) 'From professional learning community to networked learning community', in L. Stoll and K. Seashore Louis (eds), *Professional Learning Communities: Divergence, Depth and Dilemmas*. Maidenhead: McGraw-Hill International.

Lindsay, G., Muijs, D., Harris, A., Chapman, C., Arweck, E. and Goodall, J. (2007) *Schools Federations Pilot Study 2003–2007*. London: DCSF.

Lumby, J. and Morrison, M. (2006) 'Partnership, conflict and gaming', *Journal of Education Policy*, 21(3): 323–41.

Nuffield Review of 14–19 Education and Training (2007) *Issues Paper 2, 14–19 Partnerships: From Weakly Collaborative Arrangement to Strongly Collaborative Local Learning Systems*. Accessed at www.nuffield14–19review.org.uk

Powell, M. and Dowling, B. (2006) 'New Labour's partnerships: comparing conceptual models with existing forms', *Social Policy and Society*, 5: 305–14.

Rodger, J., Cowen, G., and Brass, J. (2003) *National Evaluation of Learning Partnerships: Final Report*. Nottingham: DfES, York Consulting Ltd.

Rudd, P., Lines, A., Schagen, S., Smith, R. and Reakes, A. (2004) *Partnership Approaches to Sharing Best Practice*. No. 1-903880-64-5. Coventry: National Foundation for Educational Research.

Stoll, L., Bolam, R., McMahon, A., Wallace, M. and Thomas, S. (2006) 'Professional learning communities: a review of the literature', *Journal of Educational Change*, 7: 221–58.

Stuart, M. (2002) *Collaborating for Change? Managing Widening Participation in Further and Higher Education*. Leicester: NIACE.

Styles, B., Fletcher, M. and Valentine, R. (2007) *Implementing 14–19 Provision: A Focus on Schools*. London: Learning and Skills Network.

Watson, N. and Fullan, M. (1992) 'Beyond school district–university partnerships', in M. Fullan and A. Hargreaves (eds), *Teacher Development and Educational Change*. Lewes: Falmer Press.

CHAPTER 14

Leadership and Educational Networks

Andrew Townsend

Introduction

This chapter explores leadership issues relating to the theories and practices associated with networks and networking in educational settings. Networks, it would appear, are a common phenomenon in education and the extent of this interest was illustrated in a survey of 5253 teachers (across the age ranges from elementary to high school) in the USA conducted by the National Center for Education Statistics. As many as 62 per cent of respondents reported that they had been engaged in networking with other teachers from outside their own school, a surprisingly high number when only slightly more, 69 per cent, reported that they had collaborated with colleagues from within their own institution (Parsad et al., 2001).

The notion of networks in education has been interpreted in a variety of different ways. To this end Hite et al. (2005) have identified six different uses for the term, of which three overarching applications of the term are emphasised here. The first interpretation of network refers to social network analysis. This is an approach which has been used to examine the complex nature of relationships between people in communities, businesses or even countries (Clyde Mitchell, 1969). In this context the 'term network is used to describe the observable pattern of social relationships among individual units of analysis' (Abercrombie et al., 2000). The second use, the network society, a term coined by van Dick (see, for example, 2006) and used extensively by Castells (see, for example, 2000), refers to societies in which the principal means for the transfer of information is electronically, and use of the term 'network' which has become especially significant with the invention and rapid growth of the Internet. The final use of the term refers to the creation of networks as development strategies. In this use of the term, networks are deliberately created to influence organisational management and development, a definition of which has been provided by O'Toole:

> Networks are emergent phenomena that occur when organizations or individuals begin to embrace a collaborative process, engage in joint decision making and begin to act as a coherent entity. When this occurs, a network has emerged. These new inter-organizational forms are referred to as coalitions, alliances, strategic alliance networks, consortia and partnerships. (O'Toole, 1997: 443)

Each of these uses of the term 'networks' has its own particular features but they all have aspects in common all sharing, in some way, a concern for the ways in which people interact. They have at their heart a fluidity which is intended to reflect the complexity and changing nature of social relationships in society, and in social settings such as schools and other educational organisations. They are also, in some way, interested in the influence that people have on each other derived from these relationships. The actual use of networks in education has taken a number of forms and these are explored in the following section.

The nature of educational networks

These differing conceptions of networks provide alternate perspectives on social interactions and the way in which they can be understood, enhanced and developed through networks. There have, accordingly, been a number of studies using social network methodology to research relationships associated with educational settings, but there have also been many examples of attempts to construct and develop networks in education, and to study their effects where they have been introduced.

Networks are therefore seen not only as a perspective on the social, specifically interactional, dimensions of education, but also as an approach for achieving change. These networks have different features, one being focused on networks of individuals, while the other achieves its aim through formal arrangements between organisations, in doing so providing the individuals in those organisations with the opportunity to network. A common feature of these networks, however, is a principle of voluntarism (Day and Townsend, 2009) a principle related, by Engelstad and Gustavsen (1993: 220), with concepts of ownership, collaboration and complementarity of interests: 'Network is understood to be a relationship between organizations which is not based on formal ownership but on (voluntary) collaboration and complementarity'.

Thus networks are seen as a means by which people can come together out of choice. The voluntary nature of networks and their association with ownership, are believed to satisfy a human need for interdependence, the opportunities for which have been eroded through an increasingly independent society (Posch, 1994), and which, in doing so, provide a mechanism for enhancing the agency of network participants.

> Let's argue for a moment ... that the processes and structures in social networks arise fundamentally from the 'necessity' of interdependence. Individuals in social networks are in multiple interdependent relationships with others, their origins vary depending on the network ... [Networks as development strategies] arise from the actions of individuals within the network, particularly school leaders. They therefore originate in the agency, or actions, of people who are interested in actively collaborating. (Hadfield, 2005: 177)

And so networks are based around the aspirations and actions of the individual members. This suggests something of the duality akin to structuration (Giddens, 1984; Parker, 2000); the network only exists through the actions of individual members, while the actions of those individuals are influenced by the network of which they are a part. In other words the influence of the network can be observed in participants' actions, while the common collective or collaborative features of those actions enact the network. This participant/organisation interaction in these networks is perceived as providing an opportunity for the construction and sharing of new practices which evolve from the aspirations of participants and through the mechanisms of networks, reducing reliance on interventions from outside the organisation(s) (Lieberman, 2000), for example, by consultants.

By using networks as the means of organizing and managing the work reform process, organizations could support each other in developing and maintaining their own change and local work reform effort rather than relying primarily on outside experts. Significant innovations could be fostered, for example, through collaboration between different organizations in the same ... geographical area learning ... from each other. (Engelstad and Gustavsen, 1993: 220)

A feature of these networks is, therefore, that they provide a means by which externally imposed or advocated change can not only be interrogated in local contexts but can be replaced by internally, collaboratively, driven change, associated with the common interests and actions of individuals whose work and lives are situated in the very contexts to be changed. In this model the individuality of members is not seen as a threat to the coherence of the network as a whole. Rather, relationships in these networks are sufficiently loose to make an attribute of this diversity, by fostering a multiple perspective approach to under-standing and changing those contexts.

The network is a vehicle for reconsideration of practice from many vantage points centering around a hub of common values supporting learner-centered practice. This makes connections between like-minded practitioners both possible and mutually profitable ... it expands the possibilities for the kinds of conver-sations that practitioners need to have if teaching, assessment and school structure are to be organized for school success. (Darling-Hammond, et al., 1995: 268)

The relationships created as a part of these networks, the dialogue which results, and the multiple perspectives of members all com-bine to provide a process through which, it is believed, success can be both defined and achieved. Through this process practitioners are believed to have engaged in a process of knowledge construc-tion, as opposed to the consumption of knowledge acquired from others (Little, 1993). This knowledge, however, is not constructed in isolation, and these networks are also seen as providing the opportunity to interrogate context-free imposed practices with the reality of the context in which they are being applied.

The movement organisations discussed here are more 'bottom up' in the sense that they are attempting to change schools by

changing teachers' thinking, instructional practices and professional roles, but also working at other levels to provide a complementary context of policy documents assessments, texts and
instructional materials. (Pennell and Firestone, 1996: 48–9)

This quote also suggests that these networks can facilitate bottom-
up change, although the principles of voluntarism, ownership and
participation emphasised above perhaps suggests that they would
be better seen as 'flat' or equitably participatory arrangements in
which influence derived from appointed position is replaced with
influence through dialogue and negotiation.

The general discussion of networking above provides a picture of
an approach which is believed to promise a great deal, perhaps
more than could reasonably be universally expected of any form of
intervention, let alone such a complex intervention in such complex contexts. It is unsurprising, then, that there are also caution-
ary tales around these networks. One issue, for example, refers to
the scope of networking, suggesting that in some cases the breadth
of participation of staff in schools that are members of networks
has been limited (Earl et al., 2006). Nevertheless networks are
believed to have a great deal of potential as approaches to not only
intervene and achieve change, but also to organise institutional
and inter-institutional practices in ways which encourage participant ownership, collaboration and the creation of supportive
communities. This form of organisation and interaction has implications for how leadership is understood and enacted, the issues of
which are explored in the following section.

The intersection of networks and leadership

We now need to specifically explore leadership issues relating to
educational networks. Indeed some have argued that theories and
practices of leadership would have greater sensitivity to contextual
factors were they take account of the complex networked nature of
organisations (Osborn et al., 2002). Three issues are explored here.
The first concerns the distributed view of leadership which is
encouraged by taking a networked perspective of organisations;
the second explores how those features of networks can then be
applied through the intentional formation of networks; and the
section concludes with an exploration of the role of leadership in
networks.

Networks, influence and the distribution of leadership

One use of the term 'network' refers to the pattern of relationships in social settings, and attempts at describing and researching those relationships. This research approach is believed to enhance our understanding of organisations and how leadership relates to them (Hite et al., 2005). This pattern of relationships not only describes the interactions of individuals in these social settings but also describes a web through which these individuals influence each other's practice. This web of influence operates at a personal level with members of the social context in question both leading, and following, each other (Meindl, 1995), a feature of networks noted by Mullen and Kochan in their study of the West Alabama Learning Coalition (2000). While this can be influenced by the position that these individuals hold, this web of influence is reciprocal as these influences are a product of the social context of work places, and the interpersonal relationships which define that context. Thus, in a networked view, influence is not exclusively limited to appointed leadership positions.

Viewing organisations as extended networks of social relationships challenges a centralised, arguably oversimplified view of leadership (McElroy and Shrader, 1986; Mehra et al., 2006). A networked view suggests that influences on individuals are spread throughout the wider setting of the organisation in question and do not solely arise purely from the structures of appointed leadership positions. Indeed while the management structure of organisations creates very close relationships between groups of people, these relationships (sometimes termed strong ties) are believed to be less effective at encouraging innovation (although better at ensuring the ongoing operation of the organisation) than the more flexible relationships (loose, or weak ties) associated with a wider network of contacts (Granovetter, 1973).

One perspective on networks and leadership concerns the distribution of influence connected with the range of relationships associated with the social settings of education. Bearing in mind the implications that networks provide a means for spreading of influence, distributing knowledge and sharing practice, it is perhaps unsurprising that some have attempted to establish networks to reap these perceived benefits. This creation of networks for strategic purposes is explored in the following subsection.

The strategic creation of networks

This recognition of the nature of the networks in social settings (and in particular organisations) also provides a potential strategy for the sharing of leadership. In other words the social settings of education and the leadership influence in them can be illuminated, and influenced by taking a networked perspective, but networks can also be intentionally adopted as an intervention strategy, examples of which are given later in this chapter.

These networks have been established to provide a 'bottom-up' or 'organic' stimulus for change (Mullen and Kochan, 2000) in contrast to the 'top-down' nature of central government derived policies. The creation of networks is believed to provide the opportunity for participants to learn from their network of relationships (Kubiak and Bertram, 2005). This was emphasised in a survey of network members in which the opportunity to share and exchange experiences and practice were seen by participants as the most beneficial features of that network (Veugelers and Zijlstra, 2002) a feature of educational networks also identified by Liberman and Grolnik (1996) who studied 16 educational networks, all in the USA. This was, however, not the only benefit or characteristic of the networks studied and the authors identified six main features, which are summarised below.

- Networks provide opportunities for practitioners to articulate and share tacit knowledge of their work.
- Networks are flexible; they allow structures to change and develop according to the purposes of participants. This is in contrast to bureaucratic systems which are believed to be inflexible.
- The networks studied were all concerned with practitioner inquiry. This emphasised participation was seen as being especially significant as: 'it gives voice to those who have usually been the recipients of the agendas of others' (Lieberman and Grolnick, 1996: 40).
- Networks expanded informal and formal leadership roles, providing greater opportunities for participants to engage in a wider range of leadership activities.
- Networks were believed to support the development of professional communities, challenging existing school structures which tend to encourage separation of staff rather than collaboration.
- The networks studied changed the ways in which practitioners work together, encouraging greater collaboration over new developments (adapted from Lieberman and Grolnick, 1996: 39–42).

These networks, therefore, through encouraging the kind of dialogue suggested above, are believed to encourage collaboration, emphasising inquiry and enhancing participant voices. In doing so they are believed to provide opportunities for exposing and articulating tacit knowledge. The nature of these networks also lends itself to building upon formal leadership roles by establishing informal opportunities for leadership. However, the dispersed, or distributed qualities of networks also provide a challenge for leadership, explored in the following subsection.

Leading networks, advocacy versus influence

This issue builds on the last in that it concerns a perceived tension between appointed leadership positions in schools and the 'bottom-up' aspirations of networks applied as intervention strategies (Pennell and Firestone, 1996). In one respect this challenge stems from the contradiction of educational systems which are highly centralised with linear systems of influence and accountability, but which are based upon a distributed network of education professionals who implement practices to support student learning in settings based mainly around the management of relationships. This could be seen as a tension between the common aspects of accountability measures with the diversity inherent in a distributed system.

One of the aspirations for these networks is that they are based around participants' perceptions, beliefs and aspirations; these may not necessarily align with those of their colleagues or their institutions and hence create a tension for leaders whose institutions are members of networks. A second concern is related to the pace and judgement of productivity associated with networks. Bringing together networks in and through schools associates them directly with the performance management practices of education systems. The second facet of this tension, then, is the mediation of external judgements of performance with bottom-up definitions of quality.

There is, therefore, a concern with how leaders can enhance the work of the network, and the potential benefits for their colleagues and students, without excessively influencing it in ways which might compromise its bottom-up aspirations. Kubiac and Bertram (2005) have explored some of the actions of appointed school leaders in the networks of which their institutions have been a part. Despite some leaders characterising their role as one of remaining unobtrusive, other than providing verbal support, they suggest that there are a number of roles that these leaders take on in strategically co-ordinated networks as follows:

- establishing formal communication protocols between network groups that have developed some permanence and profile
- officially recognising the teacher roles that have emerged through management points for their work, status by management, budgetary control or increased training
- providing entitlements to represent the network to external bodies or at events
- requesting the development of two- to three-year plans so emerging groups become institutionalised
- providing release time for teachers to use their own discretion to decide when to work with colleagues in other school and for what reasons (Kubiak and Bertram, 2005: 9).

These activities seem to involve appointed leaders acting as an advocates of the work of the network and directly creating the opportunities for the collaborative relationship of their staff. While their role was not believed to be directly influential they were facilitators of the network, providing opportunities for others. This suggests that while there is a potential tension between appointed school leadership positions and the operation of networks, it is being mediated, here, through the explicit recognition and authorisation of the work of the network and its relationship with other practices in member institutions. In doing so the leaders in question authorise without instructing, support without excessively intervening and are essential components in the potential success of the network. The nature of networks, their application in education and the implications for conceptions of leadership are illustrated in the following section through a brief examination of educational networks.

Examples of educational networks

The National Writing Project

The first network to be explored here is the National Writing Project (NWP). This is a well-established national network (initiated in 1974) in the USA concerned with improving the writing skills of students through collaborative teacher development. The National Writing Project is founded on a number of principles as follows:

- Universities and schools are better able to improve students' learning if they work in partnership.

- Teachers are the key to educational reform.
- Teachers are the best teachers of other teachers.
- Writing deserves constant attention from kindergarten to the university.
- Exemplary teachers of writing are themselves writers (Lieberman and Wood, 2003: 8).

The writing dimension of this network is not only seen as the intended outcome (in enhancing the teaching of writing in schools) but is also used as a part of the process. Just as practitioner writing can be seen not only as an outcome of inquiry, but a part of the process (Holly, 1989) the writing of practitioners in the National Writing Project is a means by which participants interrogate their own practice and produce artefacts which, when shared with others, encourage the transfer of the outcomes of that inquiry process. This writing is not the only feature of this network which has a number of stages incorporating centralised and dispersed features (Wood and Lieberman, 2000). The stages of participation are as follows:

1. Teachers join the National Writing Project mainly by invitation, often resulting from the endorsement of a colleague or friend.
2. Having joined, the second stage is for teachers and site directors to attend centralised network events, termed the summer institutes. These are based around a mixture of conducting small-scale research projects, presenting self-identified best practices and writing, re-writing and sharing documents of relevance to the teaching of writing in school. Completion of the institute qualifies attendees as teacher consultants.
3. The next stage of the project is dispersed across participating universities which are termed sites. Network members, and especially teacher consultants, give presentations, provide seminars and run workshops for local teachers from one of almost 200 sites (NWP, 2007). This distributes the knowledge gained and practices developed through the programme involving another 15 teachers for every teacher who leaves the summer institute as an NWP consultant (Lieberman and Wood, 2003: 37).

Through this process, participants engage in leadership in a number of ways, as described by Wood and Lieberman:

Moreover, the Writing Project authorises teacher consultants to take leadership roles in their own schools and districts. Teachers we met exercise leadership in a variety of ways. Confident about their own expertise, they volunteer for school or district curriculum committees, give frequent professional development workshops, edit teacher publications, publish their own articles, present at professional conferences, play active roles in teacher associations, and so forth. As they exercise leadership, teacher consultants feel authorised to tailor NWP ideas to their own needs and purposes. (Wood and Lieberman, 2000: 270)

The first aspect of leadership in the National Writing Project concerns the development of teacher consultants. These consultants are individuals who, having attended the summer institute, then go on to 'lead' others through the same development that they have experienced. This establishes a role for networks in creating leadership opportunities for educators beyond their own organisation. There was an additional, indirect, result to this, in that having had this experience of leadership in a different setting, these consultants were encouraged to further develop their leadership roles in other areas of their work beyond that specifically related to the network. Studies of the National Writing Project, therefore, suggest a route for participants to develop leadership other than that normally associated with taking on formal appointed roles within their organisations. By providing an alternative based around a model of developing practices through inquiry and dialogue this both broadens the potential population of educators who might become leaders, and provides those who engage with enhanced sense of professionalism. This in turn might make it more likely that they would take on formally appointed leadership responsibilities in their schools. Finally, this network also provides different forms of leadership from those normally associated with appointed positions; in one sense this is informal in the influence derived from conducting and sharing the outcomes of inquiry; in another this is formal in the development of leadership positions concerned with the facilitation of others inquiry.

The Networked Learning Communities

While involvement in the NWP was based around personal recommendation and a resulting network of individuals, without necessarily formal relationships with their institutions, the second network to be explored here, the Networked Learning Communities, was based around groups of institutional networks. This was a national programme in the UK which operated from 2002 to 2006 and provided funding for three years for groups of six or more schools willing to form a network. While each of the networks funded was based around groups of institutions working together the programme itself was a form of network, providing a medium through which funded networks could communicate, and providing opportunities for bringing together all participants in common events, such as the annual conference. This multiple tiered nature was reflected in the 'levels of learning', the aspects of education which were intended to be influenced by this programme (and around which the effectiveness of each network was judged). An early version of these levels was as follows:

- pupil learning (a pedagogical focus)
- teacher learning (with professional learning communities as the goal)
- leadership learning (at all levels, within and between schools)
- organisational, or 'within school' learning
- school-to-school learning [network wide learning] (Jackson, 2002).

This was later extended to include another level of learning, namely network to network learning, reflecting this programme's nature as both a supporter of school network and a network in itself. This, ultimately, was a large programme which included 134 school networks, involving approximately 35,000 staff and over 675,000 pupils (NCSL, 2005). The arguments used in support of the Networked Learning Communities, in common with other networking literature, emphasised the potential of networks to offer flexible systems. This feature is contrasted, by the co-founder and director of the programme, with the perceived failure of inflexible bureaucratic systems in being able to cope with the rapid rate of change in education.

> In the past, most school systems have operated almost exclusively through individual units set within hierarchically designed structural forms – typically LEAs or School Districts. Such isolation may have been appropriate during times of stability, but during times of rapid and multiple change there is a need to 'tighten the loose coupling', to increase collaboration and to establish more fluid knowledge flow in order to foster responsive structures. Networks are a means of doing this ... (Jackson, 2002)

At the heart of this work was an aspiration to establish knowledge creating networks of schools which developed practices through an action research related inquiry programme (NCSL, 2002). It was intended that the programme would establish structures and process, within and between networks, that would allow both the creation and sharing of knowledge.

> Collaboration is a more powerful, more positive motivating force than competition. Networks are about schools working smarter together, rather than harder alone, to enhance learning at every level of the education system. Strong networks make it easier to create and share knowledge about what works in the classroom, to learn from each other's experiences, to find solutions to common problems. By working together in this way, networked schools are making professional practice visible and transferable. (NCSL, 2002: 3)

The reviews of network performance by the NCSL seem to suggest that these knowledge creating aspirations were successful, emphasised particularly in reference to the national school accountability measures in which schools participating in the Networked Learning Communities programme were believed to have improved at a faster rate than schools not participating in the programme (Crowe, 2006). In one sense this highlights a challenge for these networks, to maintain their 'bottom-up' aspirations, while adhering to the judgements of the national accountability mechanism. This programme was administered and supported by the National College for School Leadership in England and so it is no surprise that leadership was a significant consideration of these networks. As well as being one of the levels of learning identified above, these networks have been identified as relating to leadership in a number of ways. A selection of these, identified in case studies of Networked Learning Communities, are outlined below:

- These networks aspired to create opportunities for institutional and organisational development through networking. This was intended to be based around the aspirations and interests of all participants (most of whom were teachers). In order to enhance this participatory principle appointed leaders adopted roles as advocates and supporters of the principles of the network, but avoided direct intervention.
- Sensitivity to the influence associated with appointed leadership positions led some networks to set up separate inquiry groups

for senior leaders. The intention of these groups was that they would inquire about, reflect upon and develop their own practices in the same way as other network members, but in their case this was concerned with their leadership rather than pedagogical roles (although, of course, student learning was at the heart of their aspirations). However senior leader support was regarded as being an essential prerequisite for schools to make a success of being members of the network and hence by extension, of the network as a whole.

- These networks provided opportunities for participants to take up leadership roles associated with the network and different from most of those in members' schools. These included network-wide roles, such as network facilitator, research-related roles, for example the role of lead researcher, or school-based roles, such as inquiry group co-ordinator.

- The principle of inquiry and the communicative structures and systems of networks provided the means by which leadership could be both distributed across networks and reciprocated by network members. (Townsend, 2010)

This programme is significantly different to the National Writing Project; first, it was a short-term initiative; secondly, as noted above, it was based around organisational participation and, finally, while the NWP aspired to improve students' writing, the purpose of Networked Learning Communities programme was to encourage networking, leaving the actual focus and purpose to individual networks to decide.

Conclusions

Because leadership is dependent on interactions between people it is always, in some way, concerned with networks, whether explicitly or not. This seems to have a particular relevance in education as a result of the complex and varied nature of relationships in the large social settings of educational institutions. This is not to claim, however, that a networked view of leadership should be the only perspective that is adopted, rather that examining leadership from the perspective of social networks leadership can help illuminate the complexity of social settings such as those in education. In addition, seeing networks as one mechanism for enhancing leadership also encourages a recognition of the influence of others on the operation and development of the organisation in question. This view encourages institutions to be seen as being more than the teams into which they are commonly structured and instead asks about the looser relationships that exist within and beyond the institution. A networked view of leadership also asks to what extent, and in what ways, notions of leadership take account of the influence derived from relationships as well as from management systems and practices?

The consideration of networks as one of the principles for educational leadership should not been seen simply as a mechanism for appointed leaders to influence others. Rather a networked view of leadership encourages a recognition of the complexity of educational institutions and the influence that members of those institutions have on each other, which can be related, but not limited to, a product of any leadership position. One consideration for appointed leaders is the extent they are influenced by, and learn from, the relationships that they have with their colleagues, with external contacts, with students and with other members of the wider community of the institutions in which they work.

Finally, the adoption of networks as an intervention strategy can provide alternative and more varied forms of leadership development. Networks are believed to enhance the development of leaders for existing leadership roles but because they bring practitioners together in different settings and with different roles than in their original institutions, they can also provide the potential for alternative forms of leadership positions. This allows networks to attract a wider range of individuals to act as leaders, including those who might have had little or no interest in taking on formal, institutionally defined, roles, thus spreading participation in educational leadership and providing opportunities for a wider range of educators to learn from each other.

Further reading

Lieberman, A. and Wood, D.R. (2003) *Inside the National Writing Project, Connecting Network Learning and Classroom Teaching*. New York: Teachers College Press.

McLaughlin, C., Black-Hawkins, K., McIntyre, D. and Townsend, A. (2007) *Networking Practitioner Research*. London: Routledge.

Veugelers, W. and O'Hair, M.J. (eds) (2005) *Network Learning for Educational Change*. Milton Keynes: Open University Press.

References

Abercrombie, N., Hill, S. and Turner, B.S. (2000) *Dictionary of Sociology*. 4th edn. London: Penguin Reference.

Castells, M. (2000) *The Information Age: Economy, Society and Culture, Volume 1. The Rise of the Networked Society*. 2nd edn. London: Blackwell.

Clyde Mitchell, J. (1969) 'The concept and use of social networks', in J. Clyde Mitchell (ed.), *Social Networks in Urban Situations: Analyses of Personal Relationships in Central African Towns*. Manchester: Manchester University Press.

Crowe, V., with Noden, C. and Stott, A. (2006) *Evidence from Learning Networks*. Cranfield: Networked Learning Communities.

Darling-Hammond, L., Ancess, L.J. and Falk, B. (1995) *Authentic Assessment in Action*. New York: Teachers College Press.

Day, C. and Townsend, A. (2009) 'Practitioner action research: building and sustaining success through networked learning communities', in S. Noffke and B. Somekh (eds), *The Sage Handbook of Educational Action Research*. London: Sage.

Earl, L., Torrance, N. and Sutherland, S. (2006) 'Changing secondary schools is hard', in A. Harris and J.H. Chrispeels (eds), *Improving Schools and Educational Systsems: International Perspectives*. London: Routledge.

Engelstad, P.H. and Gustavsen, B. (1993) 'Swedish network development for implementing national work reform strategy', *Human Relations*, 46(2): 191–248.

Giddens, A. (1984) *The Constitution of Society*. Cambridge: Polity Press.

Granovetter, M.S. (1973) 'The strength of weak ties', *American Journal of Sociology*, 78: 1360–80.

Hadfield, M. (2005) 'From networking to school networks to 'networked' learning: the challenge for the Networked Learning Communities Programme', in W. Veugelers and M.J. O'Hair (eds), *Network Learning for Educational Change*. Milton Keynes: Open University Press.

Hite, J.M., Williams, E.J. and Baugh, S.C. (2005) 'Multiple networks of public school administrators: an analysis of network content and structure', *International Journal of Leadership in Education*, 8(2): 91–122.

Holly, M.L. (1989) 'Reflective writing and the spirit of inquiry', *Cambridge Journal of Education*, 19(1): 71–80.

Jackson, D. (2002) 'The creation of knowledge networks: collaborative enquiry for school and system improvement', CERI/OECD/DfES/QCA/ESRC Forum: 'Knowledge management in education and learning', Oxford, 18–19 March.

Kubiak, C. and Bertram, J. (2005) 'Network leadership's balancing act', *Forum*, 47(1): 8–11.

Lieberman, A. (2000) 'Networks as learning communities shaping the future of teacher development', *Journal of Teacher Education*, 51(3): 221–27.

Lieberman, A. and Grolnick, M. (1996) 'Networks and reform in American education', *Teachers College Record*, 98(1): 7–45.

Lieberman, A. and Wood, D.R. (2003) *Inside the National Writing Project: Connecting Network Learning and Classroom Teaching*. New York: Teachers College Press.

Little, J.W. (1993) 'Teachers' professional development in a climate of educational reform', *Educational Evaluation and Policy Analysis*, 15(2): 129–51.

McElroy, J.C. and Shrader, C.B. (1986) 'Attribution theories of leadership and network analysis', *Journal of Management*, 12(3): 351–62.

Mehra, A., Smith, B.R., Dixon, A.L. and Robertson, B. (2006) 'Distributed leadership in teams: the network of leadership perceptions and team performance', *Leadership Quarterly*, 17(3): 232–45.

Meindl, J.R. (1995) 'The romance of leadership as a follower-centric theory: a social constructionist approach', *Leadership Quarterly*, 6(3): 329–41.

Mullen, C.A. and Kochan, F.K. (2000) 'Creating a Collaborative Leadership Network: an organic view of change', *International Journal of Leadership in Education*, 3(3): 183–200.

NCSL (2002) *Why Networked Learning Communities?* Cranfield: Networked Learning Group.

NCSL (2005) *Networked Learning Communities: Learning about Learning Networks.* Cranfield: Networked Learning Communities.

NWP (2007) *Annual Report 2007.* Berkeley, CA: National Writing Project.

O'Toole, L.J. (1997) 'The implications for democracy in a networked democratic world', *Journal of Public Administration Research and Theory*, 7(3): 443–59.

Osborn, R.N., Hunt, J.G. and Jauch, L.R. (2002) 'Towards a contextual theory of leadership', *Leadership Quarterly*, 13(6): 797–37.

Parker, J. (2000) *Structuration.* Buckingham: Open University Press.

Parsad, B., Lewis, L., Farris, E. and Greene, B. (2001) *Teacher Preparation and Professional Development: 2000.* Washington: National Center for Education Statistics.

Pennell, J.R. and Firestone, W.A. (1996) 'Changing classroom practice through teacher networks: matching program features with teacher characteristics and circumstances', *Teachers College Record*, 98(1): 46–76.

Posch, P. (1994) 'Changes in the culture of teaching and learning and implications for action research', *Educational Action Research*, 2(2): 153–61.

Townsend, A. (2010) 'Educational Action Research Networks as Participatory Interventions', in Warwick Institute of Education, University of Warwick.

Van Dijk, J.A.G.M. (2006) *The Network Society: Social Aspects of New Media.* London: Sage.

Veugelers, W. and Zijlstra, H. (2002) 'What goes on in a network? some Dutch experiences', *International Journal of Leadership in Education*, 5(2): 163–74.

Wood, D.R. and Lieberman, A. (2000) 'Teachers as authors: the National Writing Project's approach to professional development', *International Journal of Leadership in Education*, 3(3): 255–73.

CHAPTER 15

Community and Leadership in Education[1]

Tracey Allen

1 Introduction

In recent years, key national and local initiatives have emerged throughout numerous international contexts towards stronger community orientation and leadership. This chapter is concerned with the rationale and implications involved in community-oriented leadership in educational contexts. As the moral imperative in educational leadership has developed (see Chapter 3), the notion that a leader's responsibility is solely for a single institution has become almost obsolete. The idea of system leadership and the pressure for sustainability in change has ensured that leaders are encouraged to look constantly at the impact of their actions and the influence of their institutions to ensure that they extend, at the very least, into the local community and preferably further afield. It is important therefore to consider whether there are particular features of educational leadership which are necessary for success in these community contexts.

The chapter begins with a brief overview of the rationale and drivers behind these developments. Community-oriented leadership in practice is then explored as the second focus within the chapter. Tensions in such practice are also examined as it is recognised that community orientation and leadership exist alongside multiple agendas and tendencies. The chapter goes on to discuss a selection of key conceptual issues that underpin community leadership and orientation. In conclusion, some of the major implications for community-oriented leadership are discussed.

In summary, this chapter begins with an initial focus on drivers for community-oriented approaches. Second, implications for educational leadership are explored through contemporary examples of practice. Third, key concepts involved in community-oriented leadership are discussed. The chapter concludes with an overview of implications for leadership in relation to community-oriented schools.

2 Community and leadership background

This section focuses on the background to community-orientated schooling and leadership. A multifaceted relationship between education and various socio-economic outcomes is observed across many international contexts. This concern underlies many of the large-scale policy drives aimed at strengthening links between community and education. A number of local initiatives are also identified where these have arisen to address similar concerns with differential outcomes. Community-oriented schooling and leadership also aspire to enhance the resonance and relevance of the curriculum by bridging community and school cultures more effectively. These issues are covered in greater detail in the subsequent section.

In a number of countries local and national policy statements acknowledge the relationship between community and education. In the UK for example, the educational achievement of children born into high-poverty communities is far lower than those born into affluent families (Hills et al., 2009). Schools and public services in challenging circumstances also perform less effectively and local children and families in these contexts experience poorer outcomes across a range of socio-economic indices (Hartley et al., 2008; Wilkinson and Pickett, 2009). This is further amplified when other socio-economic characteristics are considered, such as ethnicity (Gillborn, 2008; Gillborn and Mirza, 2000). The premium of education also has long-term implications through boosts to employment opportunities and earnings (DCSF, 2009b). Low-education outcomes are also associated with wider levels of disadvantage and vulnerability including physical and mental well-being and contact with the criminal justice system (DCSF, 2009b; Feinstein et al., 2004; Ofsted, 2008).

Similar trends of educational inequality and community disadvantage are documented across economies as diverse as USA (Gamoran, 2007; McKinsey, 2009), Australia (Teese and Polesel, 2003), South Africa (Fiske et al., 2004), Europe (Blanden and Gregg, 2005; Bradshaw et al., 2007) and Mexico (Santibañez et al., 2005). These patterns confirm an inextricable link and interplay between home and school factors in the educational achievement and overall well-being of children and young people. In recognition of this, a number of key policy developments have emerged to encourage stronger orientation of schools towards their local communities. For example, in the USA, *No Child Left Behind* (2004) represents a significant federal policy initiative to tackle educational and social inequalities in outcomes for children and young people. The policy is manifold, encouraging and focusing on improvements in teaching and learning as well as seeking to develop parental engagement. This is aimed at encouraging parental support of those young people who traditionally spend fewer years engaged in education and achieve the poorest educational outcomes.

Community orientation is also evident at the local level in the development of full-service schools in the USA. This organisational and sometimes district-level approach aims to add value to schools through providing a range of local welfare and medical services on site (Dryfoos and Maguire, 2002; Epstein and Sanders, 2006; Fergus, 2009). This emerged from recognition that disadvantaged communities were poorly served in terms of access to amenities and services. Both *No Child Left Behind* and extended schools developments have had international ripple effects. Australia has explored the full-service school model, whereby all services are located on one site. In England, the *Every Child Matters* (DfES, 2003) national policy agenda is similar in purpose to *No Child Left Behind*, with a key aim to develop extended schools. Middlewood and Parker (2009) describe examples in England of full-service extended schools which, interestingly, cover both deprived and relatively prosperous communities. They point out that *Every Child Matters* means that the recognition of issues such as mental and emotional health issues and the impact of an over-materialistic attitude in middle-class families is also important.

Every Child Matters (DfES, 2003) is a key policy initiative that aims to meet a range of needs of children and young people. Five integral outcomes are considered and these encompass educational attainment alongside welfare and socio-economic considerations. A key focus of this important document is the engagement of local communities in both shaping and engaging in local services; community becomes participant, designer and commissioner of services. This model intends to harness community engagement for the purpose of more accurately identifying and addressing localised needs as well as increasing civic participation.

Drawing on models and findings from the experience in the USA, the English extended schools programme is designed to deliver co-located services such as childcare, adult learning, medical services and advisory services. Other recent English policy has reinforced the connection with community with a focus on the role of parents in supporting pupils' education and personal development in both the home and in school (DfES, 2005; DCSF, 2007: 2009a). This includes developments such as Parent Support Advisors (Asmussen et al., 2008; Lindsay et al., 2009) to enable stronger partnership between home and school, particularly for vulnerable learners.

Community engagement is also regarded as a key factor in developing culturally relevant teaching and learning pedagogies (Bojuwoye, 2008; Durden, 2008; Gershberg et al., 2009; Sirvani, 2007). In the case of South Africa, community engagement is considered key in addressing the legacy of unequal access to education and an ill-fitting curriculum endemic in the former apartheid regime (Bojowoye, 2008). The involvement of parents is regarded as key to developing a more representative and inclusive curriculum and school culture (Bojuwoye, 2008; Fiske et al., 2004; Jansen, 2006; Lemmer and van Wyk, 2004). The role of community is also regarded as an important accountability measure, and key to monitoring and improving educational outcomes in schools. Consequently, the South African Schools Act (1996) formalised the role of parents in schooling. This provided a role for parents as governors within South African schools and set out minimum standards for reporting pupil progress and school wide outcomes to parents. This was to serve as a platform for deeper community engagement, representation and influence on outcomes.

There is a strong body of international evidence that also supports the view that community and school partnership provides a powerful influence on improving attainment (Adams and Christenson, 2000; Allen et al., 2009; Dyson and Raffo, 2007; Gilby et al., 2008; Strand, 2007; Van der Werf et al., 2000).

For contemporary education leaders then, there are extremely strong drivers and local contextual issues that encourage engagement between community and school. The dual pressure of meeting educational needs and targets whilst addressing holistic needs creates further complexity. Managing this level of activity and beyond school relationships necessitates effective and well-resourced leadership solutions. With the ever-increasing policy and contextual pushes towards school and community engagement, this necessarily brings new opportunities as well as challenges for education leaders.

3   Community and leadership practice

In this section, issues of leadership structure are discussed. Particular reference is made to the potential for new configurations of leadership arrangements to arise when principals orientate around broader and contextualised needs of children and young people. District-level support and leadership is also highlighted as a potential means of supporting community-oriented approaches. Community-oriented leadership at the district level can enable systematic co-ordination and mobilisation of localised resources. This section goes on to focus on prospects for community leadership wherein community partners emerge as significant co-leaders.

Leadership structure

Recent studies demonstrate that leadership in extended and community-oriented contexts is associated with a focus on a broad spectrum of pupil needs (Epstein and Sanders, 2006; Griffith, 2009). These organisations are also characterised by a propensity to share leadership and responsibility along a number of axes (Harris and Allen, 2009; NCSL/NFER; 2008). This allows principals to delegate as well as develop new forms of responsibility more widely. This can manifest itself in new roles, new responsibilities, new teams and new ways of working (Cairney, 2000).

> High implementation schools were characterised by the extended use of support staff, extended leadership teams and a governing body that were well informed about ECM and had been working to support this agenda for some time. Leadership also extended to a commitment to grow young leaders in the school to support internal developments as well as providing capacity to reach out to young people in the wider community.
>
> 'Distributed leadership and effective delegation are essential; we each have to accept we "can't do it alone."' (Head Teacher) (Harris and Allen, 2009: 349)

Within schools reporting extensive connections with parents and local services, there is evidence of commitment to the community. This sits alongside a belief that more holistic approaches to development of children and young people is intrinsic to improving short-term experiences and long-term outcomes for children and the wider community (Allen et al., 2009; Craig, 2005; Cummings et al., 2007b; Edwards, 2004; Harris and Allen, 2009; Higham et al.,

2009; Leadbetter and Mongon, 2008; Leithwood and Day, 2007; Wade and Schagen, 2002).

'I think when you are working with vulnerable youngsters the impact is inevitably very much individual to them, I know there is a lot of pressures on schools to drive up overall attainment levels but in terms of the *Every Child Matters* agenda it is not always the attainment where you have the biggest impact first.' (Deputy Headteacher) (Allen et al., 2009: 7)

Those schools that embrace an outward-facing role draw on other agendas such as workforce reform, a key policy development in schools in England that involves innovative deployment of teaching professionals and administrative staff (Allen et al., 2009; Middlewood and Parker, 2009; Middlewood et al., 2005). Rather than adding to teacher workload, support staff and dedicated co-ordinators are appointed and deployed to enhance connections with the community. For example, family workers and community co-ordinators are increasingly common appointments. Other authors point to the importance of identifying personnel able to relate to community and engage effectively with needs of young people locally. (Epstein and Sanders, 2006; Griffith, 2009).

Community-oriented leadership is usually co-ordinated or overseen by a senior leader, often the vice-principal or equivalent leader. In such arrangements principal leaders often maintain an overview while delegating operational responsibilities. In the long term this is crucial, as absorbing ever-increasing responsibilities is rarely sustainable without abandoning or relinquishing elsewhere (Allen, 2008; Bryk and Schneider, 2002; Harris et al., 2007; Muijs, 2007; NCLS/NFER, 2007). This approach is also predicated on open and innovative leadership models where high levels of trust enable effective working of flatter and diverse leadership structures (Cairney, 2000; Coleman, 2006; Costa, 2003; Covey, 2006; Louis, 2007; Muijs, 2007; PricewaterhouseCooper, 2007).

Conversely, schools implementing low levels of holistic and community-facing approaches are characterised by traditional and relatively linear and narrower leadership structures (Griffith, 2009; Harris et al., 2007). The wider needs of young people and local communities are conceived as a secondary concern and detached from that of educational attainment. As a result, policy developments that encourage community and holistic orientation may remain at odds with the leadership focus and cultures pertaining in traditionally structured organisations (Gamoran, 2007). In these contexts, there tends to be a greater focus on the negative aspects of wider agendas such as additional workload, tensions with the standards agenda and difficulties in linking and working with parents and multiple agencies within the local community (Cassen and Kingdon, 2007; Shumowe and Harris, 2000; Thrupp et al., 2007; Wilkin et al., 2007).

Influencing the leadership landscape

The complexity of leadership is intensified with the 'push' from national and mandatory policy such as that surrounding extended schools in England and increasing integration of holistic outcomes in judgements concerning the progress of individual schools (Coleman, 2006; Raffo and Dyson, 2007). However, principal leaders often recognise that there must be a common set of goals between parent, community and wider partners to move forwards (Bojowoye, 2008; Epstein and Sanders, 2006; Fergus, 2009). 'You can only succeed with common goals and a willingness to take risks' (Harris and Allen, 2009: 349).

In England, the local authority has mandatory responsibilities related to extended services and multi-agency developments aimed at improving services and outcomes for local children and families. Where plans are developed with a systematic approach and through clustering of resource alongside school level innovation, the depth of progress is good (Allen et al., 2009; Huxham and Vangen, 2000). However, where local authority plans are largely formal schedules to meet minimum requirements, little consistency or depth is achieved at local level. This is especially pertinent where capacity or commitment is low; in these instances the local authority role becomes an important driver and influence on leadership and development around this agenda (Allen et al., 2009; Aspden and Birch, 2005; Epstein and Sanders, 2006; Harris and Allen, 2009; Hetherington et al., 2007; James et al., 2001; Michael et al., 2007). Individual schools that possess a culture of leadership innovation and development are less sensitive to local authority or other points of external inertia and are able to drive effective models of community orientation with their organisation as an effective locus.

Beyond traditional leadership pools

The drive towards community orientation and engagement also incorporates notions of community as active agents and this has important implications for principal leadership. The aspiration

within many recent developments visualises community stakeholders as significant partners and co-leaders. This is far removed from
traditional school leadership models. It is a model that even the most
outward facing schools express as a challenge (Allen et al., 2009;
Harris and Allen, 2009). Consequently, community-oriented activity
can too easily become interventionist; school leaders and other professional agencies tend to define needs and how these are met (Adams
and Christenson, 2000; Angus, 2009; Epstein and Sanders, 2006;
Fergus, 2009; Halsey et al., 2006; Miller and Stirling, 2004; Muijs,
2007; Tam, 2007).

Research evidence suggests that despite the challenges schools
are able to reach a stage where community is widely consulted and
included in decision-making on a systematic basis (Flutter, 2006;
Henderson et al., 2007; Hirschman, 1984; Kendall et al., 2007;
Page et al., 2007; Petrie et al., 2005; Riley, 2008).

> 'I think when you make yourself available and people see you've
> got systems in place, where you are not having casual conversa-
> tions on corridors, communication is effective, then they are all
> too willing to be involved.' (Deputy Headteacher)

> 'I run a youth workers' network forum and lots of different organ-
> isations come to that ... that are passionate about doing some-
> thing for young people and they want to support whatever goes
> on in the community. We always get together and get the police
> there and it's a fantastic forum because what we do is talk about
> the needs of young people or specific issues.' (Youth Development
> Worker) (Allen et al., 2009: 9)

Some schools have succeeded in effective and systematic engagement with community by building on long-standing good relations
with parents and community. Other approaches include developing
joint decision-making opportunities and opening up highly relevant
responsibilities (Epstein and Sanders, 2006; Harris and Allen, 2009;
Sanders and Harvey, 2002). A key influential factor in bringing
schools and community together is the development of notions of
shared purpose in meeting the needs of local children and families
(Allen et al., 2009; Epstein and Sanders, 2006; Higham et al., 2009;
Middlewood and Parker, 2009).

> 'I sit on lots of different boards that are multi agency-led so if ever
> there's an incident, say if there's a high crime rate in this area,
> then I would be able to gather the information from there, feed it
> back to the school and vice versa.' (Youth Development Worker)

'What it has done is opened up the way that we work and it has allowed us to work in a much more proactive way. I think traditionally pastoral systems are seen as reactive, it's about telling youngsters off, it's about dealing with angry parents and because of the way we've set things up I really do believe that we are working proactively.' (Deputy Headteacher) (Allen et al., 2009: 18)

In some contexts professional practice has been transformed through wholesale reconfiguration of school leadership structures and importantly, commitment to developing new professional and social cultures (Allen et al., 2009; Fergus, 2009; Middlewood and Parker, 2009; Miller and Stirling, 2004; Sanders and Harvey, 2002). Drawing in wider local services as well as young people and families has also seeded inter-professional learning between agencies, generated high levels of collaborative advantage and harnessed culturally relevant activity (Allen et al., 2009; Durden, 2008; Harris and Allen, 2009).

4   Reflections on community leadership

This chapter has considered the rationale and drivers towards community leadership, and issues arising from community leadership in practice. This section considers underlying processes and conceptualisations related to community leadership. Key concepts in remaking professional practice, reconstructing policy, and leadership innovation are highlighted.

Local and national policy are key influences and drivers in community orientation and leadership approaches (DCSF, 2007, 2009a). However, policy statements are translated and contextualised at a local level to form practice. Consequently, this raises issues of fidelity of policy implementation (Huxham and Vangen, 2000; Kalafat et al., 2007). Furthermore, collaborations and projects aimed at parental and community engagement are often based on short-term funding and entrepreneurial resources rather than on long-term funding streams (Allen et al., 2009, Hetherington et al., 2007). Where deep-seated levels of disadvantage and high levels of need exist, longer-term systematic approaches are required (Gamoran, 2007; Percy-Smith, 2004). Wider understandings of public service reform also suggest that there is an inverse relationship between the duration of the challenge and speed of reform; where challenges have been present over a long period of time, these will take relatively longer periods to redress (Hartley et al., 2008). Consequently, sustainable structures and resources are of high priority for this agenda which is characterised by long-standing differences in education and social outcomes.

'School exceeding' qualities are increasingly expected of senior leadership teams in order to address wider and more relevant needs of young people. In the English context, the make-up of senior leadership teams is increasingly expected to include wider members of the school workforce, local community and multi-agency workforce to enable more effective and relevant approaches (Allen et al., 2009; Harris and Allen, 2009; NCSL/NFER, 2008; PWC, 2007). Notions of 'system leadership' and 'distributed leadership' are now common terms in discourses characterising the broader commitment to leadership beyond the school, flatter leadership structures and strong moral purpose intrinsic to community-oriented leadership agendas (Harris, 2008; Higham et al., 2009).

With moves towards a broader focus for principal leaders beyond the school, there is a need to create sustainable leadership structures that are underpinned by meaningful opportunities for community involvement (Angus, 2009; Bojowoye, 2008; Lemmer and van Wyk, 2004). This is addressed to a large extent through flatter leadership structures with the principal retaining an overview of delegated and shared responsibilities.

There is a wide range of community-oriented action encompassing activity such as parental involvement in school events in England (Allen et al., 2009), full-service schooling in the USA and community partnership boards and multi-agency activity in South Africa. This potentially impacts positively upon both educational outcomes and wider dimensions of well-being (Dyson and Raffo, 2007; Cairney, 2000). However, there is also a key need for abandonment of those practices that no longer accord with this agenda (Leithwood and Day, 2007). It is also necessary for principals and senior leadership teams to engage in professional development and growth opportunities that will support them in developing community-oriented approaches given that this orientation has been absent from leadership models in recent history (PWC, 2007).

However, community-oriented leadership also presents challenges in terms of re-culturing the senior leadership role (Allen et al., 2009; Cummings et al., 2007a, 2007b; Jansen, 2006; Moss, 2007; Shumow and Harris, 2000). Preparation for leadership has traditionally centred on leading a single, enclosed unit often along hierarchical lines. School organisational culture is also based on time-honoured and naturalised professional paradigms that do not traditionally embrace community. Community-oriented leadership requires crossing professional boundaries as well as learning new ways of working. The shift away from traditional models does not always result in immediate or comfortable transitions (Allen, 2009; Allen et al., 2009; Ball and Maroy, 2009; Harris and Goodall, 2007; Roxburgh and Arend, 2003; Smyth, 2009). The role of the local authority is also considered important in developing sustainable approaches to community orientation and creating important frameworks and impetus. Systematic district-level support would enable coherent planning and mobilisation of local resources to meet young people and community needs.

Conclusions

There is a compelling rationale for leaders to connect with the wider community both in terms of an attainment focus and in relation to broader lifelong dimensions of well-being (Adams and Christenson, 2000; Allen et al., 2009; Bojowoye, 2008; DCSF, 2007, 2009a; Dryfoos and Maguire, 2002; Durden, 2008; Dyson and Raffo, 2007; Epstein and Sanders, 2006; Fergus, 2009; Fiske et al., 2004; Gershberg et al., 2009; Gilby et al., 2008; Jansen, 2006; Lemmer and van Wyk, 2004; Sirvani, 2007; Strand, 2007). The role of leadership is also identified as one of the most influential in-school variables in effecting educational outcomes (Leithwood and Day, 2007; McKinsey, 2007; PWC, 2007). This important dimension of community leadership requires principal leaders to construct locally meaningful activity to better connect with young people and local families. This requires the development of a shared focus, mutually beneficial approaches and inclusive leadership structures. However, there are significant challenges to this. Pupils, parents and other traditionally marginal groups continue to be under-represented in terms of their engagement in leadership and partnership roles in education and wider services. This may take time to evolve and both schools and constituent communities require support in enhancing community leadership capabilities as well as developing inclusive and significant opportunities for co-leadership (Ball and Maroy, 2009; Gamoran, 2007).

The success of community-oriented approaches is also dependent on effective localisation in its broadest sense; reconstructing national policy into meaningful and connected local practice, involving local children and families and organising school-level structures to meet contextual needs (Allen et al., 2009; Aspden and Birch, 2005; Dyson, Harris et al., 2007; Percy-Smith, 2006). Opportunities to inter-face with local communities are a potentially powerful mechanism for better identifying and meeting needs (Gershberg et al., 2009). However, creating inclusive forms of consultation and co-construction remain a challenge (Adams and Christenson, 2000; Allen et al., 2009; Asmussen et al., 2007: 2; Miller and McNicholl, 2003; PWC, 2007) For principal leaders and senior teams this entails a shift from siloed and professionally exclusive forms of leadership and focus, to cross-ing into new areas of practice and audience. This is premised on building trust and common purpose across school leadership teams and within the community.

Further reading

Dryfoos, J. and Maguire, S. (2002) *Inside Full-service Community Schools*. New York: Corwin Press.
Middlewood, D. and Parker, R. (2009) *Leading and Managing Extended Schools: Ensuring Every Child Matters*. London: Sage.
Todd, L. (2007) *Partnerships for Inclusive Education*. London: Routledge.

Note

1. Certain data used in this chapter was a result of research funded from the Economic and Social Research Council (ESRC).

References

Adams, K.S. and Christenson, S.L. (2000) 'Trust and the family–school relationship: examination of parent–teacher differences in elementary and secondary grades', *Journal of Social Psychology*, 38(5): 477–97.
Allen, T. (2008) *Developing Deep Support for Vulnerable Learners*. London: Esmée Fairbairn and Specialist Schools and Academies Trust.
Allen, T., Harris, A. and Ghent, K. (2009) *Multi-Agency Partnerships and Young People's Perceptions of Schooling*. ESRC, Final Report.
Angus, L. (2009) 'Problematizing neighbourhood renewal: community, school effectiveness and disadvantage', *Critical Studies in Education*, 50(1): 37–50.
Asmussen, K., Corlyon, J., Hauari, H. and La Place, V. (2007) *Supporting Parents of Teenagers*. London: DfES.
Aspden, J. and Birch, D. (2005) *New Localism – Citizen Engagement, Neighbourhoods and Public Services: Evidence from Local Government*. London: Local and Regional Government Research Unit, ODPM.
Ball, S.J. and Maroy, C. (2009) 'Schools' logics of action as mediation and compromise between internal dynamics and external constraints and

pressures', *Compare: A Journal of Comparative and International Education*, 39(1): 99–112.

Blanden, J. and Gregg, P. (2005) *Intergenerational Mobility in Europe and North America: A Report by the Sutton Trust*. London: Centre for Economic Performance, London School of Economics.

Bojowoye, O. (2008) 'Home–school partnership – a study of opinions of selected parents and teachers in Kwazulu Natal Province, South Africa' *Research Papers in Education*, 99991: 1.

Bradshaw, J., Hoelscher, P. and Richardson, D. (2007) 'An index of child well-being in the European Union', *Social Indicators Research*, 80: 133–77.

Bryk, A.S. and Schneider, B. (2002) *Trust in Schools: A Core Resource for Improvement*. New York: Russell Sage Foundation.

Cairney, T.H. (2000) 'Beyond the classroom walls: the rediscovery of the family and community as partners in education', *Educational Review*, 25 (2): 63–174.

Cassen, R. and Kingdon, G. (2007) *Tackling Low Educational Achievement*. York: Joseph Rowntree Foundation.

Coleman, A. (2006) *Collaborative Leadership in Extended Schools*. Nottingham: NCSL.

Costa, A. (2003) 'Work team trust and effectiveness', *Personnel Review*, 32: 605–22.

Covey, S. (2006) *The Speed of Trust*. New York: Free Press.

Craig, J. (2005) *Taking the Wide View: The New Leadership of Extended Schools*. Nottingham: NCSL.

Cummings, C., Dyson, A., Muijs, D., Papps, I., Pearson, D., Raffo, C., Tiplady, L. and Todd, L. (2007a) *Evaluation of the Full-Service Extended Schools Initiative. Final Report*. London: DfES.

Cummings, C., Todd, L. and Dyson, A. (2007b) 'Towards extended schools? How education and other professionals understand community-oriented schooling', *Children and Society*, 21(3): 189–200.

DCSF (2007) *The Children's Plan: Building Brighter Futures*. Cm 7280. London: HMSO.

DCSF (2009a) *Children and Young People's Plan Guidance 2009*. London: DCSF.

DCSF (2009b) *Children's Services Interventions Evaluation*, DCSF–RR160. London: DCSF.

Edwards, A. (2004) 'The new multi-agency working: collaborating to prevent the social exclusion of children and families', *Journal of Integrated Care*, 12 (5): 3–9.

DfES (2003a) *Every Child Matters*. Cm. 5860. London: TSO.

DfES (2005) *Extended Schools Access to Opportunities and Services for All – A Prospectus*. London: DfES.

Dryfoos, J.G. and Maguire, S. (2002) *Inside Full-Service Community Schools*. Thousand Oaks, CA: Corwin Press

Durden, T. (2008) 'Do your homework! Investigating the role of culturally relevant pedagogy in comprehensive school reform models serving diverse student populations', *Urban Review. Issues and Ideas in Public Education*, 40(4): 403–19.

Dyson, A. and Raffo, C. (2007) 'Education and disadvantage: the role of community-oriented schools', *Oxford Review of Education*, 33(3): 297–314.

Edwards, A. (2004) 'The new multi-agency working: collaborating to prevent the social exclusion of children and families', *Journal of Integrated Care*, 12(5): 3–9.

Epstein, J.L. and Sanders, M. (2006) 'Prospects for change: preparing educators for school, family, and community partnerships', *Peabody Journal of Education*, 81(2): 81–120.

Feinstein, L., Duckworth, K. and Sabates, R. (2004) *A Model of the Inter-generational Transmission of Educational Success*. London: Institute of Education.

Fergus, D. (2009) 'Dayton's neighbourhood school centres', *New Directions for Youth Development*, 122: 81–106.

Fiske, Edward B. and Ladd, Helen, F. (2004) *Elusive Equity: Education Reform in Post-Apartheid South Africa*. Cape Town: HSRC and Brookings Institute.

Flutter, J. (2006) 'This place could help you learn': student participation in creating better school environments' *Educational Review*, 58(2): 183–93.

Gamoran, A. (ed.) (2007) *Standards-Based Reform and the Poverty Gap: Lessons for 'No Child Left Behind'*. Washington, DC: Brookings Institution Press.

Gershberg, A.I., Meade, B. and Andersson, S. (2009) 'Providing better education services to the poor: accountability and context in the case of Guatemalan de-centralisation', *International Journal of Educational Development*, 29(3): 187–200.

Gilby, N., Hamlyn, B., Hanson, T., Romanou, E., Mackey, T., Clark, J., Trikka, N. and Harrison, M. (2008) *National Survey of Parents and Children: Family Life, Aspirations and Engagement with Learning*. DCSF RR059. London: DCSF.

Gillborn, D. (2008) *Racism and Education: Coincidence or Conspiracy?* Oxon: Sage.

Gillborn, D. and Mirza, H. (2000) *Educational Inequality: Mapping Race, Class and Gender – a Synthesis of Research Evidence*. Report 232. London: Ofsted.

Griffith, J. (2001) 'Principal leadership of parent involvement', *Journal of Educational Administration*, 39(2): 162–86.

Halsey, K., Murfield, J., Harland, J.L. and Lord, P. (2006) *The Voice of Young People: An Engine for Improvement? Scoping the Evidence*. Slough: NFER.

Harris, A. (2008) *Distributed Leadership*. London: Routledge.

Harris, A. and Allen, T. (2009) 'Ensuring every child matters: issues of implementation for school leaders', *School Leadership and Management*, 29(4): 337–52.

Harris, A. and Goodall, J. (2007) *Engaging Parents in Raising Achievement. Do Parents Know They Matter?* DCSF-RW004. DCSF: London.

Harris, A., Allen, T. and Goodall, J. (2007) *Understanding the Reasons Why Schools Do or Do Not Fully Engage with the* Every Child Matters/Extended Schools *Agenda*. Nottingham: NCSL.

Hartley, J., Donaldson, C., Skelcher, C. and Wallace, M. (2008) *Managing to Improve Public Services*. Cambridge: Cambridge University Press.

Henderson, A.T., Mapp, K.L., Johnson, V.R. and Davies, D. (2007) *Beyond the Bake Sale – The Essential Guide to Family-School Partnerships*. New York: New Press.

Hetherington, M., Benefield, P., Lines, A., Paterson, C., Ries, J. and Shuayb, M. (2007) *Community Cohesion for Children, Young People and their Families: A Rapid Review of Policy, Practice and Research in Local Authorities*. Slough: NFER.

Higham, R., Hopkins, D. and Matthews, P. (2009) *System Leadership in Practice*. Buckingham: Open University Press.

Hills, J., Sefton, T. and Stewart, K. (eds) (2009) *Towards a More Equal Society? Poverty, Inequality and Policy since 1997*. Bristol: Policy Press.

Hirschman, O. (1984) *Getting Ahead Collectively: Grassroots experiences in Latin America*. Oxford: Pergamon Press.

Huxham, C. and Vangen, S. (2000) 'Leadership in the shaping and implementation of collaboration agendas: how things happen in a (not quite) joined up world', *Academy of Management Journal*. 6: 1159–75.

James, P., St Leger, P. and Ward, K. (2001) *Making Connections: The Evaluation of the Victorian Full Service Schools Programme*. Canberra: Department of Education.

Jansen, J.D. (2006) 'Leading against the grain: the politics and emotions of leading for social justice in South Africa', *Leadership and Policy in Schools*, 5(1): 37–51.

Kalafat, J., Illback, R.J. and Sanders, D. (2007) 'The relationship between implementation fidelity and educational outcomes in a school-based family support program: development of a model for evaluating multidimensional full-service programs', *Evaluation and Program Planning*, 30: 136–48.

Kendall, S., Lamont, E. and Wilkin, A. (2007) *How School Leaders in Extended Schools Respond to Local Needs: Summary Report*. Slough: NFER.

Leadbetter, C. and Mongon, D. (2008) *Leadership for Public Value Achieving Valuable Outcomes for Children, Families and Communities*. Nottingham: NCSL.

Leithwood, K. and Day, C. (eds) (2007) 'The impact of school leadership on pupil outcomes' (editorial), *School Leadership and Management*, 28(1): 1–4.

Lemmer, E. and van Wyk, N. (2004) 'Schools reaching out: comprehensive parent involvement in South African primary schools', *African Education Review*, 1(2): 259–78.

Lindsay, G., Davis, H., Strand, S., Cullen, M.A., Band, S., Cullen, S., Davis, L., Hasluck, C., Evans, R. and Stewart-Brown, S. (2009) *Parent Support Advisor Pilot Project: Final Report*, DCSF-RR151. London: DCSF.

Louis, K.S. (2007) 'Trust and improvement in schools', *Journal of Educational Change*, 6(1): 1–24.

McKinsey & Company (2009) *The Economic Impact of the Achievement Gap in America's Schools*. Australia: Social Sector Office, McKinsey & Company.

Michael, S., Dittus, P. and Epstein, J. (2007) 'Family and community involvement in schools: results from the school health policies and programs Study 2006', *Journal of School Health*, 77(8): 567–87.

Middlewood, D. and Parker, R. (2009) *Leading and Managing Extended Schools: Ensuring Every Child Matters*. London: Sage.

Middlewood, D., Parker, R. and Beere, J. (2005) *Creating a Learning School*. London: Sage.

Miller, C. and McNicholl, A. (2003) *Integrating Children's Services: Issues and Practice*. London: Office for Public Management.

Miller, C. and Stirling, S. (2004) *Co-Production in Children's Services*. London: Office for Public Management.

Moss, P. (2007) 'Bringing politics into the nursery: early childhood education as a democratic practice', *European Early Childhood Education Research Journal*, 15(1): 5–20.

Muijs, D. (2007) 'Leadership in full-service extended schools: communicating across cultures', *School Leadership and Management*, 27(4): 347–62.

NCSL (2008) *What We Are Learning About: School Leadership of* Every Child Matters. Nottingham: NCSL.

Ofsted (2008) *The Annual Report of Her Majesty's Chief Inspector of Education, Children's Services and Skills 2007/8*, HC114. London: The Stationery Office.

Page, J., Whitting, G. and Mclean, C. (2007) *Engaging Effectively with Black and Minority Ethnic Parents in Children's and Parental Services*. DCSF RB013. London: DSCF.

Percy-Smith, J. (2004) 'What works in strategic partnerships for children: a research review', *Children & Society*, 20: 313–23.

Petrie, P., Boddy, J., Cameron, C., Heptinstall, E., McQuail, S., Simon, A. and Wigfall, V. (2005) *Pedagogy – a Holistic, Personal Approach to Work with Children and Young People, Across Services: European Models for Practice, Training, Education and Qualification*. London: Thomas Coram Research Institute, University of London.

PricewaterhouseCoopers (PWC) (2007) *Independent Study into School Leadership*. London: DfES.

Public Law 107–110 (2002) *No Child Left Behind Act of 2001*. Available at: http://www.ed.gov/policy/elsec/leg/esea02/107=110.pdf (accessed 7 December 2009).

Raffo, C. and Dyson, A. (2007) 'Full service extended schools and educational inequality in urban contexts – new opportunities for progress?', *Journal of Education Policy*, 22(3): 263–82.

Riley, K.A. (2008) 'Leadership and urban education', in B. McGaw, E. Baker and P.P. Peterson (eds), *International Encyclopaedia of Education*, 3rd edn. Oxford: Elsevier.

Roxburgh, I. and Arend, N. (2003) *Crossing Boundaries: New Ways of Working*. London: New Local Government Network.

Sanders M. and Harvey, A. (2002) 'Beyond the school walls: a case study of principal leadership for school–community collaboration'. New York: *Teachers Press Record*, 104 (7): 1345–69.

Santibañez, L., Vernez, G. and Razquin, P. (2005) *Education in Mexico: Challenges and Opportunities*. Santa Monica, CA: Rand.

Shumowe, L. and Harris, W. (2000) 'Teachers' thinking about home–school relations in low-income urban communities', *The School Community Journal* 10 (1): 9–24.

Sirvani, H. (2007) 'The effect of teacher communication with parents on students' mathematical achievement', *American Secondary Education*, 36(1): 31–46.

Smyth, J. (2009) 'Critically engaged community capacity building and the "community organizing" approach in disadvantaged contexts', *Critical Studies in Education*, 50(1): 9–22.

Strand, S. (2007) *Minority Ethnic Pupils in the Longitudinal Study of Young People in England (LSYPE)*. DCSF RR002. London: DCSF.

Tam, Frank Wai-ming (2007) 'Rethinking school and community relations in Hong Kong', *International Journal of Educational Management*, 21(4): 350–66.

Teese, R. and Polesel, J. (2003) *Undemocratic Schooling: Equity and Quality in Mass Secondary Education in Australia*. Carlton, Victoria: Melbourne University Press.

Thrupp, M., Lupton, R. and Brown, C. (2007) 'Pursuing the contextualisation agenda: recent progress and future prospects', in, T. Townsend (ed), *International Handbook of School Effectiveness and Improvement*. New York: Springer. pp. 111–26.

Van der Werf, G.B., Creemers, B and Guldemond, H. (2000) 'Improving parental involvement in primary education in Indonesia: implementation, effects and costs', *School Effectiveness and School Improvement*, 1 (4): 447–66.

Wade, P. and Schagen, S. (2002) *Evaluation of the Community Leadership Strategy*. Slough: NFER.

Wilkin, A., Lamont, E., White, R., Kinder, K. and Howard, P. (2007) *Schools as Community Based Organisations*. Reading: CfBT.

Wilkinson, R. and Pickett, K. (2009) *Why More Equal Societies Almost Always Do Better*. London: Allen Lane.

Glossary

ACE	Advanced Certificate in Education [South Africa]
BELMAS	British Educational Leadership, Management and Administration Society
CCEAM	Commonwealth Council for Educational Administration and Management
CCSSO	Council of Chief State School Officers [USA]
CEL	Centre for Excellence in Leadership
CIPO	Context–Input–Process–Output model of factors influencing student learning
CPD	Continuing professional development
DEA	Data envelopment analysis
DCSF	Department for Children Schools and Families [UK]
DES	Department for Education and Science [UK]
DfES	Department for Education and Skills [UK]
FCP	Flexible Curriculum Programme
FEDA	Further Education Development Agency [UK]
GCSE	General Certificate of Secondary Education [UK]
GTC	General Teaching Council [England]
HEA	Higher Education Academy [UK]
HMSO	Her Majesty's Stationery Office [UK]
ICT	Information and communication technology
ISLLC	Interstate School Leaders Licensure Consortium [USA]
KS2	Key Stage 2: School Children aged 7–11 tested at age 11 [UK]
KS3	Key Stage 3: School Children aged 11–14 tested at age 14 [UK]

NBPTS	National Board of Professional Teacher Standards [USA]
NCSL	National College for School Leadership [England]
NFER	National Foundation for Educational Research
NPQH	National Professional Qualification for Headship [England]
NWP	National Writing Project [USA]
OECD	Organisation for Economic Co-operation and Development
OFSTED	Office for Standards in Education [UK]
PRP	Performance related pay
PIRLS	Progress in International Reading Literacy Study
PISA	Programme for International Mathematics and Science Study
PWC	PricewaterhouseCoopers
QCA	Qualifications and Curriculum Authority (QCA)
SASP	South African Standards for Principalship
SBM	School-based management
SDP	School development planning
SEN	Special educational needs
SQH	Scottish Qualification for Headship
TDA	Training and Development Agency [UK]
TTA	Teacher Training Agency [UK]
UNESCO	United Nations Educational Scientific and Cultural Organisation
WRL	Work Related Learning

Author Index

Subject Index

Research Methods Books from SAGE

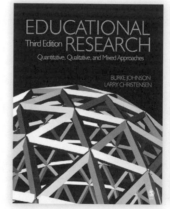

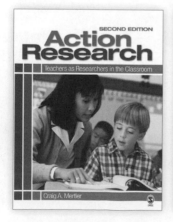

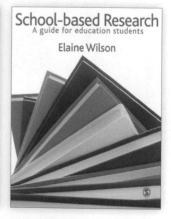

Exciting Early Years and Primary Texts from SAGE

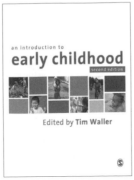

978-1-84787-518-1

978-1-84787-393-4

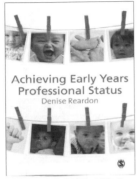

978-1-84787-190-9

978-1-84787-524-2

978-1-84860-127-7

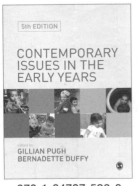

978-1-84787-593-8

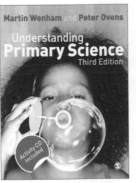

978-1-84860-119-2

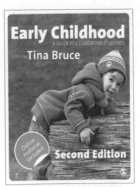

978-1-84860-224-3

978-1-84860-197-0

Find out more about these titles and our wide range of books for education students and practitioners at **www.sagepub.co.uk/education**

Exciting Education Texts from SAGE

587763

Elaine Wilson

978-1-4129-4850-0

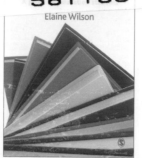

TEACHING ENGLISH

CAROL EVANS
ALYSON MIDGLEY
PHIL RIGBY
LYNNE WARHAM
PETER WOOLNOUGH

978-1-4129-4818-0

Achieving your
PTLLS Award
A Practical Guide to Successful Teaching in the Lifelong Learning Sector

Mary Francis
Jim Gould

978-1-84787-917-2

Introduction to
Research
Methods in
Education

Keith F
Punch

978-1-84787-018-6

A Toolkit
for the effective
Teaching
Assistant

2nd Edition

Maureen Parker, Chris Lee, Stuart Gunn,
Kitty Heardman, Rachael Hincks,
Mary Pittman and Mark Townsend

978-1-84787-943-1

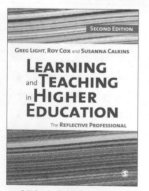

SECOND EDITION

GREG LIGHT, ROY COX and SUSANNA CALKINS

LEARNING
and TEACHING
in HIGHER
EDUCATION
The REFLECTIVE PROFESSIONAL

978-1-84860-008-9

TEACHING SCIENCE

TONY LIVERSIDGE
MATT COCHRANE
BERNARD KERFOOT
JUDITH THOMAS

978-1-84787-362-0

The Complete Guide to
Becoming an Second
English Teacher

Edited by
Stephen Clarke, Paul Dickinson
& Jo Westbrook

978-1-84787-289-0

3rd Edition

Daniel Muijs and David Reynolds
Effective Teaching
Evidence and Practice

978-1-84920-076-9

Find out more about these titles and our wide range of books for
education students and practitioners at **www.sagepub.co.uk/education**